After raping eighteen-year-old Amanda Carpova, her assailant forced her at gunpoint back to the bed in her apartment and made her lie down. He tied her wrists behind her back with cord and her ankles as well. She believed after he tied her up that he would just leave. Instead he became very quiet for a moment and then suddenly straddled her body with his own, put his hands around her throat, and tried choking her to death. Amanda thought, "He's trying to squeeze the life out of me! I know he's trying to kill me!"

One thing her attacker didn't know, however: Amanda had been on a swim team and now she used every ounce of her strength to buck him off. She twisted, squirmed and kept moving so that he could not get a good grip on her throat.

"Move, move, move!" she thought. "Do anything!" She bucked and wriggled and thrashed around on the bed with all her might. "Don't give up!" she kept thinking. Yet at one point she started to black out, and a terrifying thought came into her head, "I'm going to die!"

LUST TO KILL

ROBERT SCOTT

PINNACLE BOOKS
Kensington Publishing Corp.
http://www.kensingtonbooks.com

Some names have been changed to protect the privacy of individuals connected to this story.

PINNACLE BOOKS are published by

Kensington Publishing Corp.
119 West 40th Street
New York, NY 10018

All Kensington Titles, Imprints, and Distributed Lines are available at special quantity discounts for bulk purchases for sales promotions, premiums, fund-raising, and educational or institutional use. Special book excerpts or customized printings can also be created to fit specific needs. For details, write or phone the office of the Kensington special sales manager: Kensington Publishing Corp., 119 West 40th Street, New York, NY 10018, attn: Special Sales Department, Phone: 1-800-221-2647.

Pinnacle and the P logo Reg. U.S. Pat. & TM Off.

ISBN-13: 978-0-7860-1886-4
ISBN-10: 0-7860-1886-0

First printing: May 2009

10 9 8 7 6 5 4 3 2 1

Printed in the United States of America

Acknowledgments

I'd like to thank Larry Findling, Mike Stahlman, and Mark McDonnell for their help in gathering information for this book. I'd also like to thank my editor, Michaela Hamilton.

I've been thinking of murder lately.
                                        —Sebastian Shaw

I was a cop for thirty years, and Shaw left a real impression on me. He had no sense of the suffering and horror he was causing. It was like talking to a reptile.
                                        —Detective Mike Stahlman

Based upon my twenty-six years as a prosecutor, I have never personally had contact with a defendant who is so fixated upon the killing of other human beings.
                                        —Mark McDonnell

1

The Intruder

To everyone around them, eighteen-year-old Donna Ferguson and twenty-nine-year-old Todd Rudiger looked like a very happy couple. Donna had grown up in the Portland, Oregon, area, recently having graduated from David Douglas High School, where she had played clarinet in the marching band. The band had been so talented, Donna was able to participate in several Rose Bowl parades and at Disneyland as well. A member of the Mill Park Baptist Church, Donna was bright, attractive and in love with Todd.

Todd Rudiger had moved up to the Portland area after a two-year stint in the U.S. Navy. After the navy, he'd been a chef in Oklahoma and in California, and currently he was working part-time at a local Safeway grocery store. He also had a part-time job with his father, Edward Rudiger Sr., in the Rudiger Construction Company.

Todd and Donna had met at a Safeway store when she worked there, and they soon hit it off. By late spring 1992, Donna moved in with Todd at his residence in a mobile home park. Todd was an outgoing person, and he often mowed the lawns of elderly people in the mobile home park just to help out. Resident Geraldine Vogel said of him, "He was just one of the kids you wanted to snuggle up to and put your arms around."

People were just as enthusiastic about Donna. Todd's father declared that he couldn't have asked for Todd to have a better girlfriend. He thought Donna was very sweet and good for his son. Todd and Donna were scheduled to get married on July 17, 1993, and move to Lincoln City on the Oregon coast, where Todd planned to build their own dream home.

In midsummer 1992, Donna's cousin Rachelle Robbins came up to the Portland area with her mother to visit Donna and her mom. Normally, Rachelle would have hung out with Donna's older sister, Delani, but Delani was gone, so Rachelle spent time with Donna. She and Donna went to a party while Todd was working, and they stayed until about 1:00 A.M. The party was hosted by a young man with the nickname of "Silky." He got his nickname because of the silk shirts he liked to wear.

While the girls were at the party, some young men arrived, and Donna pointed out one of them to Rachelle. Donna declared, "That's my ex-boyfriend and he's a real jerk!"

Rachelle went out to get a six-pack of beer to bring back to the party, and when she returned, she found Donna and Donna's ex-boyfriend in the garage having a heated argument. Rachelle heard Donna clearly say, "Well, I told you I don't love you! I'm with Todd now. So let it go!"

The argument went on for another five minutes; then Donna walked away and she and Rachelle drank a beer in another part of the house. Rachelle later recalled about the argument, "Donna just kind of blew it off and seemed to enjoy the rest of the party. Her ex-boyfriend went into another room with his friends, and he and Donna didn't speak to each other for the rest of the night."

* * *

On July 17, 1992, Jeff Sutherland, who had been Todd's roommate before Donna moved in, came by the mobile home that Todd and Donna now shared. Donna was out doing errands in Todd's Jeep, and Jeff and Todd talked about having a barbecue later in the month. Sutherland left around 3:30 P.M. and Todd went over to an elderly man's yard in the mobile home park and mowed his lawn.

Donna returned home around 4:00 P.M. and spoke with her mom, Debra Adams, for a short time. Slightly after four, Todd's dad, Ed, phoned and spoke with Todd. Another phone call came in, at 4:30 P.M., from Donna's friend Christi Haner. Haner wanted to borrow Donna's old Safeway uniform. Haner had just been hired by Safeway and was to start work on the following morning. Donna told Haner that she would bring the uniform by Haner's current place of employment, Pizza Baron Restaurant, between 6:00 and 7:00 P.M. Donna never showed up with the uniform, however—which was not like her. Donna always followed through when she promised someone something. Around 5:00 P.M., Ed called his son Todd once again, but he got no answer. Since Ed and his wife were going away for the weekend, he did not call back that evening.

Sometime, just before 5:00 P.M. on July 17, 1992, a stranger had come to the door of Donna and Todd's mobile home, and Donna went to see who was there. The young man initially asked about some people he said he knew in the mobile home park, and he wondered if they still lived there. Whether Donna let him in at that point is not known, but what could be pieced together later would have to come from physical evidence and a very unusual source—the young man himself. The young man pulled out a pistol and ordered Donna into an adjacent room. Perhaps he didn't know that Todd was there at the time, but he soon had his pistol pointed at both of them, telling them to be quiet or he would kill them. Thinking they were going to be robbed, both Donna and Todd complied.

The intruder forced Todd and Donna into a back bedroom, and he had Donna tie up Todd's hands and feet with telephone extension cords. The stranger then shoved Todd into a closet and told him to not make any noise. He pointed the gun at Donna once again, and it soon became apparent that he was there to do more than just rob the place. The intruder forced Donna to lie down on the bed, and he bound her with telephone extension cords, looping them several times around her ankles and arms to make sure that she was secure. He took one of her panties, possibly from a drawer, and stuffed it into her mouth, tying it there with a sash from her bathrobe. The intruder pulled out a large knife and began slicing off items of Donna's clothing until she was completely naked and the shredded items of clothing lay around her in a heap. This was a process he seemed to savor, and it made him become erect.

When Donna's clothing was finally pushed aside, the stranger mounted her and began to rape her. He said later, "She was compliant. She didn't say anything, and she didn't fight back." One thing he did not do was cut her with the knife as he raped her, something that many sexual sadists will do to their victims. Nonetheless, the rape was brutal and persistent, and Todd, in the closet, must have realized what was happening. Todd struggled to free himself, but he also started to have an epileptic attack. Todd thrashed around in the closet, and the intruder went to check on him. At first, the intruder thought Todd was faking it, but then he could see how much distress Todd was in. The stranger even said later, "I could see he was having some kind of medical problem."

This, however, did not create any sympathy on the part of the intruder. He returned to raping Donna and there was a horrific conclusion to the rape. From what could be pieced together later—from forensic evidence and a fitting together of the puzzle pieces—the stranger violently stabbed Donna in the neck as he ejaculated. It wasn't a conventional slashing of the throat. Rather, it was him driving the knife blade clear through her neck, severing the jugular vein and carotid artery, and actually piercing the spinal cord. Donna bled out within seconds, a huge pool of blood expanding around her neck and head.

After murdering Donna, the stranger turned upon Todd, who still thrashed about on the floor. Tied up well with binding, Todd could do nothing to ward off the savage knife thrusts the stranger inflicted upon him. The stranger drove the knife blade into Todd's neck at least twice, slicing through the carotid artery, jugular vein and airway. And as if that wasn't enough, he stabbed Todd in the temple area, with a blow so violent that it penetrated the skull and the blade entered Todd's brain. Like Donna, Todd died within seconds of the lethal stab wounds.

Once the stranger was done, he cleaned himself up, stole a few items from the mobile home and let himself out. Surprisingly, even though it was late afternoon in the summertime, no one in the mobile home park had seen him come or go. One reason may have been that it was a very warm day, and most residents were inside with the air-conditioning on.

By July 19, Donna's mother, Debra, had not heard from her daughter for two days, something that was very unusual. Even more odd was the fact that Donna had not come by Debra Adams's house to babysit her younger brother. Donna was good about keeping her appointments. Debra called Todd and Donna's mobile home, but she got no answer. She phoned Leeds Shoes, where Donna worked part-time, and discovered that Donna had not shown up for work on Saturday, July 18, nor had she called in sick.

Debra stopped by the mobile home on Sunday on her way to work and noticed Todd's Jeep parked in the driveway. She also noticed all the lights in the mobile home were turned off. It's not clear if Debra knocked on the door at that point, but at any rate, there was no sign of Todd or Donna being in or around the mobile home.

On Sunday night, July 19, Todd's father, Ed, got back into Portland, and Debra Adams drove by the mobile home once again, on Monday morning. This time she did knock on the doors and windows all around the mobile home. She got no response. Debra went to work, and then at about 5:30 P.M. she phoned Todd's dad, Ed, because she was very worried. Debra's husband and Todd's father drove over to the mobile home, but they, too, got no response when they knocked. The two men broke the lock on the door and entered the mobile home. Once they rounded the corner and looked into the bedroom, they immediately saw Donna's nude body lying on the bed. There was no sign of life from Donna, and on the floor they spied two feet sticking out from beneath a blanket. Appalled by what they had seen so far, they didn't investigate any further but exited the mobile home and called the police.

The first officer on scene was M. Stevenson, and as soon as he entered the mobile home, he smelled a very foul odor. Stevenson went toward the back of the mobile home, looked through a bedroom doorway and immediately spied the body of a nude female lying on her back upon a bed. Her hands were tied behind her back, and even from the distance of the doorway, he could tell that her throat had been slashed with a great deal of blood around her neck area.

About that same time Stevenson's "ride-along," Steve Jones, entered the mobile home and briefly looked at the crime scene. He returned outside to speak with the dead female's mother, who told him that she had last spoken with her daughter Donna Ferguson on July 16, at about 4:30 P.M. According to Debra Adams, her daughter had not indicated any trouble in her relationship with Todd Rudiger.

Next on the scene was Officer Limgues, who noted that the female victim had a gag in her mouth, as well as having her hands tied behind her back. The area soon started filling up with Portland police officers, including Officers Wong, De Long and Tellis. Officer Preston Wong, like the others, did not touch the bodies while waiting for detectives to arrive, but he did look inside a purse within the mobile home and noted that there was no money present. The air-conditioning was on and an alarm clock buzzer in the bedroom was constantly sounding. All of the officers went outside the mobile home at that point, and Officer Wong secured the scene. He spoke with Todd Rudiger's father, Ed, and learned that Mr. Rudiger had discovered that the back door was still locked when he broke in. Other than that way or the front door, there were no other entrances to the mobile home.

Portland Police Department (PPD) detective Larry Findling was notified at home, around 5:00 P.M., that there was a double homicide at a mobile home park on Flavel Street. He arrived on scene about 5:30 P.M. and spoke briefly with Detectives Don Lind and George Young, who were already there. They clued in Findling about the victims and their parents. At that point Findling called for a couple of criminalists, Stan Sterba and P. Bojinoff, to come to the area. Detective Findling also told Detectives Lind and Young to start canvassing the neighborhood area, seeking information from anyone who had noticed anything suspicious, and to get more information about Todd Rudiger and Donna Ferguson and their habits.

Detective Findling learned that Todd had spoken with his father at about 5:00 P.M. on July 17, and everything had seemed fine. Findling learned that Todd's father had come back from the Oregon coast to the area on Sunday night, around midnight, and Donna Ferguson's mother had come by on Monday morning to see Ed because she was worried about Donna. Ed Rudiger Sr. told

Detective Findling about meeting Donna's parents outside the mobile home, and he and Donna's stepfather
had decided to break into the mobile home, only to find
Donna and Todd deceased.

Ed Rudiger Sr. added that two months previously his
son had said that someone had threatened him at his job
at the Safeway store, where he worked. In fact, Todd had
become so concerned over the incident, he transferred
from the store on Thirty-ninth and Powell to a store at
Eighty-second and Foster. Then Ed added, "But Todd
tended to blow things out of proportion."

Detective Findling spoke with Donna's mother and
learned that she had last seen Donna on July 16. Debra
Adams said that Donna didn't use drugs or have any
gambling debts, and she knew of no enemies that Donna
had. Adams related that Donna had seemed happy
during the month of July. Donna had told her that she
and Todd were planning on getting married and wanted
to build a house in Lincoln City on the Oregon coast.
Donna had not spoken to her of any trouble that Todd
was having at the mobile home park or at work.

Detective Findling next spoke with Todd's brother, Ed
Rudiger Jr., who said that he'd last seen Todd on July 16 at
a work site. In relation to that job, Ed Jr. added something
very interesting. He said that there had been some kind of
trouble on the work site, and Todd had phoned him later
that night of July 16, saying, "I have a friend who is a gang
member, and he can beat up anyone who has problems at
the work site." Todd's brother added that Todd tended to
exaggerate things. Despite that addition, the brother
noted that Todd did have a bad temper, and he would
scream and yell at him at times. As far as ever hitting
Donna, however, Ed Jr. said that had never happened.

Because of this "work site angle," Detective Findling
contacted Michael Woods, a man who had also been
working at the job site. Woods said that Donna had
picked Todd up there at about 4:00 or 5:00 P.M. on July
16. Just before leaving, Todd had asked Woods if he

wanted to come over to the mobile home to have a beer. Woods declined. Just like Ed Rudiger Jr. had said, Woods added that he didn't know of any problems between Donna and Todd.

Because of all the police activity around the mobile home, a small crowd of other tenants had started to form. While Officer Wong was speaking with Ed Rudiger Jr., one unidentified young man rode up on a bike and made a remark in a loud voice about Todd killing himself. Then this man snickered.

Ed Rudiger Jr. became so incensed, he ran over and knocked the man off his bike. This person took off, but Ed Jr. would not calm down, and he was eventually handcuffed by Officer Wong and Sergeant Foxworth. He was taken to a patrol car, removed from the area, and Ed Jr. eventually told officers he just wanted to go home. Swearing that he would behave himself, Ed Jr. was released to his wife and they indeed went home. The person who had made the comment about Todd killing himself was not seen again by Ed Jr. or the officers.

Criminalist Bojinoff arrived at Todd and Donna's mobile home with his kit and began fingerprint dusting both doors and four windows. He dusted an end table in the living room, a wristwatch, drinking glasses, a remote control, cordless phone and television set. He also dusted an aquarium, framed photograph, CD player and a pack of cigarettes, all of which were found in the living room. In the bedroom he dusted for prints on two tables, a Mickey Mouse phone, radio alarm clock, mirror, two pairs of eyeglasses and a prescription bottle. Bojinoff seized sheets from the bed, pillows, blankets, blue jeans, shorts, a white polo shirt, men's jockey shorts, cigarette packs and cigarette butts. He also collected bottles and cans from a trash bin.

On the same evening Detectives Findling and Connie Veenker went to the Safeway store on Eighty-second

Avenue, where Todd had worked, and spoke with Patty Brose, Todd's coworker. Brose had last seen Todd at work on July 15. At the time Todd had brought up something about sex and bondage, but she said he was just kidding. Brose added that Todd had told her that when he and Donna got married, they were going to do so in the Portland Rose Garden.

At 9:00 A.M., on July 21, 1992, Dr. Larry Lewman began an autopsy on the body of Donna Ferguson. He noted certain things even before he touched her body, such as a gag made of her underwear and secured with a pink sash-type cloth from a bathrobe placed in her mouth. Donna's wrists were bound with multiple loops of cord, and her ankles were bound with multiple loops of cord. The bathrobe sash was knotted posterior to her neck and had become partially entangled in her hair. The green bikini-type underwear in Donna's mouth was soaked with blood.

Donna's hands had been tied behind her back at the wrists with several loops of telephone cord. The cord on the left wrist had been looped nine times, and the cord on the right wrist eight times. Her ankles were also bound with telephone cord, the right ankle six times and the left ankle five times. One end of the cord had been cut, but the other end still had a plug.

Donna's hair was curly and brown, worn shoulder-length, and her eyes were brown. There were no scars on her abdomen or breasts, and there were no contusions or abrasions to her external genitalia. Donna's pubic hair was combed by criminalist Stan Sterba. A rape kit was used and two slides presented to Sterba as well.

There was a large amount of blood around the neck area that had run down upon her chest and soaked her hair, sheets and pillowcase beneath her head. Cleaning the blood away, Dr. Lewman noted a stab-incised wound to the right anterior of the neck. It was about 2⅜ inches in length, and the margin had a sharp edge with no satellite cuts. There was an exiting wound to the left posterior of the neck, meaning the knife blade had gone all the way through Donna's neck. Dr. Lewman tracked the wound length at 5½ inches. He noted in his report that this wound *completely transects the right carotid artery and jugular vein.* He noted cause of death as *a stab wound to neck with exsanguination.*

Todd Rudiger's autopsy began at 11:15 A.M. by Dr. Lewman and he noted more stab wounds to Todd than had been inflicted upon Donna. There was a stab wound to the right anterior neck, which caused a perforation of the right internal carotid artery, jugular vein and oral airway. There was a stab wound to the right temple scalp area, which perforated the skull and penetrated the brain. There was also a stab wound of the left posterior of the neck, which cut into soft tissue and muscle. The cause of death for Todd Rudiger was listed in the report as *stab wounds to neck which caused exsanguination.*

In the course of the investigation, Detective Findling discovered that one of Todd's ATM cards had been stolen, and apparently an unauthorized person had tried using it at an ATM machine in the Portland area. This person had tried using it at 8:38, 8:40, 8:41, 9:51 and 9:52 P.M. on July 17. All of the requests for $300 in cash had been denied. Unfortunately for detectives, this was an ATM machine that did not have a camera.

Detective Findling started asking different neighbors and friends about Todd and Donna's last-known movements. Rhonda Recknagle, who had been a neighbor of Todd and Donna's, said that on the night of Friday, July 17, a man named Brent Good had been at her apartment from around ten until midnight. Then three days later, on July 20, even before the bodies had been discovered, according to Recknagle, Brent had phoned her to say that Todd was missing, "and everyone was saying he was murdered." Brent then told Recknagle, "Maybe they are on the floor there, murdered." This really made the detectives' ears perk up, because, of course, Todd's body had been found on the floor. Brent added that he'd had a key to Todd's mobile home, but it didn't work anymore because Donna had changed the locks. The topic of Todd also talking about some black gang member with a large Rottweiler came up.

After these revelations about Brent Good, someone named Robert Taylor contacted detectives and said that Good had assaulted him a week earlier with a knife and had threatened to "cut [him] up!" Taylor said he had reported this incident to the police.

Since the attempted ATM withdrawals by an unknown person who had Todd's ATM card was a good lead, detectives started following that trail. They contacted a man named Ronald Prepchuck who had made a withdrawal with his card at the machine around that same time as the mystery person on July 17. Prepchuck, however, had not seen any other people at the machine. Thomas Trices-Martinez was contacted, and he recalled a black male, about twenty-one years old and five-eight, at the machine when he was there. Cindy Wilkins and Carol Hanson said they didn't see anyone when they had used the machine. It wasn't until the detectives spoke with Jan Beck that they got another possible lead. She spoke of a short woman, with brown hair, standing behind her in line. The woman was about five feet three inches tall, but that was all Beck could recall.

Michael Birnbaum was the initial person to use the machine after the first attempt of someone using Todd Rudiger's ATM card. Birnbaum said there had been an Asian man using the machine just before him. The Asian man then walked away with his wife, or at least a person Birnbaum thought was his wife.

John Harrington, Donna's principal at David Douglas High School, was contacted and told the detectives that Donna had been a good student and he'd never had any problems with her. Things went along in this vein until what appeared to be a very good lead surfaced from a man named Jason Burgess.

On July 22, Burgess was painting an apartment building on SE Courtney, at around 4:00 P.M., when he overheard two females talking in a room of the apartment building. He could hear their voices, because the window was open. Female number one, according to Burgess, said something about Flavel Street, and then added, "I think we should . . ."

"No, no, no!" female number two answered.

"If he killed them, do you think they are the same people?" female number one asked.

"Yes!" the second female replied.

According to Burgess, the girls then went to a car and got a newspaper out of the car and looked at it for a moment. Then female number one spoke of a man named Leo, who might be responsible for the murder.

Burgess said that female number one was about five-five, with long blond hair, about nineteen years old, and weighed approximately 130 pounds. Female number two was Hispanic, about five-six, weighed around 130 pounds, and was eighteen or nineteen years old. They soon left in a primer-gray Mustang, and Burgess was so intrigued by their conversation that he wrote down their license plate number and gave that to the detectives.

Detectives Findling and Veenker went to the 2300 block of SE Courtney and discovered a primer-gray Mustang parked in the apartment lot. They knocked on the door of the apartment connected to the Mustang, and a middle-aged Hispanic woman answered. They asked whom the Mustang belonged to, and she indicated that it was owned by a man named Deon Kishpaugh. Kishpaugh apparently was there at the time, because he and the detectives walked out to the vehicle, and Kishpaugh asked them what this was all about. Detective Findling answered that the vehicle may have been connected to a crime, and asked Kishpaugh where he'd been in the last four days.

Kishpaugh answered that he worked at a Wendy's on

McLoughlin Street until about midnight on July 16. He'd then gone to a place on Holgate, where he spent the night with a friend. On Friday, July 17, he was at the apartment building on Courtney until about 1:30 A.M., and at some point he slept in his car.

Detective Findling told Kishpaugh that he wanted to speak with his girlfriend to corroborate the story. Stacy Harrison came outside and spoke with the detectives, and Findling advised her that someone had overheard her recently talking about a homicide, and asked what she'd been talking about. Harrison answered she was talking about someone who was Laura Donnelly's boyfriend. The guy's name was "Merle something" and she advised the detectives that Merle had supposedly told Donnelly that "I killed a dope dealer by shooting him in northeast Portland." Harrison said that Kishpaugh was also aware of this story.

The detectives next spoke with Laura Donnelly, who said that Merle had called her and told her that he had shot a dope dealer in northeast Portland, and he was with friends when he did it. He said he'd gone to get some dope and the dealer tried to "short him, so [he] shot the guy." Supposedly, someone named Jerry had taken Merle to the address where he'd shot the guy. Jerry drove a yellow car. Donnelly added that Merle was a white male, with short, dark hair, and he worked at the Wendy's on Gladstone. She added, "Merle deals all kinds of dope."

Detective Findling contacted Deon Kishpaugh once again, and Kishpaugh told Findling that the Jerry in question did drive a yellow Chevy Nova that had a dent in the rear. The yellow car and Jerry remained elusive, however.

Returning to the area of Seventy-second and Flavel, Detectives Findling and Veenker started doing a neighborhood canvass once again. A person named Jeff Sutherland contacted the detectives and said that he'd been Todd's roommate until he'd moved out in January 1992. Jeff hadn't seen much of Todd recently, but he did go to the mobile home that Todd and Donna now shared, on

July 17, at around 3:00 P.M. Donna had been out at the time, doing errands. Jeff and Todd had talked about having a barbecue at a later date, and "Todd seemed fine. He was happier than I'd ever seen him before. He talked about getting married, and didn't seemed worried about anything. He didn't mention anyone threatening him."

Jeff told the detectives that during the time he lived with Todd, Todd had never done any narcotics. In fact, Todd had told Jeff that he'd moved up to Oregon from California to get away from drugs. As far as Jeff knew, Todd didn't keep much money in the mobile home or hide valuables there. Jeff did recall, however, someone named Bobby threatening Todd in the late summer of 1991, but he believed that Todd and Bobby had eventually ironed things out.

The detectives spoke with Ed Rudiger Sr. again, and he told the detectives they could "keep the trailer, and search it as much as you like." An alarm was installed in the mobile home to prohibit anyone from entering into it undetected. During new searches the detectives recovered phone message tapes and jewelry. They also noticed that the back door had a dead bolt lock and it had not been thrown, which indicated no one went out the back way. So the killer must have gone out the front way after killing Todd and Donna. The storage shed in back of the mobile home was searched, but no evidentiary value was found.

Jewelry from the mobile home that was still there was taken to Debra Adams, Donna's mother. These included two bracelets, a gold chain, a gold chain with a cross, two gold earrings, and a heart-shaped pin. Debra told the detectives that Donna had some other jewelry that was given to her by her grandmother, and that it was now missing.

The detectives contacted Donna's grandmother Yetta Deem, and she described an amethyst necklace that she had given Donna. Yetta also said there were amethyst earrings that matched the necklace. Besides these, Yetta had given Donna a rhinestone choker necklace with a silver clasp, and it was nearly one hundred years old.

Yetta wanted to know if the detectives had found a glass rose in a small silver vase, which she'd given Donna for her high-school graduation. The detectives said they hadn't, and Yetta responded that her brother had made the rose and had handcrafted the silver vase. While looking at a videotape of a recent birthday party, the detectives were able to see the amethyst necklace on Donna's neck. Eventually the detectives turned over all this information to the police Pawn Shop Detail to be on the look-out for the missing items.

Acting upon new information from Donna's sister, Delani, Detective Findling spoke with a man named Gary. Delani had told Findling that this Gary phoned her on her birthday, and had told her he hated Todd and was going to kill him. When confronted with this, Gary told Findling that he had called Delani on her birthday, said he didn't like Todd, but he swore he had never said anything about killing him. Findling then spoke with Gary's father and stepmother, and they recalled that Gary had been home on the evening that the detectives now thought Donna and Todd had been murdered. Findling also added one more cryptic statement to his report about this: *It appears that Gary would not be physically capable of inflicting those injuries on Donna and Todd.* As to why he wrote that is not evident from the rest of the report.

Rachelle Robbins, Donna's cousin, contacted Findling from California, and she stated that she'd spent time with Donna from June 15 to June 23. She also recounted that she'd gone to a party over at a house in Beaverton, Oregon, which was owned by someone with the nickname of Silky. According to Rachelle, this Silky and Donna had gone to school together at David Douglas High School. Rachelle then said that someone named Tony was at that party and was very angry with Donna because "Donna no longer liked him." It had gotten so bad at the party, Donna and Tony had been yelling at each other, according to Rachelle.

Now it got even murkier. According to Rachelle Robbins, "Donna had a relationship with Silky even while she was with Todd. Also, Tony really liked Donna, but she didn't like him anymore. She had told me that Tony was too into alcohol and drugs." To make matters even darker, Donna had told Rachelle that Todd was having trouble at work with someone.

Meanwhile, at the mobile home park, a woman named Dorothy Banister, who lived not far from Todd and Donna's residence, said she heard a car start near the mobile home and drive away at a high rate of speed around the time of the murders. Another tenant, Kenneth Thurston, said he had talked to Todd on Thursday, July 16, and Todd was going to come over to mow his lawn, but he never did. However, another tenant in a space on the 30 row told the detectives that Todd had mowed his lawn in the early afternoon of Friday, July 17.

Fern Taylor, who lived two spaces away from Todd and Donna, recalled that their front shades had been drawn on Saturday, July 18, and Sunday, July 19, and Todd and Donna never did that for two days running. Other neighbors also remembered suspicious vehicles around Todd and Donna's place. Claire Olson recalled a large mustard yellowish car slowly driving by Todd's mobile home early one morning before he was murdered.

One of Donna's closest friends, Tessalie Brault, contacted the detectives and said she was receiving strange phone calls and they had only begun after she contacted Donna Ferguson on July 17 and had left her new phone number on the answering machine. The detectives had the telephone company put a trace out on these calls.

Carlyn Robbins spoke with the detectives and said that she had been with a psychic, who lived in Fresno, California. In the psychic's vision, three men had overpowered Todd, and these men had gone to Todd's high school. The psychic added that keys to the Safeway store were stolen, along with Todd's wallet and Donna's purse. Silver was a key element in the case, and a girl who had warned Donna *not* to move in with Todd knew more than she was saying. Just who this girl was, was not revealed. The detectives took this with a grain of salt, but nothing was being dismissed at this point.

It wasn't until September 8, 1992, that the detectives released the crime scene back to the care of Ed Rudiger Sr. Debra Adams and Vicky Johnson, Todd's mother, were also present. Detective Findling told them that there was a rumor going around that Todd had been involved in drug use and dealing, and he asked them to be on the lookout for any drug paraphernalia, drugs or hidden money. If they discovered any of those items, they were to contact him immediately.

All the parents wanted to start a reward fund for information regarding the murders. Detective Findling discouraged this action, but they were determined to set up a reward fund, anyway. Findling attempted to draw up an agreement where he would be involved in the decisions regarding the disbursement of funds for pertinent and provable information. He said that it was understood that funds would be collected before any reward amount was posted. However, before this went into effect, Vicky Johnson and Debra Adams began distributing 1,500 flyers about the reward fund. When Detective Findling contacted them about this, they admitted they didn't have any money in the reward fund at the present time, but if someone was arrested, they could raise the money to cover the fund. Detective Findling told them that neither he nor the police department would be involved any longer with a reward fund, and that they would have to do this on their own.

By October 1992, new information came in as well. Someone contacted Detective Findling and said that a man named Jerry Allen, who worked at a gas station near the Safeway store where Todd had worked, knew about a fight between someone named Floyd and Todd just a few days before the murders. This informant said that Allen had actually witnessed the fight. When Jerry Allen was contacted, however, he told Findling that the only person named Floyd whom he knew had quit working at the gas station in June 1992, and he knew nothing about any fight between Todd Rudiger and another man at or near the gas station.

Jeff Sutherland came to the Detective Division and once again told the detectives that in the fall of 1990, he had met Todd Rudiger at the Safeway store at SE Thirty-ninth and Powell. He became a coworker with Todd for about a year, and according to Sutherland, Todd had told him, "I came to Oregon to get away from the fast life in California." Sutherland added that Todd had said to him that he'd worked for the Marriott Corporation in California, and used to do cocaine there. Todd also intimated that he'd gotten into debt down in southern California.

Sutherland moved in with Todd in August 1991, and by then, Todd was no longer doing drugs. Sutherland claimed that Todd was a real penny-pincher and did not go out a lot. Asked if he and Todd had ever gotten into an argument, Sutherland said only once and it wasn't a big deal. Sutherland also noted that Todd always locked the doors of his mobile home and was very concerned about that, to the point of paranoia. On one occasion Sutherland had not locked a sliding door on the mobile home, and when Todd found out, he became very upset with Sutherland. Sutherland said that if anyone knocked at the door, Todd would always look out through the window first before opening it.

Sutherland recalled that when he first moved in, Todd wasn't dating anyone, but later on he began to date a girl named Heather. Sutherland believed that Todd was the one who broke up with Heather. Sutherland added that when Todd and Donna got together, he realized that Donna would be moving in with Todd after she graduated from high school, and that the mobile home would be cramped. Sutherland said that he didn't know Donna very well, but she seemed very sensible for someone her age. Todd had told Sutherland that he really liked Donna, that she was a sweet girl, and that he wanted to settle down with her.

Once he moved out, Sutherland didn't see Todd very often, but they kept in contact by phone every two or three weeks. On July 17, Sutherland had gone over to Todd's mobile home at about 3:00 P.M., and as he already told the detectives, stayed for a half hour. Todd was the only one at the mobile home at the time, because Donna had taken the Jeep and was doing errands. Sutherland and Todd sat at the living-room table, and Todd seemed very happy, saying that he was engaged to Donna. They talked about Todd's business plans and the possibility of Todd leaving Safeway. Todd was only working there about twenty-four hours a week and not making much money. Sutherland believed that Todd was supposed to go into work that night, but that didn't happen. When asked if Todd was good about calling Safeway if he wouldn't show up, Sutherland said that he was.

When asked about Todd's personal habits, Sutherland said that if Todd knew people well enough, he would just wear boxer shorts around the mobile home. Sutherland couldn't think of any reason why Todd had been killed. He wasn't aware of Todd dealing any drugs or owing anyone a large sum of money. To see if Sutherland was telling the truth about all of this, he was scheduled for a polygraph test on November 16, and he apparently passed the test.

The psychic business was still going strong as well. Because Todd and Donna's pet cat had been taken in by Todd's parents, the cat was given to a psychic named Beatrice Lydecker, who "read animals." After "reading" the cat, Lydecker informed Detective Findling that "there was a lot of arguing and fighting and that hands were tied behind backs. Todd opened the door and a guy pushed his way in." She described the suspect as a tall, dark-skinned man, about six-two or six-three, with fine features, wearing a jean jacket. She related that Todd tried to get the intruder out of the mobile home, but the man was strong. The person hit Todd and killed him right away, while Donna was still alive. He then tied up Donna, looked through things in the mobile home and then killed Donna. Lydecker said that Donna died instantly.

From psychics to vehicles, the detectives next looked into the history of Todd's Jeep and several interesting things appeared. It was determined that on December 3, 1991, Todd had traded in a Buick Century for the Jeep. Todd had agreed to make some payments on the Jeep, but he defaulted on the payments because he was not satisfied with its performance. The salesperson who had sold Todd the Jeep was a guy named Greg, and Greg had once worked with Todd at a car dealership. Greg said that Todd seemed to be happy with the Jeep at the time of sale. When Todd bounced a check on the Jeep, the matter was turned over to a collection agency.

The sales dealership told the detectives that Todd had originally paid some money for the Jeep in installments, but then he bounced the last check. When the dealership tried to reprocess the check, Todd put a stop payment on it. That's when the collection agency had become involved.

So did Jeff Sutherland—once again. It turned out that Sutherland's dad worked for a bonded credit agency (apparently not the one that was trying to collect money from Todd on the Jeep). Todd spoke with Jeff's dad about the situation and complained that the Jeep was a lemon. Todd said there were problems with the transmission and the power windows, and he refused to make any more payments until the dealership fixed these problems.

While the stories about the Jeep percolated along, the detectives contacted the Safeway on Eighty-second

Avenue once again about Todd. Mike Sept, who was store manager during the time Todd worked there, said there were no sexual harassment charges filed against Todd at the Eighty-second store, as one rumor had it. Nor did he know of any drug problems on Todd's part. However, someone named Ken was mentioned in connection with Donna having made a sexual harassment claim against him at one point.

The detectives were able to trace Ken, and discovered he worked at a Vancouver-area Safeway. On July 17, 1992, the probable date of the murders, Ken worked from 11:00 P.M. until 8:00 A.M., and wasn't there from 1:00 P.M. until 2:00 A.M. the next day. Checking even further, the detectives discovered a letter from Donna to the Safeway management dated March 10, 1992, alleging sexual harassment by this Ken. According to Mike Sept, Ken then transferred to the Vancouver store, but it was a routine change and not because of any proof of sexual harassment. Ken was later able to prove to them that he had a viable alibi for the time in question.

The detectives spoke with Wade Robertson, who had been Donna's boyfriend in late 1991 and early 1992. Wade had first seen Donna while she was staying at an apartment on SE Powell Street and then had seen her at a party around November or December 1991. According to Wade, he and Donna started dating, and he would stay at her apartment on different occasions. Wade said they were boyfriend and girlfriend for only about a month, and he told her it wasn't working out. Wade described Donna as a sweet girl who was sensitive. He did admit she smoked marijuana on occasion, but she didn't use any stronger drugs. Wade also said he had never been to the mobile home park where Todd and Donna lived, and he only learned of her death through his girlfriend.

Dan Klettke was contacted, and he said that during a period of time in 1991, he called Todd between six and ten times, because he was trying to have a man named Bobby Hammond arrested on warrants. Klettke said that Hammond had threatened him, his daughter Regina, and his son, as well as Todd. Klettke was trying to have Hammond arrested.

Regina Klettke told the detectives she cleaned house for Todd for about four weeks at some apartments where Todd had lived. Regina declared that Todd told her that he had been threatened by Bobby Hammond and that "this thing was getting out of hand." According to Regina, Todd told her, "Bobby knows where I live, and he could hurt me or you!" Then Todd added that he didn't want her to clean his place anymore. Just what all the trouble was about, she didn't say. All of this had occurred in the summer of 1991.

Tantalizing clues kept surfacing, but nothing concrete, and the detectives took the step of phoning people listed in Todd Rudiger's personal telephone directory. As Findling's report noted: *An attempt was made to contact everyone in that directory regarding their contact with Todd and to see if they had any information about his homicide.*

Ray Burns was contacted in Palm Springs, and said that he'd dated Todd's mother, but he hadn't seen Todd for two years, and had no idea why someone would want to kill him. Shelly Crabtree replied that she'd known Todd a long time ago, and had met him at a church camp. She, too, had no idea why he had been murdered. Annette Hanson worked for the Chamberlain Insurance Company and spoke of Todd as a "sweet guy"; as did Marcia Drew, who added, "He seemed to be happy-go-lucky." Corinne Gibson, on the other hand, had worked with Todd, and said he was not "a personable person." Tim Won, who worked with Todd at the Thirty-ninth and Powell Safeway, also took up this theme. He called Todd "a loner."

Michelle Grimm had actually dated Todd in Portland, Oregon, in 1990, and knew of no drug usage on his part. Andre Washington stated he had last seen Todd about a month before he was murdered, and Todd seemed very happy to be getting married. They drank a few beers, and Todd had told Andre that he used to do cocaine in California when he was younger, but he'd given it up.

This angle of drug use in California had the detectives contacting people who had known Todd down in Palm Springs. Brian Tuggle had some interesting stories to tell. He said that Todd was a "nice kid, but troubled." Tuggle had let Todd live in his house for one month and said, "Todd had a hard life growing up." According to Tuggle, Todd had told him that Todd's uncle had beat him when he was younger. During the time at Tuggle's house, there had been no problems, and Todd moved out within a month. Apparently, he moved away to Oregon, and then out of the blue, Tuggle got a phone call from Todd in 1992. Todd said he was happy and had quit the drug lifestyle in which he'd been involved.

Sue Richardson had worked with Todd in Palm Springs, and also called him a nice guy. She added that "he had a tendency to piss some people off, though." Tracy Lyneis had dated Todd in the Palm Springs area in 1987, and she spoke of a motorcycle accident he had been involved in. Tracing this motorcycle connection back to Oregon, they found Cindy Harris, who had dated Todd in Oregon. She said that "after his motorcycle accident, he was not tactful. He would go too far in his humor. I last saw him in the summer of 1991, and he could be irritating. He was a big talker."

B. J. Worzack was contacted and responded that Todd had lived with him for a while, but Worzack ended up "booting him out." Worzack said, "He was lazy around the house, and always sleepy." Worzack did admit this might have been due to Todd working such strange hours.

Switching over to people who had known Donna Ferguson, the detectives contacted Chad Lanning. He had known Donna at David Douglas High School and had seen her at a party, but he had no idea who someone named Silky might be. Brian Luggerway also knew Donna from high school, and he'd heard a rumor that her death was drug-related, and someone named Jason was involved.

Delani Ferguson, Donna's sister, spoke to the detectives and said of Donna that "she was quiet and reserved—someone with low self-esteem and smoked pot. Donna changed when she started going with Todd." Delani also told the detectives that when the mobile home was released back to the Rudigers, she went inside and noticed that some of Donna's clothing seemed to be missing. These items included an Eddie Bauer–type pair of khaki pants, a pink polo pullover and two tweed sweaters.

The first new lead, for a while, that looked promising came from Patrick Pen-Martinez. According to Martinez, he had been sitting in his living room with Brent Good and Bill Selleck when Patrick got a phone call from his cousin, and the conversation, according to the police report, was *about getting 28 months in the penitentiary.* Just who got the twenty-eight months was not noted. After that conversation was over, Patrick started talking about some gang shootings. Brent Good stood up, looked at Bill Selleck and said, "I'll tell ya how I took this one shithead out! I stabbed him a lot of times, hammered on the guy with a knife!"

Patrick said to Brent, "Oh, bullshit!"

Selleck, however, turned to Patrick and said, "No, man. Straight up, it's true!"

According to Patrick, Brent Good added, "I was over there visiting, and the guy and the girl were arguing. So I went over to the kitchen, got a butcher knife, and started stabbing this guy, and the guy fell over something. I turned back and looked at the girl, because I thought she'd love me for it. But she freaked out and I had to take her out too!" According to Martinez, Good's next remark may have meant that he raped her as well: "I got mine from that bitch!"

Patrick started to ask Good how many times he had stabbed the guy, but Patrick's wife called him from the kitchen and said, "Get him out of here!" because she had overheard the conversation. Brent came in and told her that he was sorry she'd overheard the conversation, because he didn't know she was there. And then he left.

Brent Good was asked to take a polygraph test about the Rudiger/Ferguson murders, and he passed. Not only that, he asked for his blood to be drawn to run a DNA test, proving he didn't rape or kill at the Rudiger/ Ferguson mobile home. Eventually the DNA test proved that semen recovered from Donna Ferguson's body did *not* match that of Brent Good.

And so it went, one clue leading into another, and going around and around in circles. Henry Yoder contacted the detectives because he said he knew a security guard who had seen a blond man standing over a woman named Helen at a nearby mobile home park. The man had been carrying a knife. Supposedly, this had happened on the same afternoon that Donna Ferguson and Todd Rudiger were murdered.

The Rudiger family somehow got new information from someone named Scott, who had supposedly met with another person who knew about the murder. When the detectives contacted Scott, he was reluctant to talk about what he'd heard, but eventually said that on Super Bowl Sunday, he'd been talking to a guy named Les. Les said that some people had ripped him off of a quarter gram of dope and he'd had them killed. Les described the people killed as "the manager of a trailer park and his wife." Todd and Donna were not managers of a trailer park, but Todd's grandmother had been. Not only that, Todd sometimes told people he was the manager of the mobile home park, even though he wasn't. Scott described Les as a white male, with gray-streaked hair, six feet tall, weighing about 180 pounds, and had a two-inch beard. Even though the detectives tried finding this Les, they came up empty.

* * *

By March 1993, the detectives were once again reduced to taking information from psychics. One psychic named Karen Miller advised them that she'd had a dream where Donna came to her. Donna told Miller that she'd been on a bus and met a white male in his forties, with shoulder-length gray hair and a full gray beard. He also wore glasses. He was a big guy, about six feet tall, and chubby. This person was on a platform with Donna and two other people, and they were all cordial to one another. Then things changed, and in the dream Donna told Miller that the guy with the beard and glasses was the one who had killed her and Todd. It remained to be seen, however, if Karen Miller or any of the other psychics were right about the description of the person who had murdered Todd Rudiger and Donna Ferguson.

2

"My Life Will Never Be the Same"

By the spring of 1993, the families of Todd Rudiger and Donna Ferguson had raised reward money in the amount of $20,000 for information on the double slaying. Debra Adams, Donna's mother, told a reporter, "Somebody knows what happened, and I'm basically pleading with them. I know they are afraid they are going to be knifed or get a bullet in the head, or whatever, but I'm pleading with them. If my daughter had been killed in a car accident, I could deal with it. But this way, not knowing—well, if I knew, it would be one hundred thousand times better."

Because of all the stress from the murder, Debra Adams no longer worked as a radiographer, a job she'd had for six years. She did draw strength from Donna's sister and five-year-old brother. Adams then added how it had changed all their lives, and her five-year-old spoke of getting the "bad guys who did it." He also brought up his fears, saying, "Nobody can get us. We have alarms and we have guns."

This issue of safety and crime often haunted Debra Adams, who, as a single mother, had raised Donna for five years in the Los Angeles area of California. Adams said, "I wanted to move out of L.A. to get away from crime. Isn't that a joke? There's crime everywhere and you can't get away from it!"

Ed Rudiger Sr., Todd's dad, spoke of Donna in glowing terms and said, "I could have looked for a thousand years and could never have met anybody more perfect for Todd than her. She was the sweetest thing. They were so content. Completely happy. When we didn't hear from them that weekend, we hoped they had hopped on a plane and went someplace to elope. They had a wedding date of July 17, 1993, exactly a year to the day from the date that they were murdered."

Todd Rudiger's mother, Vicky Johnson, also spoke with a reporter, and noted, "It's surprising to me how this ricochets through the whole family. The murderer moves into your home. That person moves into your family, into your life, and every day is spent trying to cope with that person." Then she added something that was a lot closer to the mark than she knew at the time. "I would bet that the person who killed Todd didn't know him well. I don't think anyone who knew him would kill him."

As far as newspapers of the area went, the detectives had told them some of the facts about the case, and withheld other information. For instance, the newspapers reported that Donna had been found naked, sexually assaulted and her hands tied behind her back, all of which was true. What was used to tie her hands, however, was withheld. Todd Rudiger was reported to have been lying on the floor beside the bed in a position that made it hard at first to tell who it was. Information was not released whether he was clothed or if he had been tied up as Donna had been. It was reported that $100 in cash was missing from a wallet, driver's licenses stolen and credit cards as well. A one-of-a-kind purple amethyst necklace was missing and matching earrings. Left in the mobile home were a televison set, VCR and stereo. The mobile home had not been ransacked.

By the six-month anniversary of the crime, the Portland *Oregonian* noted that detectives had questioned three hundred people, given lie detector tests to a dozen people, tested the blood of six persons, and the casebook had grown into multiple case binders, each one six inches thick. Detective Findling told a reporter, "It is the most baffling and frustrating case I've worked on in my years in homicide. This case is killing me. I have come up with a thousand different scenarios. Which one of them is right? Are any of them right? I have no idea."

The detectives were wading through Rudiger and Ferguson's financial statements, anything they'd ever written. They talked to friends of friends of the couple. Even false leads came in, such as a coworker of Rudiger's who said that he had seen Todd and Donna in Rudiger's Jeep between 7:15 and 7:30 P.M. on July 17 at a stoplight. According to this person, Todd and Donna had waved, and "everything seemed fine." Of course, by 7:15 P.M., they were already dead.

Donna's parents advised that she had been getting crank phone calls a few weeks before she was murdered. At first, the caller would call and hang up. Later a female caller would get through to Donna and yell and curse incoherently. Who this person was, Donna didn't know.

One Crime Stoppers caller had an intriguing story to tell as well. It seemed that her husband had picked up a hitchhiker in the Columbia River Gorge about two weeks after the murders, and the hitchhiker said he was on his way to Montana and only had $14, but he had an amethyst necklace. The hitchhiker offered to sell the necklace to the driver, but he didn't want it and never asked to see it. The driver dropped the hitchhiker off in Cascade Locks, about thirty miles from Portland. He described the hitchhiker as a young man, about five-seven and weighing 150 pounds.

Also intriguing was the woman who had been at the ATM machine at the Lloyd Center Cinema right around the time that Todd Rudiger's ATM card had been used by someone there on July 17. This woman described the person behind her as a short woman who stood about five-four. The detectives dismissed this woman as the killer of Todd and Donna because of her size and the fact that a rape had been involved. But they did wonder if she had any connection to a male killer. The detectives ran theories that up to three people had killed Donna and Todd, but they also admitted that one person with a gun could have overpowered them.

Detective Mike Stahlman, who was also working the case by now, later told a reporter, "We've gone through all other residential robberies/rapes since mid-May of 1992, and this thing was the only one of its kind. I wake up at three in the morning and think about this stuff. What's this mean? What's that mean? Did I read that or just think that? With all the paperwork we could be looking right at it and just haven't put it together." He admitted that it was all very baffling, but the next phone call could have someone on the line who said, "You know there's something I've been thinking about and . . ."

Detective Findling backed Stahlman up about this. "If I'm on the phone for the next week, twelve hours a day, with people giving me humbug crap, fine. Let me decide what's important and what isn't. It could be something we need."

The weeks turned into months, however, and the one essential lead that was "something the detectives needed" never came. By the advent of the one-year anniversary in July 1993, the capture of the killer of Todd Rudiger and Donna Ferguson was just as elusive as ever. By that point the detectives had interviewed over four hundred people, the homicide unit had found no evidence that either Todd or Donna were involved in drug dealing, all of the psychics had come up empty and the detectives couldn't say for sure if the Rudiger/Ferguson case was related to some others that were somewhat similar.

One case that did have some similarities was the Wheatley case in nearby Washington State. On August 29, 1988, sixty-one-year-old Robert Wheatley and sixty-nine-year-old Frieda Wheatley were discovered by a relative, days after they had been murdered. They were found in the basement of their home, strangled to death. A television set had been stolen, along with costume jewelry and credit cards. The person who had killed them managed to withdraw $200 per day for three days, using the Wheatleys' stolen ATM card.

The Wheatleys' car was also stolen and later found abandoned at Jantzen Beach on the coast. A car stolen from Sauvie Island on the day Todd and Donna were murdered was found parked in a lot near to where their mobile home park on Flavel Street was located. Another similarity was that there didn't seem to be much sense as to why the Wheatleys were killed, or why Todd Rudiger and Donna Ferguson had been as well. Detective Tom Nelson told a reporter, "If you just want to burglarize them, tie them up and gag them and leave. There's something else that we don't know. Something else is involved."

For the families of Todd Rudiger and Donna Ferguson, "the something else" was extremely frustrating. Donna's mother said, "I would be planning for my daughter's wedding now. It was to be a joyful time. My daughter was cheated out of her life, and my life will never be the same."

Debra Adams kept a scrapbook on her daughter and a collage of photos of Donna that measured three by five feet. The collage depicted a smiling dark-haired girl who washed and curled her grandmother's hair. Her grandmother had said of Donna, "She loved all old people, young people, dogs, cats and animals."

Todd's mom, Vicky Johnson, related, "I know I will

never get over it, and I will never accept it, but what I've learned to do is manage my feelings. I want to see justice. I want this to come to an end. It's an open chapter, and there's nothing shutting it off. Not knowing the answer, the motive, keeps things stirred up."

The families were still seeking help from psychics. In fact, by the one-year anniversary of the murders, they had been contacted by a dozen psychics. Perhaps the most famous one was Kebrina Kinkade, who was known nationally and had a (900) telephone number advertised on television. Kinkade had visions of a trio of hired gunmen who killed Todd and Donna. Kinkade told Todd's mother, "I want to set your soul at rest. Todd was guiltless. He threatened a drug dealer, and that's what did him in."

Yet, once again, Detective Findling told the press that he'd found no involvement by Todd or Donna in drug dealing. Even though Findling was skeptical of psychics, he didn't dismiss them totally. Findling said, "I'll check out any information anyone gives me. I'm waiting for them to bring me a name, though."

Seeking some kind of solace, Donna's mother joined a group called Parents of Murdered Children. She went to a national congress of that organization, which met in Portland; the title of their conference was, "Come Hold My Hand." It brought crime professionals and parents of murdered children together. The crime professionals included police detectives, court personnel and mental-health therapists.

At the conference Debra Adams spoke about the loss of her daughter, Donna, and the impact it had on her family. Her youngest son had to have counseling, and Adams said it was her faith in God that helped her carry on. Sitting next to Debra was a teenager who spoke of her friend who was stalked and murdered by a former employee. The teenager said that she couldn't comfort the victim's mother, and declared, "We need help!" Another mother of a victim shared how her son had been murdered by his best friend.

One of the panelists, Greg Kammann, a Portland Police Bureau chaplain, spoke of the organization as one of the few outlets that would constantly listen to the problems of the victim's loved ones. Kammann said, "Other people they had hoped would support them, abandon them fairly early. Family, friends, coworkers—nobody seems to understand or accept people who have been through it."

As 1993 went on, news items about Donna Ferguson and Todd Rudiger disappered from the local newspapers. The killer of Todd Rudiger and Donna Ferguson, however, was not through with his depredation of the Portland area. In 1995, he was agitated and in a murderous frame of mind once again. He even wrote in his diary, *I've been thinking about murder lately.* He began stalking a very attractive young college woman who lived near him. In fact, the woman he began stalking looked a lot like Donna Ferguson—just the type the killer liked.

3

The Survivor

Amanda Carpova was a pretty, dark-haired eighteen-year-old girl who lived in Portland and attended a local college. She was studying French philosophy at the university, as well as taking liberal arts courses. Not only a bright student, she danced in a local dance troupe as well, performing modern dance. She had been in performances with the Ballet of Oregon, American Dance Theater and Pacific Ballet Theater. She also played the flute and cello. Amanda worked at a local restaurant, the Bread and Ink Cafe, as a waitress, and was popular there. She had a boyfriend, Dan, who was about her age, and they often walked around the neighborhood, and once in a while, they had a few drinks and shot pool at a tavern named Claudia's, which was in the neighborhood.

Amanda lived in an apartment complex that was U-shaped, with three apartments on each side of the U, separated by a small garden. Each person entered his or her apartment from the center passageway. Sometime in the last week of May 1995, a young Asian man showed up at Amanda's front door and inquired about the FOR RENT sign out front. Amanda was studying for finals at the time, and she was curt with him, telling him he shouldn't bother the tenants but rather call the phone number listed on the sign. The Asian man agreed that he would do so and left without another word.

Later, probably on May 31, Amanda and her boyfriend were walking home in the late afternoon, down Thirty-seventh Avenue near Harrison. Their path took them right in front of Dorothy Connet's residence. Connet was a retired music teacher who had taught school from 1968 to 1993. She did a fair amount of yard work at her place on Thirty-seventh Avenue, and was aware of the pretty girl with dark hair who often walked by with her boyfriend. On that late May 1995 afternoon, Connet was painting the side of her porch. She happened to look up to see the dark-haired girl and her boyfriend coming up the sidewalk, talking and laughing. Connet recalled later, "I thought to myself, 'I wish I had that kind of relationship.' I had just moved to Portland and was lonely.

"Then I looked down the sidewalk and saw a young man following them. When they slowed up, he slowed up. They stopped abruptly near the corner, and he stopped abruptly. He was about fifty feet behind them, right in front of my house. And then he saw me. He went into a trance on me, and he looked right at me and stared. I raised my paintbrush and walked slowly back into the house, but he stayed frozen in a glaring trance on the same spot. I went into the house, locked the door and watched him.

"Up the street, the girl and her boyfriend split up. He went one way and she went the other. The young man in front of my house broke out of his trance and followed her. He went around the corner and turned her way."

Around 11:00 P.M. on May 31, 1995, several people who were sitting and watching television in an apartment in the same complex where Amanda Carpova lived were startled by a young Asian man peeking in the front window. When he spotted them, a sheepish grin spread across his face. He came to the door, claiming that he once knew a family who lived in the apartment complex and wondered if they still lived there. The people noted that the young Asian man was about five-seven or five-eight in height and they seemed to think he was Polynesian, Hawaiian or possibly a mix of Japanese and Caucasian. He seemed to weigh about two hundred pounds. When they said they didn't know anything about the family he was inquiring about, he left and headed back out toward the street. One of the women inside, who had dark hair, said later that he'd had a very weird stare when he looked at her. She wondered if the other people hadn't been there, would the young man have forced his way inside to rape her.

On the night of June 1, 1995, a former boyfriend of Amanda's named Adam Smith came to visit her and they talked and listened to music into the early-morning hours. They were only friends now, so Amanda went to her bedroom and Adam slept on the couch. The next morning Adam left for work and Amanda got out of bed sometime after Adam left and peeked out the window. There was a clear blue sky and the temperature promised to get up into the mid-80s by afternoon. Amanda's friend Maya lived across the courtyard in another apartment, and Amanda went over and asked if Maya wanted to go out to breakfast. Maya declined and Amanda went back to her own apartment and had breakfast there. Later, dressed only in underwear and a nightgown, she sat down on her sofa and began studying for an upcoming final. It was a warm morning and she kept her front door open. Normally, she would have locked the screen door, but Maya had come over with something after breakfast, and Amanda hadn't bothered latching the screen door.

While she was absorbed in her studies, a young Asian man wearing sunglasses suddenly walked right into her apartment and pointed a pistol at her. The stranger had a grin on his face, and he told Amanda not to scream or he would kill her. He closed the front door behind him and walked toward her. Once he closed the front door, it locked automatically. The intruder asked Amanda where her bedroom was, and when she indicated the direction, he told her to go in there. Then he followed her, telling her to do exactly as he said, or he would shoot her.

Once they were in her bedroom, the intruder told Amanda, "Take your clothes off!" With a gun pointed right at her, she did as she was told. Once she was naked, he unzipped his pants and said, "Give me a blow job!"

"I didn't want to do it, but he had the gun at my neck. I tried to do what he wanted, but I kept gagging. It wasn't working and it made him very angry. All through this he kept telling me not to scream or he would kill me," Amanda recalled.

Since oral sex wasn't working, the man made Amanda lie down on the bed and then covered her face with a pillow to blindfold her. She told him she couldn't breathe and he removed the pillow and substituted a T-shirt as a blindfold. He forced her to manually stimulate his penis while he talked to her. He asked her why she was wearing a knee brace and she replied that she had hurt her knee. He asked if she had hurt it doing sports, and Amanda replied that she'd hurt it dancing.

The man fondled her breasts and constantly reminded her to keep masturbating him, even though he remained only partially erect. After a while, he grew tired of this, and he demanded to have vaginal sex with her. Amanda was worried about sexual diseases and asked him, "Do you have protection?" He answered no, and then added, "What do you and your boyfriend do?" From this remark she believed he knew that she had a boyfriend.

Amanda said that she had a diaphragm over at her boyfriend's place, and that he was coming over soon. The man did not believe that her boyfriend was going to show up soon and demanded to have vaginal sex with her. Once more, Amanda insisted on having some kind of protection because she was afraid of sexual diseases. In frustration he answered, "I don't have any diseases!"

Still, she was persistent on this issue and said, "Raping me is one thing. But how do I know you don't have AIDS? You can't come inside me!"

Her assailant straddled her body and put his penis into her vagina, and once more, Amanda insisted, "You can't come inside me!" He replied, "I wont, I won't, I won't!"

Even when he was inside her, Amanda could barely feel his penis. Later she would say that he had an unusually small penis and he seemed to have trouble keeping it inside her vagina. This made him more and more upset, and this frightened her. He wanted to kiss her on the mouth, but she didn't want him to. This made him even more angry and he placed the gun muzzle up beside her head. He growled, "You have to do what I say, or I'll kill you!"

Through all his shifting moods, she tried to match the way he was feeling at the moment. One thing she determined was not to let him see her cry. She didn't want him to think she was out of control. He finally seemed to become erect enough, then pulled out and ejaculated on her stomach. Amanda wasn't certain, but she thought he might have then wiped up his semen with an article of clothing.

Amanda realized that as soon as he ejaculated, her assailant had become more cold and calculating toward her. She would later describe this as his going into a "pyscho/rapist mode." He tied an article of her clothing more tightly around her eyes and told her to get up. When she said, "I don't know where I'm going," he responded, "Shut up! I'll lead you there!"

He led her to the bathroom, told her to get into the shower and stand there with the shower curtain open. She turned the shower on and he handed her a bar of soap and told her, "Wash your crotch really good, and be quick about it!"

Amanda did as instructed, and after she was done, she

turned the water off and he led her back to the bedroom. He had barely let her dry herself off and she was very cold and still wet at this point. He told her to lie facedown on the bed and repeated, "I have a gun. So do as I say." Then he asked her if she had anything to tie her up with and she answered she had some scarves in the closet. He got those and then he yanked some telephone cords out of the wall as well.

He tied her wrists behind her back with cord and her ankles as well. He told her, "You have a really beautiful back." Then he began pushing and poking her buttocks with his fingers. He said, "It's too bad you're tied up now. It would be good to do that too." (He meant anal sex.) She thought to herself, *Oh, no! Not that too!*

She believed, after he had tied her up, he would leave. Her assailant became very quiet and then suddenly he straddled her body with his own, put his hands around her throat and tried choking her to death. Amanda recalled later, "He was trying to squeeze the life out of me. At that point I knew that he was trying to kill me. Even though I was tied up, I used to be on a swim team at school. I had done the butterfly in swimming and so I did that now. I kept trying to buck him off, and he kind of fell to the side. The one thought I had was if I could keep him off me, he couldn't kill me. I thought, 'Just move, move, move! Do anything.' He kept trying, though, and it went on and on."

The intruder would climb on her back, Amanda bucked and wiggled and squirmed, and he could never quite get a good grip on her throat as he slid off her. They thrashed around all over the bed and their actions were so erratic and violent that the mattress moved around as well. Amanda recalled, "I tried pinching him, but it was hard to do since I was tied up. He put a pillow over my head, trying to smother me, and I thought I'd try playing dead. But it didn't work and I almost blacked out. I thought I was going to die then, but I kept fighting back. We were moving around a lot, and there were some suitcases I used for a nightstand and there were some drinking glasses on that. They got knocked to the floor and shattered. The mattress actually fell to the floor at one point, and to me it seemed like we were really making a lot of noise.

"This went on for what seemed like twenty minutes. I thought to myself, 'I can go on as long as it takes.' My window was partially open and we heard people outside the apartment. My gag came loose and I tried making noise that way. But he told me not to scream and said if I did, he would kill me. I told him, 'You're already killing me!'"

More desperate fighting and struggling ensued, but then both Amanda and her attacker thought they heard voices right outside her window once again. There seemed to be a man and woman out there. Amanda managed to snap the bindings on her hands and pull her blindfold off. Amanda recalled, "He got off me, and I thought I heard someone next door say they were going to call the police. When I got my blindfold off, he was standing above me, pointing the pistol at my head. By then I was on the floor, and he kept saying, 'Do what I say, or I'll kill you.' I think both of us at that point thought the police were coming. I asked him to give me the pistol, but that only made him angry again. I begged him not to kill me, and he finally answered, 'I can't kill you now. If I get caught, it will only be for rape and not manslaughter.' When he said that, I thought he knew what he was talking about concerning the law.

"By now, he was sweating and seemed kind of tired. He sat down against a wall and he had me put his sandals on. My ankles were still bound, and I was still naked, but I did it. Finally he asked me how to get out of the apartment building the back way, and I told him. He left out the bedroom door, and as soon as he did, I closed the door. But I was afraid he would shoot right through the door, so I scooted up against a wall.

"Unfortunately, the police did not come. When I thought time enough had passed, I tried to get my ankles untied. It was very tight and there was a lot of blood around my feet and ankles. I had got my feet bloody from the glass on the floor. I had lots of cuts and abrasions around my ankles and wrists, and my face was cut, my lips were cut, and there was a lot of bruising on my neck and back. I finally got untied and crawled out my bedroom window and ran over to Maya's apartment. I just had a T-shirt kind of wrapped around me. When I got there, Maya called the police."

Not only had Maya called the police, but a neighbor next door to Amanda did as well. An officer arrived on scene within about fifteen minutes of being dispatched. Officer Chilen took Amanda Carpova to the hospital in his vehicle. Once there, she had photographs taken of her numerous wounds and bruises. A rape kit was used and there was hope that some of the attacker's semen would still be present, despite his having made Amanda wash herself thoroughly after being raped.

Amanda spoke with Detective W. Carter at the hospital in an interview room, and Amanda's mother joined them, along with Maya. Before even speaking with Amanda and the others, Detective Carter had noticed all her cuts and bruises and wrote about them in his report. Then Amanda told the detective that she had been bound tightly with lamp cord and phone cord. The red marks on her neck, she explained, were there from the assailant trying to choke her to death. Criminalist Roger O'Brien arrived and began taking 35mm photographs of all the bruises, cuts and marks on Amanda's body.

In talking to Detective Carter, Amanda said that her attacker had pulled a "silver handgun with black grips" on her. She reiterated that every time she hesitated or questioned his demands, he shoved the gun up against her neck or head and told her he would kill her if she didn't do exactly what he said.

As far as the suspect went, Amanda said, he was possibly Hawaiian or of mixed Japanese/Caucasian descent.

He had a round face, black ear-length hair, was "flabby in body tone," and about five-seven or five-eight. He'd worn black wraparound sunglasses with a foam strap, a white T-shirt, khaki shorts, Fruit of the Loom–type underwear and black sandals with Velcro straps. She also mentioned that he had a very small circumcised penis. In fact, at first when she was being raped, she hadn't realized that he'd already penetrated her.

Amanda had bruises all over her body and especially her neck area. She also had severe cuts on her feet, from having walked and struggled around on the broken glass on her bedroom floor. Four oral swabs were obtained from her, as well as vaginal swabs. Then criminalist O'Brien went to her apartment and collected two swabs containing suspected human blood from the bedroom floor. Even though it was probably Amanda's blood, there was always hope that she might have scratched her attacker and made him bleed, or he might have cut himself on the glass. O'Brien collected two white towels from the bathroom floor, and a purple towel and maroon towel from the bedroom floor. O'Brien also collected a lamp from the bedroom and telephone extension cord.

Officer Chilen wrote a report about the rape after talking with Maya, Kim Gillespie and Mike Harpole. Maya told him that Amanda had come running over to her apartment, wearing only some kind of white T-shirt or robe, and a scarf around her neck, which appeared to have blood on it. Maya said that Amanda had been screaming when she arrived and wouldn't calm down. She was still very agitated when police first arrived.

Both Gillespie and Harpole said that they'd heard noises when they first arrived at the apartment complex and were passing apartment number 3. The only reason they were there at all was because Gillespie had forgotten something at her apartment before going to a gym. They discussed whether or not to call the police about all the noise coming from the next apartment. Finally Gillespie thought it was a domestic situation gone out of control and she did call 911. The police eventually arrived, and detective work was done, but as in the case of Donna Ferguson and Todd Rudiger, all the clues seemed to go around and around in circles and never became connected to any one individual.

In fact, the person who raped and attempted to kill Amanda Carpova was the same person who had raped Donna Ferguson, then killed her and Todd Rudiger. He was not Hawaiian, Pacific Islander, or a mix of Japanese and Caucasian. He was twenty-eight-year-old Chau Quang Ho, who now called himself "Sebastian Shaw." He had been born in war-torn Vietnam, and in an incredible juncture of fate and history, he was one of the children helicoptered off the roof of the American Embassy just before Saigon fell to the Communists. From the embattled streets of Saigon, to a dark and bloody trail up and down the West Coast of the United States, Sebastian Shaw's story was one that bordered on the margins of incredible.

4

"The End of the World"

Chau Quang Ho was born on November 28, 1967, at Phuoc Tuy, in the Republic of South Vietnam, to Van Ho, a father who was in the army, and a mother who stayed at home. Unfortunately for Chau, his mother had severe medical problems related to heart disease and she died when he was only ten months old. Since his father was serving far away in the provinces, attached to a military unit, he could not come back and raise Chau. This was initially done by some neighbors of his mother, but for whatever reason, the people designated to take care of Chau didn't do a good job. In fact, their neglect had serious consequences down the line.

Anna Ho, Chau's paternal aunt, Van Ho's sister, went one day to check up on young Chau and was horrified by what she saw. Chau's legs were covered with red-ant bites and he was becoming very ill from the effects of the untreated bites. In outrage Anna told the people who had Chau that she would take him into her own household from now on and take care of him.

Anna lived with her three daughters in one of the outer sections of Saigon, and two of her sons were away fighting in the South Vietnamese army. Her husband had also been a soldier, but recently he'd been killed in combat. Anna said later, "My brother, Van Ho, Chau's father, had joined the military in 1957 and he would go off into remote villages to try and help them develop. He would go into these villages to try and tell the villagers the difference between the South Vietnamese government and the Communists. He would also try to learn who had sympathy for the North Vietnamese and the Viet Cong. He was away from home a lot in very dangerous areas.

"My own husband was killed in battle in 1968 when I was thirty-three years old, and even our own neighborhood of Saigon was attacked that year. I had originally been a small merchant, but my shop was destroyed in the fighting. A friend gave me a job working in a mail room, but I didn't make much money there. Times were very hard.

"When I learned that Chau had been bitten by red ants, I was outraged. I brought him home so I could take care of him, but he was very badly bitten. I knew what that was like. I had a fruit tree and there were two red-ant nests in the tree. When I picked the fruit one time, I must have shaken the branches because they came down and bit me. I kept shaking them off, but they kept on biting. It itched very bad and I got chills and had a fever afterward.

"For Chau, it was worse. He was so young, not yet two years old, and I thought he might die. From his crotch down to his ankles, he was all red and swollen, with lots of pusy sores. I took him to a local doctor, and the doctor told me that Chau's body was infected by disease. All the doctor could do was give Chau medication to lessen the pain.

"I came home early one day from work and Chau had a bad fever and was very hot. He cried and cried all day and night. I had a good friend who was an electrical engineer who worked for the Americans. I told this friend, 'You must take us to a U.S. military base hospital.' When we got there, they put Chau in a cold room and didn't allow anyone else in there. For a while, they thought the fever would not go down, and if it didn't, they told me they would have to amputate one leg."

Luckily for Chau, it never came to that, but the trauma of this incident would stay with him for a long time. Even when he went back home, Chau had a great deal of trouble walking. One of Anna's daughters recalled later that Chau had to hold himself up with the use of his hands by grabbing onto objects, because his legs were so weak.

In 1971, Chau's father got married once more, but Chau remained with his paternal aunt and her daughters. Van Ho and his new wife eventually had two daughters of their own, but Chau did not see his father again until he was nearly five years old. One day a strange man came to the door of the house where Chau lived and asked to come inside. Chau was on the floor, sitting and eating a bowl of rice, and said to the stranger, "Who are you?" In response the man said, "I'm your father."

Van's visit was of short duration, however. Soon he was off to a remote area once again, leaving Chau behind with his paternal aunt. Chau didn't lack for company, however. Besides Anna's daughters, another boy, named Kiet (pronounced Kit), who was Chau's cousin, joined the household. Kiet's mother (Anna's sister) had been able to make her way to France from Vietnam, but for some reason Kiet was not allowed to follow her at that time. At least Chau now had a male cousin about his own age with whom he could play and relate to.

One of Anna's daughters, Thuha Tran, recalled that Chau had a lot of problems with his legs as a young boy. She added, "He never complained, though. Never cried about them. It took years for his legs to heal, and we kept having to take him back for shots."

By 1975, however, Chau's legs were the least of everybody's problems. By that year the United States troops had been gone from South Vietnam for two years and the war was going very badly for the South. Just how badly was attested to years later by ABC journalist Ken Kashiwahara—

a man whose own journey in South Vietnam would bring him unexpectedly into contact with Chau Quang Ho (Sebastian Shaw) thirty years later in Portland, Oregon.

Ken Kashiwahara had been in the United States Air Force from 1968 through 1969 in Vietnam, and after his military duties, he became a correspondent for ABC News. As the situation in South Vietnam deteriorated, Kashiwahara was sent back there in March 1975. What he saw firsthand not only impacted him but the family of Chau as well.

Kashiwahara recalled, "The South Vietnamese Army was in disarray. Maybe not in full rout yet, but certainly in disarray. Morale was very low and soldiers were going AWOL. The troops would run from a fight, and the North Vietnamese were in effect marching straight down from the North to the South. One of my first assignments was to go to Qui Nhon, near Da Nang. We went to the town, and most of the residents were in the process of fleeing. The next day when we went back to the airport to wait for a charter plane, it never showed up. The reason I found out later was because there was nobody in the control tower. They had fled as well.

"The next place was Da Nang. There was news of the last flight out of World Airlines, and this executive who in a show of bravado had said, 'I'm going up there with my civilian airplane, and I'm gonna get as many people out as I can.' He landed at the airport, and people just mobbed the airplane. He wasn't going to be able to take off again, so he started kicking people off the plane. And as the plane started taxiing, the people were hanging onto the wheel wells and back stairs of the plane, and those people fell to their deaths."

Chau's aunt Anna also knew that things were unraveling quickly—and she and her family were in danger—because by that time she worked for the American Embassy. Anna recalled, "If you worked for the Americans, you knew you were on a list held by the Communists. I began plans to leave the country, in late March, but it wasn't until April that someone at the embassy told me that they would try and help me, Chau, Kiet and my daughters leave the country. I was not supposed to tell anyone else, including my sons, who were serving in the army.

"The Communists were outside of Saigon by then, and I told my daughters, Chau and Kiet to be packed and ready to go. The mood in Saigon was one of fear, hope and despair. There was so much tension because of a sense of not knowing what was going to happen next."

Ken Kashiwahara, who was in Saigon at the same time as Chau and his aunt, also sensed the extreme tension within the city. He recalled, "At five P.M., on April twenty-eighth, we were all at the presidential palace to witness the swearing in of a new president—a Vietnamese general named Big Minh. It took about an hour, and we got back to our office at six o'clock. As soon as we got back, it seemed like all hell broke loose, as if every single weapon in Saigon started firing at something. My cameraman and I went out to try and find out what was going on. What we learned later was that the North Vietnamese had bombed the airport and effectively closed it. All the South Vietnamese soldiers were firing into the air or at anything that moved. That night as we stood on the roof of our hotel, we could see the explosions going on."

Not far away that same evening, Anna, Chau and the others were huddled together, packed and ready to go, when Anna got a call from her supervisor to get on a bus. She recalled, "We were going to be flown out of Than Sa Noot Airport, but on the way there, it got rocketed and everything changed." Turned away from the airport, they were driven back into a city on the verge of collapse.

Just what Saigon was like on the morning of April 29, 1975, was vividly recounted by Ken Kashiwahara many years later as Chau Quang Ho sat not more than twenty feet away from him in a Portland, Oregon, courtroom. Kashiwahara related, "My cameraman and I went out that morning, and the people were packed up and going here and going there. Everyone was on the move. We went to an American commissary, and hundreds of Vietnamese were looting everything they could carry out. There was a sense in the city that early morning that something was going to happen.

"I interviewed Vietnamese nationals who had worked for the Americans, and if you had worked for the Americans, their feeling was that their lives were at great risk. The signal to evacuate was playing on the embassy radio station, and it was the song 'White Christmas.' So we knew it was time to leave. The drill was, we were to go to a predesignated evacuation pickup point, and the first buses that came, it was fairly orderly. But when my bus came, my cameraman and bureau chief got on, and I was right behind them. At that point there was a huge surge of Vietnamese people who became a mob. They started pushing and shoving, and obviously they felt if they could get on an American bus, they could get out of the country."

Anna, Chau and family were in similar straits, not knowing when their turn to depart would be as mobs swirled around them near the embassy. Looting was going on everywhere, and there was a constant background din of automatic-weapon fire and artillery in the distance. Just as had happened to Anna and the others, who had been turned away from the now-burning Than Sa Noot Airport, Ken Kashiwahara's bus was in the same predicament. He recalled, "At that point the evacuation plans fell apart. Our bus driver, he was just a guy who worked at the American Embassy, he wasn't a regular bus driver. He started driving around the city, and he had no communication with the embassy or anyone else. Not being a bus driver, he smashed into fruit stands alongside the road, making people very angry. A lot of Vietnamese, knowing the Americans were leaving, were yelling 'Yankee, go home!'

"Finally someone suggested, 'Let's go down to the port and see if we can get a boat out of there!' We went down there, the bus stopped, and Vietnamese were piling on barges, boats, anything that would float. We decided this was not a good idea, and decided to get back on the bus. Unfortunately, I was the last one to get on the bus, and before I could, the bus started pulling away. I started running, and I felt someone grab the straps of my backpack and pull me back. I looked around and there were angry faces of Vietnamese, who were probably thinking, 'If I can't go, you can't go!' I immediately threw off my shoulder straps, ran and got on the bus. Just as I did, a Vietnamese man ran up, holding a baby. As he ran beside the bus, he was yelling, 'Take my baby! Take my baby!' He tripped and fell, and the bus ran over the baby. We just kept going and everyone on the bus was absolutely stunned."

Only a few miles away, Anna and her family waited in mounting fear and doubt. When the time finally came, it arrived in the form of a friend who drove them straight down to the embassy area. Luckily for her, she was still wearing her embassy uniform, because no one without an identification card or uniform was even getting on the grounds. Anna recalled, "Helicopters were constantly flying overhead and a big wall around the embassy was surrounded by people. I could hear fighting and bombs on the margins of the city. We waited and waited for our turn. It was all very frightening." In fact, there was a swirling mob surrounding the embassy—people trying to climb over the walls, only to be pushed back down by United States Marines.

Ken Kashiwahara became just as aware of the embassy wall and the mob surrounding it. "There were thousands of Vietnamese trying to climb over the walls. As they tried climbing over, U.S. Marines were on top of the wall, kicking them down. I thought to myself, 'I've been mistaken many times before as Vietnamese. One of those guys is going to mistake me for Vietnamese and I'm gonna get a boot right in my face.' So I wedged myself right in between two white journalists, and we pushed our way to the wall. I decided that if a boot came toward my face, I would yell, 'The Dodgers won the Pennant!' Fortunately, when I reached the wall, the marine recognized me as an American. He reached out a hand and pulled me over the wall."

For Anna and Chau, the waiting and chaos went on all afternoon and into the night of April 29. Finally, at around 1:30 A.M., it was their turn to be helicoptered off the roof of the American Embassy. Anna recalled, "Our helicopter flew right out to an American ship, the *Blue Ridge*. Military jets were flying overhead and everything was very frightening. We set foot on the ship, and just as we did, one helicopter did not make it. It fell off the ship in front of our eyes. I don't know how many people died on that helicopter.

"There was no space for us, except to stand. Eventually one of my daughters and I were taken to a lower deck. Down there I heard a loud explosion and I felt as if the ship was going to roll over. I was told later that two helicopters had collided and one must have banged into the ship. At the time I thought it was a bomb."

Kashiwahara's own escape from the American Embassy was just as chaotic and filled with drama and pathos. "Inside the embassy it was wall-to-wall people. They were sitting, standing, waiting around. The ABC crew took off about sunset, and we got ten feet into the air, and the helicopter started shaking. It was too heavy a load, so we landed again and kicked people out. We took off again, got a little higher, and the helicopter started shaking again. We came crashing back down, opened the door and kicked more people out. Finally, on the third try, we made it. I personally thought we would be shot down, either by North Vietnamese or by angry South Vietnamese soldiers. As we took off over the city, the sun had just set. I looked to the north of the city and there was an ammunition dump going off. As we flew out over the South China Sea, there were fires everywhere. It really struck me, this was a country going up in flames. I was witnessing the disintegration of a country."

* * *

Years later, Chau Quang Ho, or Sebastian Shaw as he was calling himself by then, would write of the experience of escaping a war-torn country amidst chaos when he was only seven years old. He wrote it as fiction, but the resemblance to his own situation was striking. Clearly, the story line revealed the depth of the psychic trauma the events had had upon a seven-year-old boy. Chau named his protagonist Captain Powers, and depicted him as an adult, but it is evident that Captain Powers was Chau.

Chau wrote:

It was chaos as he was looking over the heads of the crowd, and all he saw was a sea of humanity. The air was thick with the smell of bodies, washed and unwashed, all comingled to create the unmistakable smell of desperation. Their eyes were all frantic with the question of what's going to happen to us? The end of the world was here. The bitter taste of defeat was on everyone's tongue. They jostled each other trying to get their papers cleared and their families out of harm's way.

Chau went on in the story about a low-flying enemy aircraft that strafed the crowd, its pilot leering at his helpless victims down below. There was no fear of retaliation on the pilot's part; he knew his comrades dominated the skies over the embassy grounds. Chau wrote of *sizzling flesh and screams of agony* by those wounded in the crowd. To the pilot, the fleeing mass of refugees, aligned with the *Southern Freedom Fighters*, didn't deserve mercy. For all he knew, they were soldiers who had thrown off their uniforms to mingle with the crowd.

Captain Powers was not one of those who had thrown away his uniform—he still proudly wore his officer's uniform, even though it was stained and dirty by now. Yet, the flyby had a horrible consequence for Powers:

*In the panic that ensued, the air lousy with the smell of
human misery and death, he was separated from his
family—his mother and two sisters.*

They were now lost somewhere out there in the sea
of humanity, and Powers knew he had to find them because he had their papers. It was their only means of
escape, and without his family he would never leave the
war-torn country, *which had suffered 10,000 days of war.* He
could hear death knocking at the door. *What could you do
when your side has lost the war?* Chau penned.

Suddenly, there was a thunderclap above his head, and
a loud *whoosh* sound of another "hovercraft" taking
refugees from the embassy to allied ships at sea. Captain
Powers could only scratch his dusty, sweaty head and
wonder how many more there would be taking refugees
from the stricken city. Once the refugees reached the ves-
sels of the Southern Freedom Fighters' last ally, they
would be safe. But on the journey over, they were sitting
ducks for the enemy aircraft.

Captain Powers pushed his way through the crowd,
calling out his mother's name. His fear of not finding
her or his sisters was eating away at his reserves of energy
and confidence. It was like searching *for a life line in an
ocean of bodies,* Chau wrote. He wondered how he could
be seen or heard in this shifting tide of people.

Off in the distance near the embassy gate, he spied a
sergeant trying to keep people from plunging through
the gate or climbing over the wall. The sergeant's sweat-
stained uniform, caked with someone's blood, was
Powers's only means of getting his family out of the country. *His heart beat as if it was being chased by the devil,* Chau
related. Powers zeroed in on the red-bearded sergeant,
but when he got there, the stressed sergeant didn't even
acknowledge him—he was so busy pushing civilians back
into the crowd as they tried climbing over the fence into
the "Promised Land." After seeing Powers's dirty uni-

form, the sergeant saluted, but he would not let him pass without first seeing his papers. Powers was startled when the sergeant told him he had to give up his red-smoke grenade. Too many infiltrators had tried sneaking in, using captured uniforms and carrying weapons.

Powers wouldn't give up his grenade, however, and he wandered back into the crowd, searching for his mother and sisters: *It was like wading through water in a tuxedo.* As he made his way through the crowd, he saw all manner of people—rich and poor, young and old. *They all wanted out of the killing zone, away from the dead bodies,* Chau narrated. Powers was so intent in looking for his family, he almost tripped over an old man who had fallen and been trampled on the ground. Powers thought to himself: *A stampede is indiscriminate, no matter what kind of animals are in the stampede.* Captain Powers picked up the old-timer and placed him on his feet, making sure the elderly man was not badly hurt. He comforted him for a while, and then moved away to try and find his family.

Near a lamppost he found a boy, dressed in blue overalls: *Hanging on a lamppost, by one hand, and one foot dangling over the edge, he was a miniature version of King Kong, hanging on the side of the Empire State Building.* The boy appeared to be looking for his family as well. And yet Powers had one advantage the boy didn't have—the red-smoke grenade that he wouldn't hand over to the sergeant at the checkpoint. Powers now pulled the pin with his teeth, and held it aloft, hoping that his family would spot it. A light breeze was blowing the smoke sideways into his face, but he didn't care. He knew if they saw the smoke, they might recognize it and come to him. It was his only hope. As minutes ticked by, the heat of the grenade almost burned his hand, but he held on to it with all his might. It was all he could do to keep from crumbling under the futility of the situation.

Then like the sound of an angel coming to the deathbed of a dying man, he heard his name being called. Suddenly he saw them, his mother and sisters struggling through the crowd, frantically waving. His mother ran over and embraced him, and then his sisters. He stood in the middle of the small group, hugging them, *the center of their life. As it should be, as it always will be,* Chau imagined.

Time was of the essence, however, so he herded them toward the gate, and it took almost an hour to finally reach a guard, who politely but firmly asked them for their papers. Captain Powers reached into his jacket pocket and found nothing. The tickets to freedom were gone. He rummaged through all his pockets, but they were nowhere to be found. The guard's face turned from friendly to cold, thinking that Powers was only trying to fool him. Powers's uniform meant nothing, it could have been stolen or taken off a dead Southern Freedom Fighter. All his cajoling, blustering and pleas fell on deaf ears. The guards' weapons were locked and loaded, ready to repel any intruder.

He closed his eyes so as not to see the anguish and fear in his mother and sisters' eyes. Anguish at their plight, and fear for their future. If captured, he knew he would be summarily shot for being a captain in the Southern Freedom Fighters Army, while his mother and sisters would be taken to a reeducation camp. He died twice that day—once when he lost his family in the crowd, and now when he discovered his papers were gone.

They slowly drifted toward an exit gate, and in his grief he didn't hear that someone was calling him: *"Captain! Captain!"* Calling out from the crowd was an old man, waving frantically and trying to make his way through the mob. Captain Powers suddenly recognized the old man. It was the same man he had helped off the ground. The old man's smiling face seemed out of place in the frantic crowd, until he pulled a set of papers out of his pocket and handed them to Powers. With trembling hands Powers opened them and saw that they were his papers: *It was like a door opening up in a musty old palace, letting in fresh spring air.* His act of kindness to the old man had been repaid in spades. Captain Powers knew the effort it must have taken the old man to make his way through the mob. He wanted to thank the old man, but the old man had already faded back into the crowd:

He had his family now, and nothing was going to stop him from getting them away. Out there, beyond the horizon, was a chance to start things afresh. A new life of freedom.

Chau's story—written years later when he was already calling himself Sebastian Shaw—still echoed the panic and chaos of one of the darkest days in Vietnamese and American history. It also spoke of a fictional hero, Captain Powers, whom Chau may have wished his father had been. Chau/Shaw would have a very difficult relationship with his father in the years to come.

For Chau, Kiet, Anna and her daughters, they slowly sailed away from their homeland, enduring incredibly cramped conditions. Anna recalled, "We were packed so tightly, we could hardly move. We were like fish in a can. After a while, we transferred to a different ship and we were taken to Guam, but it was too crowded there, so we were shifted to a different area that only had embassy employees. Someone shared a can of food with us, and even though Chau was so young, he had a good appetite. He started to eat, but then he said, 'Mom, there's no food for you.' He was concerned for me. My daughters and I went hungry some on Guam, but then we got army food. We were there for a couple of weeks and then we were sent to Wake Island.

"At Wake Island, Catholic Social Services and the Red Cross helped us there. I told them I had relatives in France, but it turned out we could not go there. We waited and waited and waited, but we could not go to France. It was on Wake Island that we met my brother, Chau's father."

Van Ho's own journey from Vietnam had been incredible in its own right. He had wanted to bring his new wife and young daughters out of the country with him, but with the situation crashing down before their very eyes, his superior officer ordered him to leave. The officer knew that Van, who had worked against the Communists, was probably on a death list. Escaping by military helicopter, along with other army officers, Van was taken aboard a United States Navy ship in the South China Sea. When Van eventually ended up on Wake Island, he reunited once more with Chau. Van Ho's wife and children remained in Vietnam.

Just as before, however, Van Ho wanted Chau to stay with his sister and her daughters. Van planned to go off to mainland America with his army comrades. Even Anna agreed to this. She later said, "Van was too used to military ways to raise a son. He was very hard on himself and others."

When Chau, Kiet, Anna and her daughters were finally allowed to depart to mainland America, they were first sent to Marine Corps Base Camp Pendleton in California. One part of the base was set aside for Vietnamese refugees. From August until November 1975, Chau and the others lived in an army tent and ate army food. It wasn't until November 30, 1975, that a group in Port Arthur, Texas, sponsored them to come out to that state to live. Even though they were now leaving a military base behind for civilian life, for Chau and the others, the adaptation to their new country would not be an easy one.

5

The Promised Land

Chau's aunt Anna remembered the move to Texas as being filled with both fear and hope. Fear for what their new life would entail, and hope that they could eventually fit into the fabric of American life. Anna's daughter Thuha Tran recalled that just because Van Ho was also in the area, things were really not any better between him and Chau. Thuha remembered, "Chau's father never was around very much. When he was around, I remember him being drunk and yelling at Mom. He seemed to be angry a lot."

Thuha also recalled that period in Texas as being frightening and chaotic. "I spoke very little English then. We were like strangers in Texas. Many people there were prejudiced against us. One time my family and I went to church and there were empty seats. People who were sitting on the same bench got up and moved away from us. We tried to say hi to them, but they just moved away. They ended up sitting behind us. At other times people would just stare at us or make fun of us."

Thuha remembered during this time that Chau would be teased a lot about his weight. He was hefty for his age, and he became the butt of jokes about being a "blimp" or "pig." Even when taunts and insults weren't blatant toward Chau and the girls, Thuha said, "I can remember the teasing behind my back. I couldn't hear it, but I could feel it."

As far as Chau's father went, Thuha recalled that she saw him drunk many times, although he didn't seem to drink at her mom's house, but rather he would show up there that way. Van went out drinking with his friends and then came over inebriated. One particularly traumatic event stuck in the mind of Thuha, and she said later, "My uncle (Van Ho) had a girlfriend in Texas, and he stalked her to work, where she worked with my mother. He went in there to beat her, and I saw him strike her. I was very scared.

"He used to beat his girlfriend a lot. The cops came to look for him one time, and my mom begged and begged and begged the woman not to press charges against my uncle. This incident is one of the reasons my uncle moved from Texas to Oregon," Thuha added.

Chau's aunt Anna said later that there was another reason as well. She had been taking care of Chau, Kiet and her daughters at the time on very little money. Van Ho told her that it was too much stress for her, and that he wanted Chau and Kiet to come live with him in Oregon. Even though it made sense economically, Anna was afraid about this move. "Van was short-tempered and had a military mentality. I was worried about him and Chau being together. But then I thought maybe that father and son would take care of each other there. Chau didn't want me to let him go with his father. I was a mother to him. But in the end, he and Kiet went with Van to Oregon," Anna said.

Anna was right about one thing—Van not only had a military mentality, but also a very strict code about how a boy should be raised. His ideas were not those shared by Americans in the 1970s, but rather traditional old-style Vietnamese ideas that included harsh discipline when a boy acted up. One woman who would witness the interaction of Van and Chau firsthand was Ly Do.

Not unlike Anna and her family, Ly Do and her daughter had escaped Saigon in the last terrifying days of its downfall. Ly Do and her daughter ended up living on a military base in the San Francisco Bay Area, and from there they moved up to Mount Angel, Oregon, and lived in temporary housing for a while. Ly Do and her daughter, Cong Lee, eventually moved into an apartment in Mt. Angel, right next door to Van Ho, Chau and Kiet.

Since Chau had no mother, and Van was away at work a lot, Van asked Ly Do if she could watch Chau on many occasions. Ly Do felt sorry for Chau, since his mother had died at such an early age; she agreed to have the boy come over to her place often. Ly Do recalled, "Chau was left alone a lot. He was only in second or third grade. He would come over to our apartment a lot in the after-noons."

Set in a hilly rural area, Mt. Angel is dominated by a Benedictine monastery resting atop a nearby hill. In fact, many Catholic institutions are built within the framework of the town, and the church there has the appearance of a medieval European cathedral, rather than a church built for a small town in Oregon. Young Chau attended that church and it became part of the fabric of his life.

Chau initially had a hard time fitting in at the elementary school at Mt. Angel. Fourth-grade teacher Carol Piatz remembered Chau very well and said, "In the third grade Chau had temper tantrums now and then. We didn't have a counselor at the school at that time, but the principal worked with him. By the time Chau got into my fourth-grade class, he had adjusted very nicely and I didn't have any disruptions from him. He was a happy, diligent student, and always had a smile on his face."

Smiles or not, there were by now more changes in Chau's life. Ly Do and Chau's father, Van, saw so much of each other that they eventually got married—despite the fact that Van was still married to his wife back in Vietnam, and they had two children together. Ly Do said later, "Van was calm and nice originally, but he also had a bad temper and could easily snap. He wanted to live by the old Vietnamese ways, and he had his ideas about disciplining children. Van told me, 'If you love the child, then you hit them. If you don't like the child, you spoil them.'

"He had a hard personality when he drank. This made him very mean at times. If Chau did something wrong, Van didn't try to explain things to him the American way. He hit him with a board or a rock so that he would remember the pain and not do it again.

"Van would hit Chau with a belt so hard he could not sit down later. He left marks on Chau's buttocks and I had to put on ointment later. Van was not interested in my input on how to raise a child. He wanted the old Vietnamese style where a wife was to obey her husband's wishes. The mother might be a counselor to the children, but she could not discipline them. If a child wanted to go somewhere, he had to ask his father first."

Teacher Carol Piatz at Chau's school added, "Back then, we didn't address things about problems at home or from neighbors or relatives. Now we tell children that if someone harms them, they should tell a teacher. But even back then, I felt that for many children, school was the only happy and safe environment."

Piatz also recalled that around this time Chau was baptized at her Catholic church. "His sisters asked that I sponsor him and I was glad to do so. He became a faithful altar server at St. Mary's Catholic Church in Mt. Angel." Chau seemed to like being an altar server and enjoyed the company of Piatz and others there. Besides school, it was the one place he fit in.

One person who would become a lifelong friend of Chau's was his sixth-grade teacher, Suzanne Garman. She saw a lot of potential in the boy and knew of his hard life, both in Vietnam and America. Suzanne was a very kind person and loved all her students, especially her "special kids," as she called them, those like Chau who had problems at home. In the years to come, Suzanne would stay in touch with Chau, and he with her. In fact, she would remain his friend when his other friendships soured.

* * *

Chau and his family moved to Woodburn, Oregon, in Marion County, when he was just starting high school. Woodburn was a very interesting community, especially because the "Old Believers" of the Russian Orthodox Church had emigrated there in great numbers. This sect had split from the Russian Orthodox Church in the 1660s because of theological differences. Even by the twentieth century, they still wore traditional clothing and were much like the Amish in their farming practices and exclusive lifestyles. Unlike the Amish of Pennsylvania, however, they could operate machinery and have electricity, but many of their beliefs were in conflict with modern life. At home, and with each other, they still spoke an old style of Russian, and in every public building in Woodburn, there were signs in English and old Russian. One good aspect of this for Chau was that he wasn't the only person outside the mainstream in the Woodburn area.

When Chau and family moved to Woodburn, he soon made a friend there named Jeff Krier. Krier remembered Chau: "He was very intelligent and friendly. He got along with everyone at high school. There were some who gave him a hard time, but then they did that to everybody, just to try and be cool. In one way it was easier for Chau at Woodburn High, because there was a large population of Hispanics and Russian immigrants."

The guy who gave Chau the hardest time of all, however, wasn't some school bully, but rather his own father. Chau was good at wrestling in gym class and wanted to go out for the team, but Van would not let him do it. Ly Do recalled, "I also wanted Chau to go out for the high school wrestling team, but his father said no, because he might get hurt and then could not help him at work. Chau liked sports where strength was involved. He was very disappointed not to get on the team."

Chau's aunt Anna and her daughters drove up once in a while to visit him in Oregon, and those were happy times for Chau. He liked Anna's daughters and still thought of Anna as his mother. Thuha remembered that Chau was always nice to her and laughed a lot. Beneath the surface, however, Chau was a very troubled and unhappy young man. At one point he took an overdose of aspirin in a suicide attempt. Chau later told Ly Do that he didn't feel well and had taken too many aspirin by mistake, but she always believed he had attempted suicide. She recalled, "I wouldn't go into it later with him, to dredge up bad memories. In Vietnam we didn't have mental-health clinics like in America. If you were troubled there, you went to an older relative to talk about things, but Chau had no older and wiser relative in Oregon. One time a mental-health agent who spoke Vietnamese came to speak about things to Chau, but Van would not allow him to do so. I wanted to help Chau, but I would not go against Van's wishes.

"Things got very bad for Chau. One day he did not go to school but rode his bicycle thirty miles to Portland and went to a police station. He told them how his father mistreated him. The school contacted me about letting Chau live with another Vietnamese family and go to school from their house. But Van would not give permission, so it did not happen."

Though some of the details are unclear, it seems that Chau called his former sixth-grade teacher, Suzanne Garman, from Portland and told her what he had done. She went up to Portland and picked Chau up in her car and brought him home to the area. He may have even spent the night at Garman's house, before being returned home. Suzanne always felt sorry for the way Chau was treated by his father.

The final break for father and son came in 1985. Van wanted Chau to accompany him to work at midnight and help him, but Chau said that he had a test the following day and couldn't go. Enraged, Van took a piece of wood from the woodpile and savagely beat him with it. Chau yelled at his father, "You treat me like an animal!"

Van replied, "If you don't want to listen to me, you can't live in this house!"

What happened next comes in two versions. In one, Chau grabbed some clothes and left immediately for southern California, going to live at a friend's home. In this version he went to high school directly from the friend's house, even though he was still too young to be legally on his own. In the other version Van drove Chau down to southern California. Whichever happened, life for those left with Van soon deteriorated as well. Ly Do said, "One time we were eating, and Van became angry. He got mad at something I said and threw a can of V-8 juice at me. It cut my head and made me bleed. I said to myself, 'I don't want to live anymore with someone who is like a tiger!' I wanted to take my children and go to a neighbor's house and call the police. But then I thought, the police will come and arrest him, but he'll be back in a day or two and it will be worse than ever."

It was finally Van that rearranged their household by kicking Ly Do out. Ly Do left for good and initially spent some time in a shelter before moving on to her own residence. Even though life was initially very hard, she eventually got back on track and was able to live in her own apartment with her daughters.

Down in southern California, Chau enjoyed living once again with his aunt Anna and her daughters. He went to Redondo Union High School and did well there. Thuha recalled, "I knew there had been a bad problem between Chau and his father. He did not really talk about it much." Thuha added that, as always, Chau was fun to be around and "very lovable."

Chau's aunt recalled of this period, "When Chau came back to live with us, I felt so bad for him because he had no mother. His father didn't take care of him. He didn't know how to raise a son. Chau's situation required more love in the family. My own children would ask me, 'Why do you love Chau when you don't love us?' I said, 'I do love you, but he has no mother.'"

Chau worked for a company in the area for a short time after he finished high school, and then he joined the United States Marine Corps. Perhaps he wanted to thank the country that had given him a new home. Perhaps he wanted to prove to his father that he was tough and disciplined. Whatever the reason, Chau passed through marine basic training and was stationed around the United States, and later to Okinawa and Japan. Whether it is true or not, Chau would later relate that he wanted to be in a combat unit, but access was denied for him because he still had relatives in Vietnam (Anna's sons). Chau said that the marines only let him serve in support units, and this frustrated him.

Chau was eventually stationed at a marine base out in the desert of southern California, at 29 Palms. He began to frequent the Sandy Hills Bowling Lanes there in his off-hours, and he was a fairly good bowler. In fact, he was good enough to participate in local tournaments. As in many things, however, Chau had an uncontrollable temper. Jo Ann Koster, who also frequented the Sandy Hills Bowling Lanes and remembered Chau, said later, "He was a hothead. When he lost his concentration, he would be abnormally mad at himself, which would completely throw off his game."

Unlike others, however, Koster thought that Chau was popular around the bowling alley. She said, "I often saw him kidding with girls around the snack bar." She thought it was all harmless and that Chau was "okay."

Chau did keep a clean record while in the marines, and no criminal activity on his part came to the surface when he was later checked by law enforcement. However, he was disillusioned with where life had led him and he felt trapped and sullen. In 1990, Chau applied for and received an honorable discharge from the marines. Or at least that was his version of why he left the marines. According to a file from the marines, however, they discharged Chau because he would not or could not keep his weight down. It constantly fluctuated well above what was deemed fit to be a marine, and it may have affected his work performance.

Chau returned to civilian life in Oregon and got an apartment on Thirty-third Avenue in Portland, right next door to Ly Do and her daughters. For some reason, Ly Do was now suspicious of Chau and his intentions with her daughters. She told them not to ever be alone with Chau, and she changed her locks so that he did not have a key to their place. Very murky details of Ly Do's suspicions would later surface about his conduct with her daughters.

On October 5, 1990, Chau was hired as a security dispatcher for the Paragon Cable Company, which was located on Sandy Boulevard. He also did one more very interesting thing around this time—he legally changed his name from Chau Quang Ho to Sebastian Alexander Shaw. When Thuha heard of this, she said, "I don't think he was proud of his father's name. In the Vietnamese culture, to disown a father's name is a very bad insult."

Chau, who was now Sebastian, had picked an intriguing choice of names. Sebastian Shaw was an actor from Great Britain who played Anakin Skywalker in *Return of the Jedi*, in the *Star Wars* trilogy. In the movies Anakin Skywalker would go over to the "Dark Side" to become the villain Darth Vader. Within this context were subtexts of a troubled relationship between father and son, good and evil, life and death. Just as Anakin Skywalker went over to the Dark Side, Chau Quang Ho, now Sebastian Alexander Shaw, would soon go to the Dark Side as well. He would pick a helpless paraplegic as his first victim, and leave him murdered in a blood-soaked residence.

6

The Devil's Face

Forty-year-old Jay Rickbeil may have had cerebral palsy, but it certainly didn't keep him inactive. In his electric wheelchair Jay was constantly on the go around the streets of Portland, Oregon, shopping, exploring and meeting with friends. He'd been born in Klamath Falls, Oregon, in 1951 to parents who owned a jewelry store in that city, which they'd managed since 1936. Jay was born with cerebral palsy, but despite his condition, he had parents and two sisters who loved him and helped him as much as they could. And for Jay's part, he strived to be as normal a student as possible at Klamath Falls Elementary School. There were constant interruptions, however, due to surgeries and visits to the doctor. Jay was eventually sent down to Vallejo, California, to a school where his special needs could be addressed more adequately.

During his younger years Jay could still get around without a wheelchair by using steel braces on his legs— the bulk of his power becoming centered more and more in his upper body and arms, which he used to pull himself along. His sister Tamara recalled later, "He was left-handed, so he was much stronger on that side.

He could sign his name to a certain degree, but it was hard for him to write. His arms turned inward, and he couldn't straighten out his right arm very well at all."

The round of surgeries continued for Jay as he grew older, because of the continuing curvature of his legs, and eventually the doctors knew that drastic steps would have to be taken concerning the worsening problem. When Jay was in his early twenties, the tendons in his legs were cut and he was permanently wheelchair-bound from that point on. Jay's dad moved him to Portland, Oregon, in 1969 so that Jay could interact with its larger population of handicapped people. Both Jay and his parents agreed that he could have a more fulfilling life there. Jay received a small amount of money through the Veterans Administration, because his father had been in the service, and he also made ends meet by working part-time at Goodwill Industries and doing bell ringing for the Salvation Army during the holiday season. As Tamara put it, "Jay didn't like to think of himself as handicapped."

Even though Tamara didn't live nearby, she spoke to Jay by phone three to five times a week, and related, "He was a real chatterbox." In fact, Jay was extremely sociable and had lots of friends in the Portland area. He eventually moved into an apartment on Raymond Street in Portland, which he shared with roommate Sherman Polley. Each had his own bedroom and shared a common kitchen, dining area, bathroom and living area. Polley was a painter and handyman by trade and was often gone during the daytime. Tamara said of this living arrangement, "They were kind of like *The Odd Couple*, but they got along well together."

To make matters easier for Jay, an automatic lift was created so that he could get in and out of the bathtub/shower, and Tamara came by about once a month to visit, do laundry and clean up around the apartment. Jay's aunt also lived nearby and stopped in on occasion to visit and check up on him. As time went on, one of

Jay's friends, Victoria Taylor, helped out with cleaning and cooking.

Victoria also noted that Jay had a lot of friends, and many of them dropped by his place, day or night. Many of these people were what she called "street people." "By the spring of 1991, the place was practically public domain. There was a constant stream of people coming to the door. In fact, Jay did not lock his front door, because it was hard for him to unlock it. It got to the point where it started to wear him out, what with all the people coming over, and he got to where he wanted some people pushed out. So I began answering the door. Lots of times I'd tell people that Jay was too tired and to come back later," Victoria recalled.

Most of the people who came by understood and left without any trouble, but that was not the case with one individual, according to Victoria Taylor. She stated that "it was about two P.M. when a Chinese or Vietnamese guy came by and he acted like he ought to be there. He had thick glasses and his eyes looked really bad. He acted like he had some kind of deal going with Jay, but I told him to come back later. He got really upset and made some improper remarks. He was cussing, but he finally left."

On July 2, 1991, Sherman Polley went to work as usual, this time not far away on a painting job. Just before he left, he gave Jay a blanket because Jay was cold, even though it was a warm day. Jay lounged around the apartment and sometime during the late-afternoon hours an individual came to the door. This individual had just been fired from his job at the Paragon Cable Company in Portland and he was extremely angry. He had been out drinking all afternoon, and it had made his mood even darker. He was so angry, in fact, he felt like killing somebody. The individual was Sebastian Shaw.

In June 1991, Shirley Philip worked at Paragon Cable Company in Portland, dispatching workers to various sites. Philip's main shift was from 2:00 to 10:00 P.M., but she would work other shifts as well. Her work area was a small room with five other desks, and it brought her into close contact with other employees at Paragon. One employee in particular kept bugging her, making inappropriate comments that Shirley thought were overly sexual in nature. That employee was Sebastian Shaw. It eventually got so bad that Shirley twice reported his remarks to her supervisor; warnings were given to Shaw to knock it off. Despite the warnings, Shaw kept harassing Shirley.

One of the supervisors above Shirley in the chain of command was named Elaine and she knew about Sebastian Shaw very well. In March 1991, Elaine had warned him to quit harassing a different woman named Lisa, who also worked for Paragon. In response Shaw told Elaine, "My mom (aunt) said don't be friendly with women." (She probably meant at work with coworkers.) "I never mean to make women uncomfortable."

Yet, he did make them very uncomfortable, and after one incident—it's not clear if this was with Shirley Philip or Lisa—he was given another verbal warning and really took offense at it. He went into the office of the personnel director of human resources, Linda Aday, and told her, "It's out-of-the-blue backstabbing!" (He meant the report by the woman about harassment.) A few days later, he told Aday, "I was so angry, I went to a police station and said, 'Lock me up for the weekend!'"

Aday didn't check if Shaw was telling the truth about this or not, and in years to come, law enforcement could find no Portland police station that had taken a report from Shaw in this regard. As others would discover later, Shaw on occasion fabricated wild stories of things he had done.

By the end of June 1991, Shaw went over the line with his sexual innuendos concerning Shirley Philip. With the latest incident Shaw was given a written warning and told not to retaliate against her in any way. He didn't say much at the time, but silently he was seething. Shaw had joined the U.S. Marines and it hadn't worked out; he felt trapped in a job where he was going nowhere. Even when he tried to be friendly to a woman, he discovered that his words came out menacing rather than funny. If America was the land of opportunity, it certainly didn't seem that way to him. He was constantly turned down on dates, had few friends and always felt like an outsider. All of his resentments started to boil over, and he decided to get even with Shirley Philip in a very graphic manner.

Shaw bought a red balloon and painted a devil's face on it. Then he wrote a note and attached it to the balloon. The note stated: *69 makes a coven, spread out all below heaven. One foolish god in death adorned by a bestial goat's head. Death is too final, but to live and suffer before dying, that's damnation.*

He left it on Philip's desk, where she would find it in the morning.

On July 2, 1991, Shirley Philip approached her desk and was stunned by what she saw there. After all the warnings Sebastian Shaw had been given, this was his response to her! She said later, "It was very scary. I didn't even want to touch the balloon. The first thing I thought of was satanic cults, suffering and sacrifices. It was freaky."

Shirley was pretty sure that Shaw had left the balloon on her desk, but she confronted him, anyway, just to make sure. Surprisingly, he told her point-blank that he had, and seemed in no way apologetic. Irate and afraid, Shirley turned the balloon and message over to her supervisor, Elaine. When Elaine looked at the balloon and attached message, she was equally stunned and furious that despite a clear directive, Sebastian Shaw had seen fit to retaliate against Philip. Elaine made a copy of the message and balloon, then brought Shaw into her office, confronting him with the evidence. Asked if this was his handiwork, he admitted that it was, and Elaine told him to go home to await a decision about what would happen to him next. Shaw left Paragon Cable without making a fuss.

Within the next few hours, Elaine and other supervisors got together to decide what to do about Shaw. They finally agreed that he had gone too far over the line this time, and they decided to terminate his employment. Documents were written up and his last paycheck was cut. Human resources director Linda Aday phoned Shaw and told him to come back to Paragon after noon. She didn't let him know at that point that he was being terminated.

When Shaw entered Aday's office, she closed the door behind him and began to explain that he was being fired and the reasons why. Aday said later, "He was quiet at first, but then he jumped out of his chair, tore his watch off and threw it against a wall. He went over to the window and he was so worked up I thought he was going to put his fist through the window. At that point I stood up and said, 'Sebastian! Stop it!' He began pacing back and forth in front of my desk, and I realized that he was between me and the door, and I became very uncomfortable. I finally called a male supervisor to come in and show him off the property. Sebastian kept saying, 'I can't believe this! This is wrong! I can't believe this!'"

Shaw was taken outside and didn't come back to Paragon. Even though he felt like killing Shirley Philip and Linda Aday, he realized that would be too obvious and he would quickly be caught. Instead, to vent his rage, he chose another victim—one who would have a hard time fighting back and had very little connection to him, and absolutely none to Paragon Cable.

A few miles away, Jay Rickbeil spent a quiet afternoon on a very warm July day. For once, there were no visitors, and peace and quiet pervaded the apartment. Suddenly, at some time in the late afternoon, his bedroom door swung open without warning and an intruder stood there. The intruder was Sebastian Shaw. Whether he knocked at the door is unknown. Rickbeil's door was generally unlocked and Shaw could have walked right in.

Jay was either sitting in his wheelchair by his bed or just starting to get into the wheelchair when Shaw pulled out a large knife and advanced across the room. What words were spoken between the two of them remains a mystery. Only mute evidence would tell the story of what happened next. Shaw swung the knife at Jay, and in a defensive move Jay raised his arm, and the knife blade sliced into it. Shaw kept stabbing at him, one blow after another, as Jay tried warding them off, suffering severe wounds to his hands and fingers. One blow nearly severed his thumb. The intruder was strong, but so was Jay, at least in his upper body, as he warded off one blow after another, receiving superficial wounds to his chest. As Jay moved about, parrying the blows, blood flew from his hands and spattered onto a back wall. His hands and arms became bloody and wounded from numerous cuts; still, he fought on for his very life.

Jay may have been strong, but one thing he could not do was run away. The attacker was no weakling either, and slowly he got the upper hand, pushing Jay back onto the bed. Then in one savage stroke, Sebastian Shaw completely sliced through Jay's neck, jugular vein and carotid artery. Jay slumped over on the bed, a huge pool of blood gushing out onto the blanket and pooling beneath his body. Because the carotid artery carried blood to the brain, Jay lost consciousness and within seconds was dead from the lethal wound.

After Shaw had murdered Jay Rickbeil, he walked down a hallway to the bathroom, dripping some of Jay's blood onto the hallway rug. In the bathroom he attempted to clean off blood that had spattered onto his hands and shirt by washing them in the sink. He left droplets of blood on the sink surface, and swirls of blood around the sink rim. Using some toilet tissue, Shaw dabbed at various places on his hands and arms, throwing one piece of toilet tissue into the toilet. He may have even attempted to flush the tissue, but it did not flush. Whether he knew it or not at the time, that one bit of tissue contained not only Jay Rickbeil's blood, but some of his own as well—because Jay had scratched him during his desperate struggle. After cleaning up as best he could, Shaw left without anyone knowing he had been there or had savagely killed Jay Rickbeil in a brutal attack.

Sherman Polley returned from work in the late afternoon but found that he couldn't open the front door to the apartment he shared with Rickbeil. Polley went to apartment manager "Mac" MacCartney and told him of the problem. They both went back to Polley's apartment and managed to open the door. As soon as they stepped inside, the two men looked into Jay's bedroom and saw his bloody body half-sprawled across his bed. MacCartney immediately called 911, and he seems to have said that Jay was injured at that point and not dead.

Marilyn Donner, of the Portland PD, was a patrol officer on July 2, 1991, cruising through the streets of her beat in the southeast district. She got a call on her patrol car radio at 5:42 P.M. that an individual "is injured with lots of blood at the address listed on Eighty-second Avenue, near Raymond and Colgate."

When Donner arrived there, paramedics were already on scene, and they advised her that a male in the residence was suffering more than just injuries, he was deceased. Officer Donner entered the front part of the residence but did not cross the threshold into the deceased man's bedroom. She knew that detectives would be arriving shortly and would want the room to be as untouched as possible. Of course there was a problem in that the paramedics had already been in there, but that couldn't be helped. From the threshold Donner was able to view the body of a male victim sprawled out of a wheelchair, his upper torso lying on the bed. The victim's legs were on the wheelchair, his arms were splayed out on the bed, and there was a clearly visible slash on his throat. A large amount of blood had pooled beneath his upper body on top of a blanket.

The weather was very hot that day, in the high 90s, and Donner noticed curtains blowing from an open window in the decedent's room. She found herself wondering if the killer had come in through the window. Waiting for detectives to arrive, she contacted the manager of the apartments and found out that the deceased male was forty-year-old Jay Rickbeil.

When the detectives arrived, Donner spoke with them, filling them in on what she had observed, and then she let them take over in the interior. Officer Donner went around behind the apartment where the open window was located. There was a parking lot back there, but the screen on the open window did not appear to have been tampered with.

Portland PD detectives Jim Bellah and Lloyd Higgins arrived at the 8000 block of SE Raymond about fifteen minutes after Officer Donner. Both of them had been to hundreds of crime locations by then, and dozens of homicide scenes by 1992. It soon became apparent that they were on one more homicide scene. Higgins would take over as lead detective on the case; they both entered Rickbeil's bedroom. Detective Bellah noted later, "The first thing I saw was the wound on Mr. Rickbeil and it was a huge cut, almost all the way through the neck. It was a grisly-looking scene, and blood had pooled underneath his upper body. There wasn't much blood on his lower extremities, but he had cuts on his chest and defensive wounds on his hands.

"The apartment was fairly messy that day, but that may have been its normal state. There was blood spatter on one wall behind him and to the side. I think those blood spatters happened when his hands were cut by the knife and he threw blood onto the wall as he moved around."

Detectives Bellah and Higgins observed everything they could in the bedroom, taking numerous notes, and then they started following a trail of blood droplets down a hallway to the bathroom. Since they were both sure that Jay Rickbeil was not able to move, once his throat had been cut, they surmised the killer had walked down the hallway with a sharp weapon and it had dripped blood onto the rug. Once they were in the bathroom, they noticed blood on the faucet, on the sink, and blood droplets on a roll of toilet paper. There was also a bloody tissue in the toilet bowl, as if the killer had deposited it there, intending to flush it down the toilet, but he had not succeeded.

Criminalist Roger O'Brien received a call about 6:00 P.M. to respond to the address on Raymond Street, and it took him almost forty-five minutes to assemble a crime scene kit, which included toolboxes filled with swabs, chemicals, envelopes, Baggies and other items. O'Brien recalled, "When I arrived at the scene, officers had responded and I was walked through the apartment by Detective Higgins. Higgins was the primary detective and I was the lead criminalist. Back then, one criminalist did a scene from start to finish. Detective Higgins pointed out items that he thought were important and wanted photographed. I had a thirty-five-millimeter camera and took two rolls of film."

Some of the photos O'Brien snapped included exterior shots of the apartment, the living room, Rickbeil's bedroom, his body, wheelchair and blood spatters on the wall. O'Brien moved down the hallway, taking photos of the blood droplets, and he recalled later, "The blood droplets hit the floor at an angle, so there was movement into the bathroom to make them that way. Someone was not just standing in there." (He was referring to Jay Rickbeil or Sherman Polley, who might have cut themselves shaving.) "There was diluted blood in the sink, as if someone had washed blood off [his] hands there. And a toilet paper roll between the toilet and sink had a blood droplet on it."

After taking 35mm photographs, O'Brien videotaped the same rooms and the exterior of the residence. All 35mm film and videotapes were eventually handed over by him to the Portland PD photo lab. When O'Brien was done videotaping, he met with Detective Higgins once again, and Higgins discussed what physical items he wanted taken from the scene. O'Brien started by collecting blood evidence from the walls of the bedroom using cotton swabs. Wherever the blood was dry, he used a canister of distilled water that he'd brought along to moisten the cotton swab, and then swabbed the dried blood area. He was very conscious of not cross-contaminating any of the swabs, and he used a small wooden rack with holes punched into it to separate each swab from the other. These swabs were then allowed to air-dry before they were placed into separate envelopes.

O'Brien seized a roll of toilet paper from the bathroom, placed it into a paper bag and labeled it. As for the toilet tissue in the bowl that had some blood on it, he fished it out with a swab and let it air-dry before placing it into an envelope. He carefully labeled each and every bit of evidence that was seized.

Detective Higgins asked O'Brien to collect and package a paring knife that lay on an end table. The letter *J* was written on the handle. Even though it had no apparent bloodstains on it, it was seized, anyway. A pocketknife from the bedroom was also taken. Neither Higgins nor O'Brien saw any other sharp instruments in the rooms that they felt could have caused the injuries to Jay Rickbeil.

When the swabs he had collected earlier had dried, O'Brien placed them into manila envelopes and labeled them. He sealed the envelopes shut and knew that each one would eventually either make its way to the Portland PD Crime Lab or the Oregon State Police (OSP) Crime Lab. After he had dealt with those items, and Jay Rickbeil's body had been removed, O'Brien had the crime scene to himself. It was time to try and lift fingerprints from an apartment that had seen people coming in and out of it like a train station.

O'Brien applied a fine gray powder by brush to different areas, and then he applied a very high-quality Scotch tape to the locations he had just dusted. He processed the living room, hallway, bathroom and bedroom. He processed the wheelchair, a TV tray next to the wheelchair, a telephone and door handles of the bedroom. He processed the handles inside and outside the bathroom, the sink top and sink handles. It was hard to get good prints of any value, even prints of Jay Rickbeil and Sherman Polley, much less anyone else. Criminalist O'Brien was at the crime scene for over five hours, and when he was finally done lifting prints and collecting items, he locked the front door and placed a police tape across the entrance.

Medical examiner (ME) Karen Gunson had done nearly one thousand autopsies by the time Jay Rickbeil's body arrived at the coroner's office. Gunson had graduated from Whitman College in Walla Walla, Washington, and then had done postgraduate work at a medical school in Oregon. Not only was Gunson trained in doing autopsies, but she specialized in the study of blood and fluid forensics. In 1991, DNA typing was still in its infancy, and a lot still depended on serology, the study and typing of blood.

Gunson started out by observing Jay Rickbeil's clothing and the surface area of his body. She made a note that his pants were quite large and seemed to be that way for ease of removal, since his arms had limited capacity. There was some blood on the waistband of the pants, but none below the waist. She surmised this may have been caused by Rickbeil being on his back on the bed while receiving the fatal cut to his neck. In a case like that, the blood would not have sprayed out onto his pants and elsewhere, but would have immediately pooled below his upper body. This scenario suggested the killer may have been pinning Rickbeil down when the fatal knife wound was incurred. It suggested an attacker with a fair amount of strength.

There was a gaping injury on the right side of Rickbeil's neck, and Gunson wrote that it was *caused by a sharp force injury*. There were tissue bruises in that area as well. The main wound cut through the trachea and larynx, across the muscle and across the thyroid gland. It severed the jugular vein and carotid artery, which carried blood to the brain.

Gunson noted *satellite cuts* nearby, which were shallow and nonlethal. She also noted in her reports, *There would have been copious amounts of blood flow. Someone would die quickly from this because the brain requires a large amount of blood. The carotid artery carries about eighty percent of the blood to the brain and he would have become unconscious in about ten seconds.*

Besides the obvious wound to Rickbeil's neck, Gunson found stab wounds on his chest, but these were superficial in nature, the knife point not having gone through the sternum. There was a small wound in the right bicep area and a cut on the right wrist as well. She posited these were defensive wounds. Since Rickbeil was left-handed, there were many more defensive wounds on his left arm and hand. One of these sliced between finger and thumb, possibly when he tried grabbing the knife blade to protect his chest and head area. The knife wounds to the left arm and hand were more severe than those to the right arm and hand.

In her final assessment about the cause of death, Gunson wrote, *An incised wound on the neck caused exsanguination. Classification—Homicide caused by the hands of another.*

Crime tech O'Brien was also at the autopsy of Jay Rickbeil, and his job was to collect and bag all the clothing and items taken, and photograph each one. He also photographed wounds on Rickbeil's body. O'Brien took fingernail scrapings from Rickbeil, just in case epidermal cells from the attacker were underneath Jay's fingernails. He also collected some foreign hairs that had become attached to bloody areas of Rickbeil's body, with the supposition the hairs did not belong to Rickbeil. After all the items were collected, they, too, eventually made their way to the Portland PD Crime Lab and Oregon State Crime Lab.

* * *

Detective Bellah had Sherman Polley come down to the station and Mirandized him, not because Bellah immediately thought Polley was the killer, but because he wanted to cover all the bases. After questioning, it was obvious that Polley had been at work, seen there by others, and could not have killed Jay Rickbeil in the time frame that the ME spoke of. Detective Bellah also contacted one of Jay Rickbeil's old girlfriends. Apparently, she had made a threat against him at some point. This may have been over the fact that there were a lot of other young women coming and going from Rickbeil's apartment.

Detectives Bellah and Higgins talked to people who had known Jay Rickbeil, including Victoria Taylor. They discovered that Jay never locked his front door. Bellah recalled, "I checked the door to see if it would open easily and it did. There was no evidence of damage to the door and no pry marks. The windows had been open, but there were screens on the windows and no evidence that they had been removed or damaged." Detective Bellah concluded that it could have been very easy for anyone who knew about Rickbeil's unlocked door to simply walk into the apartment and attack him.

Another thing the detectives found was that there was a virtual parade of people coming and going from Rickbeil's apartment over the last several months. One thing they did not learn, and it wouldn't come up until much later, was that Victoria Taylor had encountered one particularly angry young Asian man not long before the murder whom she had turned away from Rickbeil's door.

Instead, the investigation went down an unexpected avenue when the detectives discovered that Jay, who was an amateur photographer, had recently put an ad in a Portland newspaper asking for models. This modeling would include nude modeling by young women, but apparently he got no responses to his ad. Nonetheless, it made the detectives wonder if this angle had anything to do with his murder.

A neighbor in the apartment building, Vera White, said, "I told Jay, 'Not everyone who comes to your place has to be your friend.'" Then she added that Rickbeil "had New Age religious philosophies. He'd often politely proselytize to strangers, give them a card with his name and address on it and invite them over to his apartment. The first time I ever met him, he gave me his New Age pitch. He would invite over people who he met on the bus or at a store. Then he would complain about people coming over and stealing things."

As the days of summer went by, Detectives Bellah and Higgins were no closer to solving the murder of Jay Rickbeil. Bellah said later, "The case dead-ended pretty quickly."

Sebastian Shaw had been right about one thing: it is very difficult for law enforcement to catch a killer when the victim is chosen at random, and there were no witnesses who viewed the murder. Perhaps he began to think, *If I can get away with one murder, why not another?*

Sebastian Shaw, of course, did murder again the very next year, after having been terminated as a Pinkerton guard, and this time his victims were Todd Rudiger and Donna Ferguson. Not content to just murder, he raped Donna first in a very brutal fashion. After killing them, he soon left for southern California and went to live with his aunt Anna once more. With at least three murders to his credit by 1994, Shaw was far from staying out of trouble. In fact, he would soon be having difficulties at work once again, and as usual, his difficulties concerned the way he treated women.

7

Journey into Darkness

It wouldn't come to light until many years later just exactly what new trouble Sebastian Shaw got into concerning work and women in southern California. He just couldn't seem to hold a job for very long, either because he irritated coworkers or harassed women in the workplace. And a curious thing happened to Bruce Campbell and his parents living in San Ramon, California, in 1994. Even though San Ramon is in the San Francisco Bay Area of northern California, an incident happened there soon after Shaw was terminated from yet another job.

Someone broke into the Campbells' home, while the parents were on vacation in Europe, grabbed some keys from inside the house and stole the parents' car. The intruder also stole two .22-caliber rifles. When Bruce, who was living in Bakersfield at the time, came over to his parents' house to check up, he discovered that a window was broken in the middle bedroom, and the items gone. The car in question was a four-door green 1978 Pontiac Bonneville. Bruce Campbell had knowledge of the stolen rifles because he had used them as a boy and knew that one of the rifles had a bent sight.

Not long after this incident, twenty-year-old Michelle Lewis, of Redding, California, who lived about 250 miles north of San Ramon, was working at the Shasta Mall, a short distance from Interstate 5 on the direct route from California to Portland, Oregon. She was a pretty young woman, with dark hair, and had a lot of contact with the public at her job. At some point in time, she discovered that she never received her primary voter booklet. In fact, the booklet had been stolen by Sebastian Shaw. It had Michelle Lewis's name and address written on it.

At 4:35 A.M., on August 30, 1994, while sleeping in the stolen car from San Ramon, at the corner of Fifty-first and Klickitat in Portland, Shaw was arrested by Portland PD officer Wagenknecht. The license plate on the stolen vehicle was different from the original license plate that should have been on the car. Because of the seemingly minor nature of a stolen car, and the amount of paperwork and judicial proceedings it would take, Contra Costa County, California, decided not to prosecute Shaw for the stolen items and stolen car. Soon thereafter, Multnomah County, Oregon, dropped charges as well. Shaw spent only about two weeks in jail.

Incredibly, after being arrested and released, Shaw called up the Portland PD auto theft office and spoke with Officer Terry Long. Shaw said that he had been arrested in a stolen car—not admitting that he was the one who had stolen it—and had a lot of items in the car that he wanted back, including overdue library books. Officer Long agreed to meet with Shaw at the impound lot and take a look at what articles he was talking about.

Officer Long read the initial arrest report and discovered that the stolen vehicle belonged to Dean Campbell, of San Ramon, California. He contacted Mr. Campbell and got verbal permission to search the car for two rifles that had also been stolen. When Officer Long and Shaw both arrived at the impound lot, Officer Long told Shaw that he was going to look at all the items in the car and take photographs of them. Shaw didn't seem to have any problem with this. Once Long started looking at the items and photographing them, however, the officer was absolutely stunned.

Long found duct tape and black plastic wire ties that could be used as handcuffs. There were two ski masks and binoculars, a box of .22-rifle bullets, a claw hammer, nunchakus, a throwing knife, pepper spray and surgical gloves. A single sock contained a heavy weight inside it, as if it was to be used for a sap. There was a book about making keys, a book on first-aid training, a book on lethal poisons and *The Anarchist Cookbook*. Along with these was a *Hustler* magazine, several *Playboy* magazines and a *High Society* magazine. Long later related, "All of this stuff was like a rape/murder kit."

One more item in the car was Michelle Lewis's sample voter ballot from Redding, California. Officer Long agreed to give Shaw the library books, but all the other items were kept in law enforcement control. The items were so disturbing, Officer Long kept this file and photographs even after he retired years later. In fact, he began to keep a file on Sebastian Shaw. As far as Long was concerned, there was something just "not right" about Shaw and the items with which he was found.

Shaw soon got temporary employment with Oregon Staffing Services, and colleague Becky Black thought "there was something just not right" with Shaw. Black had numerous contacts with him, starting in August 1994, and said later, "He often asked me personal questions and wanted to know about my Christian beliefs. I couldn't get rid of him and I had a strange feeling about him. Eventually I asked my manager, Gary Helton, to come to work early because of Shaw. Sebastian would come in early and was waiting for me at work before anyone else was in the building. It was strange that he wouldn't leave until other people started showing up for work. He was always trying to prove that my beliefs in God and Jesus were wrong. He'd bring up verses of the Bible and then question those verses."

Shaw was questioning a lot of things by then, and his journal attested to that. He wrote on November 12, 1994, that he had been working hard all day. (Apparently, he was at a bakery at the time, because he wrote of taking a cigarette break outside of a bakery.) Then he wrote, *The passing of events and regrets just seem to add to the heaviness of my soul. I realize that everything I've done seems to come back and haunt me.* He noted that he lost jobs out of stupidity and felt like a failure since being discharged from the Marine Corps. Then he wrote:

> *No one knows my secret, and it is to my eternal shame that I shall probably keep the secret until my grave. The blows to my self worth seem continuous, one after the other, until there is nothing left except a nearly conscienceless time-bomb. Once I wouldn't have harmed a rodent, but now I would nuke a city without blinking. Damn this creature I have become, for it is a dark beast just waiting for the unwitting fool to come by and release it.*

Shaw wrote that he felt nothing anymore. Then he spoke of completing some task, though he didn't say what the task was. He said that he felt for his family, but that he would have to walk a road alone from now on. Then he asked, *I love them, but is it true love? Or just what's expected of me?* He also wrote that he had strayed far off the beaten path. He likened his life to a house of cards that could fall at any moment.

By 1995, Sebastian Shaw began work at a Safeway store on Hawthorne Avenue in Portland. One person who remembered him from there was Anne Roland. Shaw was a courtesy clerk at the time, and he trained her in that capacity when she joined Safeway stores. In time Shaw moved up to checker, and Roland remembered him as a hard worker who kept his uniform of dark slacks, white shirt and navy blue tie always pressed and clean. At least for Roland, Shaw was easy to get along with, but some of the other female coworkers were wary of him. He tried dating almost every woman in the store who was single, and they all turned him down.

Shaw eventually moved up to the position of a night manager at the store, and he proved to be an exacting boss. Given to fits of bad temper, he was constantly ragging other workers about being too slow or not keeping their work areas clean.

On March 5, 1995, he wrote in his journal:

In a moment of startling clarity I saw what I need to do to escape my present situation. I really don't think my family gives a shit whether I live or die. I'm starting to lose my hold on the bright side. Like in Star Wars, *I have only one more step to go before I am completely gone over to the Dark Side.*

Then he spoke of having no regrets about the things he had done in his life, which, of course, included rape and murder. He wrote, *Fuck them all!* though he didn't specify who "they" were. Perhaps he meant society in general. He said that he would go the way that others of his tempermant had gone: *My cynicism is terribly advanced. My soul, now rotten, only wants to spread rottenness to others.*

Once again, in later diary entries, he likened his life to a house of cards. He wrote, *Just one touch of the cardhouse, and it would send us all to oblivion. The charade must go on. The play and the acting is the same, wherein we keep our conscience from the king.*

Despite his dark and moody diary entries, Shaw was just about to be cast into an unforseen role as a "hero." On April 18, 1995, at 2:58 A.M., Portland PD officer Paul Jensen received a call in his patrol car that there was a home invasion robbery either in progress or had just happened at a residence near Thirtieth and Market. Officer Jensen, who was nearby, sped to the scene. Being that his windows were rolled down, he was able to hear some banging and crashing noises near a cedar fence close to the property in question. When Officer Jensen pulled over to the curb, he saw a head pop up over the fence, and a person obviously spied his squad car, because the head immediately popped back down again. When Jensen got out of his squad car, he heard multiple footsteps of people running down an alleyway.

Other patrol cars soon arrived on scene and the officers set up a perimeter around the whole block. When they were organized into a sufficient cordon, the officers, with a police dog, started moving into the interior of the block. At that point they still had no contact with the victims of the robbery, but they were pretty sure they had the suspects trapped within a perimeter.

While this was going on, Officer Jensen made his way to the victims' residence and he encountered Sebastian Shaw there. Shaw was a renter at the house and he had an upstairs bedroom there. He had been awakened by loud, strange noises downstairs around 2 A.M. The house was owned by an elderly Vietnamese couple, and when Shaw went downstairs to investigate, he discovered that several unknown men were in the residence. Shaw stealthily made his way out of the house, ran to a next-door neighbor's residence, then called 911.

As Jensen talked with Shaw, he learned that the elderly Vietnamese couple spoke almost no English. Jensen asked Shaw to be an interpreter, and Shaw willingly agreed to do so. Through Shaw, the elderly woman related that she was in the basement watching television, while her husband slept in a main-floor bedroom. She heard noises near the back door and went to investigate. When she got there, someone spoke to her in Vietnamese, saying that they wanted to speak to her son. Even before she could react, several young Vietnamese men burst through the back door, which was unlocked. The intruders pushed her back down into the basement and placed her on her hands and knees. They attempted to gag her by putting a cloth in her mouth, but when that didn't work, they simply draped some clothing over her head. Then they placed a gun next to her neck and told her not to scream.

Some of the young men went to the main-floor bedroom, where her husband was sleeping, woke him up and proceeded to ransack the place. They opened drawers, looked under the bed and totally ransacked the closet. In their quest they found jewelry and $1,400 in cash. There was a large amount of cash in the house because the elderly couple neither understood nor trusted banks.

Because of Shaw's timely intervention, three of the five intruders were eventually caught in the perimeter that the officers had established. And when it came time for a grand jury on the matter, one of the witnesses who was called was none other than Sebastian Shaw. Amazingly, Shaw was interviewed by Officer Preston Wong, the same Officer Wong who had been one of the first policemen on the scene at the Todd Rudiger/Donna Ferguson murder scene in July 1992. Officer Wong had no idea in April 1995 that the "hero" of the Vietnamese home invasion, Sebastian Shaw, was the same Shaw who had raped Donna Ferguson and then murdered her and Todd Rudiger. Despite Shaw's good deed in this situation, his role as hero was short-lived. Within a matter of months, he would return to the Dark Side.

By the late spring of 1995, Sebastian Shaw no longer seemed to care about his work habits or appearance at the Safeway store. He told Anne Roland that he was going through a breakup at the time. Just who he was talking about is not known, or whether he really was breaking up with someone at all. Shaw often seemed to fantasize that he was in a relationship with some woman. What was certain was that he now dressed in a more slovenly manner, didn't polish his shoes, and often showed up late for work. He also went out more frequently at lunchtime to have some drinks. One of the bars he frequented was Claudia's, the same tavern that Amanda Carpova went to on occasion. Before long, all vestiges of Sebastian Shaw being "the hero" of the home invasion robbery would be gone. He set his sights on another dark-haired young woman, and that woman was Amanda Carpova. It was only by her grit and tenacity—and luck—that she survived her brutal rape and attempted murder at the hands of Sebastian Shaw.

8

"You'd Better Kill Me!"

Even after Amanda Carpova's rape and near murder—
and Shaw's close call at not being seen at her apartment
when he escaped—he couldn't stay out of trouble for
long. He still worked at Safeway and continuously tried
dating one woman after another there, with no success.

By January 1996, Sebastian Shaw was living in a large
house on Eighty-sixth Avenue SE, which he shared with
several other young men. Each had his own room, and
they shared a common living area, dining room and
kitchen. The other men there were Robert Prince, Brandon Sours, Russ Sperou, John Reynolds and someone
known by the others only as "Shiloh." Of all of these, Russ
Sperou had the most checkered past, except for Shaw
who was keeping his dark secrets to himself. In the 1970s,
Sperou served prison time for various crimes, and he was
in the penitentiary long enough to know how such places
operated. In fact, he had served quite a few of his adult
years in prison.

When Sperou was back in civilian life by 1996, he lived
with the others in the large house on Eighty-sixth Avenue
and constantly reported to his probation officer (PO).

Sperou recalled later, "There was tension in the house for about a week. The others said that Shaw was bullying them about keeping the kitchen clean. Since it was a common area, I figured he was just as responsible as the others, so I didn't know what he was complaining about.

"There was some kind of argument (on January 19, 1996) going on between Shaw and one of the other guys in the kitchen. I went there to see what was going on. I told Sebastian, 'You can't be pushing these people around.' He came up and shoved me, and I shoved him back."

Brandon Sours, who was also there at the time, recalled, "Shaw and Russell got into an argument. Shaw pushed Russ, and then Russ pushed Shaw. I jumped in between them, and Shaw took a swing at Russ. That pissed Russ off, and he hit Shaw, knocking his glasses off. Then Russ put him in a headlock."

Even though Russ Sperou was six inches taller than Shaw, and weighed 205 pounds, Shaw weighed 200 pounds and had been a good wrestler in high school. It was no easy match for Sperou. Russ said later, "I'd been in a lot of fights, but he felt even stronger than me. I knew I was in a real fight this time."

Brandon Sours was also amazed at how long the wrestling/scuffling match went on. He said, "Russell kept Shaw in a headlock for a long time. Shaw kept saying, 'You'd better kill me! Because if you don't, I'll kill you!' This went on for five minutes. Then I thought to myself, 'This is really stupid,' and I left to go take a shower."

Even after Sours left the room, the wrestling match went on for another five minutes. Russ Sperou recalled, "I finally felt his strength begin to sap. I asked him if I could let him go, and he said yes. When I let him up, I asked, 'Are you okay?' He said, 'I'll let you know if I'm okay.' As exhausted as I was, he must have been the same. He went upstairs to get something and I was absolutely sure he was going to get a weapon, so I ran out of the house."

Sperou's instincts were right on the mark—Sebastian Shaw had gone upstairs to his room and had retrieved two pistols to shoot Sperou. When he came downstairs to try and find him, Sperou was gone, and it sent Shaw into a rage. He walked into Sperou's room and began blasting items within the room.

Brandon Sours, who was just drying off after a shower, recalled, "I heard gunshots, and the first thing that entered my mind was 'Oh, Jesus, this is not where I want to be, naked in the bathroom!' So I ran to my bedroom, grabbed some clothes and threw them on. When I got to the head of the stairs, Sebastian put two pistols to my face and asked where Russell was. I said I didn't know. I was scared to death, but Sebastian let me go. I walked over to my friend John's room, which was right across from Russ's room, and John was back, hidden in a corner, freaking out. We headed out of the house and tried to chase down a police officer."

Russ Sperou spoke of his own adventures while away from the residence. "I was out of the house for maybe five minutes and I ran by a construction crew, and they asked me what was going on. I told them some guy in my house had a gun. Then I went back to the house and waited underneath my window, which was on the first floor. I listened, and I thought Shaw was smashing something in my room. I took a chance and went inside, and there was Sebastian. He said, 'Russ, let's talk about this,' but he had a gun, and I bolted out of the house, went past the construction crew again and told them the guy did have a gun. I ran to a phone booth on Foster and called 911, but I felt vulnerable in the phone booth out in the open. So I ran to a second phone booth and called 911 again, but it was taking too long—giving the information—and I still felt too vulnerable. So I left it, and finally called my probation officer and told him to call the police, which he did."

Brandon Sours also had his take about what occurred when Russ Sperou returned to the house. He said, "John and I came back to the house and we were picking stuff up and getting ready to leave again, when Russell came back. Russ probably thought that Sebastian was gone, but he was still there. Shaw pointed the gun at Russ, and in my mind the only reason he didn't shoot him was because he shot so many bullets and the gun was empty. Russell turned around and ran right back out.

"John and I left, and we went to my girlfriend's house in Milwaukie. A police officer called and said he was going to the house." (At some point they apparently had gotten in touch with a police officer who returned their call.) "We gave the police officers some statements."

Portland PD officer Paul Kennard arrived at the house shared by Shaw and the others, and he met fellow officer Boedigheimer and Sperou's probation officer, Ed Gurgurich, and the landlord of the house there. They were all out on the sidewalk in front. It might be that Russ Sperou met them there as well, or at least Gurgurich had the pertinent information, because Officer Kennard learned about the argument in the kitchen, the wrestling match and Sebastian Shaw grabbing a gun afterward. Kennard also went into more detail about what occurred when Sperou returned to the house the first time.

Kennard's report noted that Shaw came out onto the porch after Sperou and yelled, *"You're dead! I won't do that much time in the pen! I'm gonna get my rifle and wait for you!"*

Also in Kennard's report, he noted that Sperou said he'd waited about twenty minutes at the second phone booth when calling 911, got cold and decided to take his chances back at the house for the second time. Apparently, Sperou did go back, found that the front door was locked and sneaked into the residence through a window. He didn't see Shaw there, so he called his PO Ed Gurgurich from the house and told him what had happened.

Officers Kennard and Boedigheimer eventually went into the house with Sperou and noted that he was still visibly shaken, even though the shootings had happened hours earlier. Sperou told Kennard that he had no doubt in his mind that Shaw would have killed him, had there been bullets in the gun the first time he came back to the house. Officers Kennard and Boedigheimer made a walk-through of the residence with Sperou as he pointed out where each incident had occurred. One interesting thing in Kennard's report was: *As we stood outside the house, where Mr. Sperou had stood and listened as his audio/video equipment was shot, I couldn't help but marvel at how fortunate he was that none of the bullets penetrated the wall and struck him.*

When they entered Sperou's bedroom, Officer Kennard saw a television, JVC video recorder, cassette deck and radio cabinet that had all been damaged by gunfire. Officer Kennard also found a .22-caliber shell casing and what appeared to be a .38-caliber bullet in the room. These finds seemed to confirm what the others had said about Shaw having two guns.

It's not clear when Officer Kennard wrote in his report what both Brandon Sours and John Reynolds said of the incident, but John added that sometime after the shooting, he saw Sebastian Shaw leave the area in a silver-colored van, which Shaw had told the others belonged to his sister. (It was actually a stolen van, as later noted in a police report.) Officer Kennard radioed another unit to search for the van at Shaw's stepsister's house, and at the Safeway store on Hawthorne. Both of these checks, however, came up empty.

After Officers Kennard and Boedigheimer made their reports and left, something incredible occurred, at least according to Brandon Sours. He stated later that no one had bothered to check Sebastian Shaw's room; they assumed he was gone in the van. Sours said, however, that Shaw was there the whole time the police were in the house, and he spent the entire night there, perhaps in the hope that Russ Sperou would return and he would kill him. Luckily, Russ Sperou had decided to spend the night over at his girlfriend's residence.

Even more amazing was the fact that when the police

came back the next morning on a follow-up check, Sebastian Shaw was still there. Why he didn't make a run for it is a mystery. Maybe he was so arrogant at this point—having murdered three people, and raped and nearly murdered one more without being caught—that he surmised he could talk his way out of anything. He certainly tried. When asked by a policeman why he had pointed a loaded pistol at Russ Sperou and then shot up Russ's room, Shaw blatantly replied, "I don't own any guns."

The police looked around for the pistols, and didn't find any. However, they had statements from everyone else that Shaw did own two pistols, and there was all the evidence of a room that had been blasted as well. Even further than that, John Reynolds told the police that Shaw had a .22 and a .38, the same kind of weapons that matched the bullet and bullet casing found in Russ Sperou's room.

As Sebastian Shaw was arrested for "menacing/criminal mischief and unlawful use of a firearm," he didn't help his cause any by shouting at John, "You'd better hope I don't get out of jail, because I'll kill you!"

Sebastian Shaw was taken down to a jail and was booked on the charges, had his fingerprints taken and mug shots snapped. Perhaps the charges weren't as bad as they could have been, but he was at last in the criminal justice system, and that fact alone would have far-reaching and unforeseen consequences for him later.

His name was written down on a form as Sebastian Shaw, and also as Chau Quong Ho. He was listed as being twenty-eight years old, five-eight and weighing two hundred pounds. Yet, once again, Shaw did not serve much jail time, just as had happened after being arrested for stealing the Campbells' car in 1994. He was able to plead guilty and got probation, in which he had to see a court-appointed counselor.

Psychiatrist Paul Leung originally saw Sebastian Shaw

while Shaw was incarcerated in the county jail awaiting trial. Dr. Leung spoke English, Vietnamese, Mandarin Chinese and Cantonese Chinese. Because of a large community of refugees from Vietnam, Cambodia and Laos that lived in Oregon, he treated many of them as clients. Dr. Leung first saw Shaw because of an evaluation request by Shaw's defense attorney concerning the Russell Sperou shooting.

The visit between Dr. Leung and Shaw occurred as a noncontact visit, which meant they did not have a private room, but rather they spoke through phones with a thick Plexiglas screen between them in the jail. There were many other inmates and visitors in the room as well. Dr. Leung had already read the police report on the matter, and Shaw told him that he was currently working as lead checker and part-time manager at a local Safeway store. In his position as supervisor, Shaw said, he often had to tell other employees to keep their work areas clean. Some did not follow his rules, and it upset him. When one of his roommates, according to Shaw, accused him of not keeping the kitchen area tidy, it set him off and led to a fight.

Shaw admitted to grabbing a gun and going to that person's room and shooting some of his personal belongings, but Shaw left out the part where he had threatened to kill Russ Sperou. Shaw did mention that he didn't try to flee the scene, and he was there the next day when police talked to everyone. Shaw also said he tried to tell the officers the truth about what happened, but they arrested him, anyway (at least the truth according to Shaw).

Delving into Shaw's past, Dr. Leung learned that when Sebastian was only ten months old, Shaw's mother had died. What was curious now was that Shaw lied and said that his mother's maiden name had been Shaw, when, in fact, it was not. Shaw went on to say that he was raised by a paternal aunt, and that he could remember being evacuated from Saigon. He did not bring up anything about having been bitten by fire ants as a child or the trauma of being a refugee on Guam and Wake Island.

Shaw added, "In my grade school years, my father demanded me back. I left my aunt with sadness." He then related that living with his father was hard, and there was a lot of verbal and physical abuse. Shaw said he was beaten with a belt or firewood for even the most minor of infractions. He also recalled that he had come home from school one day, only to find that he had lost his key to the residence. He ended up spending the afternoon and evening out in the cold until his father came home. Instead of being sympathetic to his plight, Van Ho punched out a window to get inside and dragged Shaw through the broken glass and proceeded to beat him with a belt. Shaw said his father beat him until he got tired and couldn't continue. And Shaw related that he had not only been covered with bruises from the whipping, but he was also covered with cuts from the glass.

Shaw then spoke of another time when his father left him alone for a number of days and Sebastian didn't have warm clothing to wear to school. It was his next-door neighbor Ly Do who gave him some clothing that was appropriate for the cold weather.

Shaw also brought up an incident with Ly Do, and this seems to have been when he was either a teenager or already out of the Marine Corps. Shaw said that there was some kind of allegation against his stepmom that she was defrauding the welfare system, which was not true. Shaw was asked to act as an interpreter with an official, and he got some wording wrong, which caused his stepmom to be found guilty of fraud and fined $20,000. Shaw said he felt very guilty about this. In fact, when he related this incident to Dr. Leung, he began sobbing. Dr. Leung later said he felt sorry and embarrassed for Shaw, since there were other inmates sitting nearby and visitors as well.

Shaw also told Dr. Leung he hadn't been very happy in the marines. He wanted to be in the infantry, but according to Shaw, he had been denied the posting because he still had stepbrothers in Vietnam. Instead, he was forced to stay in a supply unit, and he felt frustrated and said that he didn't fit in. Shaw did not mention that he had really been booted out of the marines because he could not keep his weight down.

Dr. Leung did a follow-up about Shaw's father, Van Ho, and discovered that the man had been arrested and convicted of crimes and placed in a state hospital for a while. Then Van Ho had ended up serving seven years in the Oregon State prison system. According to Shaw, his father had been convicted of kidnapping and some violent acts.

Dr. Leung made a diagnosis of Sebastian Shaw and noted that he suffered from chronic depression, had post-traumatic stress disorder (PTSD) in chronic form and an alcohol problem. Dr. Leung did not have an opinion whether Sebastian Shaw suffered from a personality disorder. Of course, at that point, Dr. Leung had no idea that Shaw had killed three people.

Sebastian Shaw eventually pled guilty to assault charges against Russ Sperou and served a very short amount of time. As part of his plea agreement, he was to see Dr. Leung again for follow-up treatment. Shaw also had to see a social worker as part of the release program. This program concerned Shaw's abuse of alcohol and lack of control when it came to his anger. He had to submit to a formal evaluation by Steve McNamara, who did drug and alcohol evaluations for the Department of Corrections.

McNamara spoke with Shaw and learned that Sebastian had been born in Vietnam and his mother had died before he was a year old. Raised by a paternal aunt, Shaw described his father as an abusive alcoholic. Then Shaw added one more thing that had not come up before—and would not come up later. He said that while he was in the third grade, he was sexually abused by two of his dad's friends. McNamara later said that Shaw seemed to be telling the truth about this, as far as he could tell, as there was no benefit to Shaw at the time to bring up this kind of thing. McNamara was trained in psychotherapy, and he believed that Shaw was telling him the truth on this and other matters.

Shaw told McNamara that his childhood had been very chaotic, and he had been dragged from one town to another, which often disrupted his schooling. He also admitted to one suicide attempt when he was a teenager. He had told Ly Do at the time that it was an accident, but he told McNamara that he had really tried to kill himself. According to McNamara, Shaw seemed depressed and anxious when it came to family relationships. McNamara assessed that Shaw no longer had a need for alcohol treatment, but that he should seek counseling for anger management. This report was sent on to Shaw's probation officer.

Back on the street, Shaw just couldn't stay out of trouble, however, and the next incident occurred between himself and stepsister Lan Do. On June 5, 1996, Shaw got into an argument with her. He pushed her very hard and threw an onion at her. According to Lan Do, "the onion exploded against the side of my head." A restraining order was put out against Shaw not to come within one hundred feet of Lan Do.

Dr. Leung saw Shaw from September 1996 into February 1997. Shaw went to a place where Dr. Leung worked part-time, the Chinese Mental Health Care Facility in Portland, Oregon. Because Shaw later waived his rights to doctor/client privileges, just what he and Dr. Leung talked about became a matter of record. Shaw told Dr. Leung he always felt like an outsider. Dr. Leung noted a lack of an ability on Shaw's part to have an emotional tie with his father. Shaw also said that he didn't hate his father, but that he did fear him.

Shaw told Dr. Leung that he felt "ugly," and that no female wanted to have a relationship with him. Over the course of the sessions, Dr. Leung wrote, *It is my opinion that Mr. Sebastian Shaw needs mainstream psychiatric attention in order to deal with his depression and PTSD, specifically addressing the raging issues and hypervigilance. If the conditions are left untreated, the risk of seeing Mr. Shaw get into similar conflicts in the future is quite high, and the outcome may be less fortunate than this one.* Because of Shaw's symptoms, Dr. Leung prescribed Paxil, an antidepressant medication.

There were several key things that Sebastian Shaw never told Dr. Leung or Steve McNamara, and these included the facts that he had murdered Jay Rickbeil, Donna Ferguson and Todd Rudiger, as well as raping Amanda Carpova and nearly killing her. Then suddenly, in March 1997, Sebastian Shaw quit going to see Dr. Leung. In some ways it didn't matter—the charade of normalcy that he had tried portraying to the outside world was about to come to an end. There were two police detectives who by now had an inkling that Sebastian Shaw had done a lot more than merely shoot out Russ Sperou's audio and video equipment.

Despite all his troubles with the law, and the need to keep a low profile, Sebastian Shaw did not refrain from putting down in print exactly how he felt about violence and murder. In a remarkable story that he entitled "The Time Is Right!" Shaw wrote of a young man and woman being chased in the dark woods by a killer. The killer Shaw named the "Hunter," and remarked that life went from bacteria to worm to frog to snake to eagle and back to bacteria again when the eagle died.

In the story a man and woman ran through the woods, where they spotted a cabin. They dashed inside, hoping it would give them enough time to concoct a plan against their pursuer. It was here that Shaw described the woman as having *midnight ebony hair and green catlike eyes.* They propped a chair up against the door, but within minutes the Hunter smashed his way in, and the man and woman ran to opposite corners of the cabin. Shaw wrote, *The Hunter drew his left sleeve across his lips, his saliva already tasting their hot, fevered blood.* The Hunter had first targeted these two at a Saturday market in the city, and then followed them as they went on a camping trip out into

the woods. In fact, just before leaving the city, the Hunter
had sneaked up on a police officer, who was sitting in his
patrol car and eating a doughnut, and ripped the officer's
throat apart with one quick motion.

Now with the prey at his mercy, the Hunter had to
decide whom to kill first. He quickly glanced at both.
Shaw wrote:

> *The female of the species tasted better, more aromatic, like the
> difference of a fresh apple pie coming out of the oven to the
> store bought variety that has already cooled. With unbeliev-
> able speed, he rushed the female, pinning her to the dilapi-
> dated wall of the cabin by her neck, savoring the moment
> before he sunk his teeth into her flesh. He grabbed a handful
> of blouse and ripped it away from her body, exposing a pair
> of perfectly shaped globes topped by the pinkest of nipples.*

Suddenly the Hunter felt the male jump on his back,
but he tossed him backward across the room. Then he
threw the man through a window with an explosion of
glass. The woman took this opportunity to escape out
the door, but the Hunter smiled, knowing that this was
just a chance to *play with his food*.

Unexpectedly, however, the night sky lit up, and the
Hunter realized that he was becoming the hunted. "Two
predators" were coming out of the woods to hunt him,
bent on vengeance. He had killed their young, and now
they were after him. In the last few seconds of his life, the
Hunter realized how quickly tables could turn *as his last
sight was a brown and gray blur heading for his exposed throat.*

Amazingly, Shaw had just written a record of sex, violence and the slashing of throats. And whether he realized
it or not on some level, there were two detectives who
were about to begin a long and detailed quest to put Sebastian Shaw's deadly rapes and murders to an end, once
and for all.

9

Tracking Leads

Sebastian Shaw entered the Oregon criminal system database in 1996, and while he was out on probation, he set in motion a long string of events, which on the surface seemed to have no connection. However, as time went on, they did connect one dot to another of his past crimes. It started way outside of having anything to do with the shooting of Russ Sperou's room or Shaw's assault of his stepsister.

What started the whole process was an update check on cold cases, using the DNA database at the Oregon State Crime Laboratory. On September 5, 1997, there was a positive DNA match between a sperm cell taken from the Donna Ferguson case and a sperm cell from the Amanda Carpova case. The labs didn't know who the contributor of the sperm cell was, only that the person was the same contributor.

Detective Larry Findling, who had been the chief investigator on the Rudiger/Ferguson case, just happened to see a photo of Amanda Carpova and thought, *Wow, this girl looks like Donna Ferguson!* They both had dark hair and shared many similar aspects. The fact that both Carpova and Ferguson had been raped by the same person, according to DNA results, was a breakthrough for Findling. Carpova had lived to tell about her attacker. She had described not only the clothing he was wearing, but his mode of assault and his facial features and overall body proportions as well.

Findling went to the captain of detectives at Portland PD, hoping to do further detective work, but initially this person didn't want resources and time spent on an old and *very* cold case. Luckily for Findling, Assistant Chief of Police Lanae Berg just happened to be there that day. When she heard Findling say, "He's a hunter!" that was enough for her. She knew those types and knew they wouldn't stop raping and killing until they were stopped. She allocated the money and time needed.

By now, Findling was a lieutenant in the police department and couldn't do the day-to-day investigative work trying to discover who the "sperm donor" rapist was. So he chose one of the detectives who had worked on the Rudiger/Ferguson case to do more investigation, and this brought the Sebastian Shaw matter onto the desk of Portland Police detective Mike Stahlman. Stahlman had been a policeman with the Portland PD for eleven years, by 1997. He had been on the original Donna Ferguson/Todd Rudiger case, and he later did some work on the Amanda Carpova case. Knowing that there was some kind of connection between Donna Ferguson and Amanda Carpova, Detective Stahlman noted that both women had dark hair, had been raped by an intruder, plus the intruder had used a pistol to gain access into Amanda's apartment and forced her to do what he wanted. He wondered if that might have been the case with Donna Ferguson as well.

On September 9, 1997, Stahlman began the process by reading police reports written three months before and after the crimes of Donna Ferguson and Amanda Carpova. He was looking for prowlers and suspicious persons who had been seen in the area and matched the description of Amanda's attacker. Nothing popped up on his radar about this, so Stahlman ran computer searches for prowler reports, trespass reports, burglary reports and sex crime reports in the areas where the crimes had occurred. Once again, nothing stood out about a possible suspect.

On September 16, Stahlman sent a teletype report to police agencies in eleven states in the West, concerning details and the MOs of the Ferguson and Carpova cases, along with a description of Carpova's rapist. It took only one day for Officer Merino, of the Steilacoom, Washington, Police Department, to respond by saying a Japanese male named Derrick Nishmura might fit the profile. Officer Merino related, "Nishmura is extremely violent and has assaulted his wife numerous times." Officer Merino said he would attempt to find out where Nishmura had been in 1992 and 1995.

That very same day, Stahlman also received a response from Detective Garcia, of the Fresno, California, Police Department. Detective Garcia was investigating a rape/sodomy/homicide that had occurred in August 1996. In that case a white twenty-two-year-old female college student was killed in her apartment sometime between noon and 7:00 P.M. Her wrists and ankles had been bound with duct tape, as well as her mouth. She had been both vaginally and anally raped. Her cause of death was from duct tape being placed over her nose and mouth; she had suffocated.

A few days later, Detective Jack Archer, of the Costa Mesa, California, Police Department, responded to the teletype by saying that he was investigating a rape/sodomy/homicide of a twenty-six-year-old female college student. She had been killed in her apartment around 3:00 A.M. She had not been bound, but she had been manually strangled. DNA had been recovered, and Detective Stahlman gave Archer the phone number of Terry Coons at the OSP Lab. (These would later not come back as a match to Shaw).

Possible crimes came from as far away as Iowa, and Special Agent Joe Motzinger, of the Iowa Department of Public Safety, informed Stahlman that a twenty-one-year-old female housekeeper at a motel was bound with insulation tape and murdered. She had not been sexually assaulted, but she had died from stab wounds to her throat. DNA had not been recovered from that crime scene.

On September 27, Detective Stahlman met with Detective Tom Nelson in Portland and they sat down with Terry Coons at the Oregon lab. Coons told them that twelve states now had computerized DNA databases that could be easily checked for a match. In fact, by that date, the DNA information from the Ferguson and Carpova cases had been checked against DNA databases in California and Washington State, with no matches. Stahlman later asked Bill Wesslund, of the Portland Police Bureau (PPB) Data Processing Unit, to provide him with a list of all robbery and rape/homicide cases that contained the words "Hawaiian," "Japanese" or "Asian."

A few days later, Detective McCann, of the Los Angeles Police Department, contacted Stahlman about a white female who in 1989 had been raped and strangled in her residence. She had been bound with extension cord, and a Hispanic man had been arrested, but was later released. The man now lived in New Orleans. Detective Nikki Poole, of Colorado Springs, Colorado, told Stahlman that a case in her jurisdiction involved a woman who had been tied up, raped and beaten to death with a hockey stick.

Following an interview on Crime Stoppers on televison, regarding the Rudiger/Ferguson case, Detective Stahlman was contacted by a woman named Lori Kohler. She knew some people with the last name of Jordan, and they had lived in a trailer park in the southeastern portion of Portland. Mr. Jordan had threatened his wife with a knife and also stolen credit cards during their marriage. Kohler thought Jordan was violent and could be responsible for the Rudiger/Ferguson homicides. Detective Stahlman checked Jordan's photo and decided that he did not match the description given by Amanda Carpova about her rapist.

In October, Randy Ireson, who was a data analyst at the Department of Corrections in Salem, Oregon, ran a computer check of all inmates between January 1, 1980, through June 1, 1995, who were between the ages of twenty-five and forty-two, and incarcerated for rape/sodomy. Detective Stahlman also contacted Dick Steiner, a retired Seattle Police Department homicide detective who supervised the Washington State Homicide Investigation and Tracking System (HITS) Unit, which did computer analysis of major crimes in western states. Stahlman asked Steiner to research files of cases similar to the ones he was looking at.

Detective John Bocciolatt, an important member of the team, joined Stahlman on November 1, 1997. From that day forward, Stahlman and Bocciolatt devoted countless hours in trying to find the connection between the rape and murder of Donna Ferguson and the rape and attempted murder of Amanda Carpova. They sometimes worked together, and at other times went their separate ways in the investigation, but they always got back together at some point and compared information. Stahlman and Bocciolatt met at the property room that contained evidence concerning both cases, and Stahlman thought the stocking cap left at the scene of the 1995 rape might contain DNA evidence, so he submitted that to the crime lab for testing.

A very interesting contact came in to the detectives on November 5, 1997. Detective Bryan Costigan, of the Montana Department of Investigation, reported that a white male burglarized a mobile home of a female in his state, tied up the female with athletic tape and raped her. The rapist at that time had referred to his penis as his "nub," and even said he wanted to go to Oregon. The comment about "nub" was interesting, because Amanda Carpova described her attacker as having a very small penis.

On November 6, Detective Stahlman spoke with De-

tective Casey Nice, of the Alameda County Sheriff's
Office (ACSO), about a case in Alameda County that
had occurred on May 27, 1994. In that case a fourteen-
year-old Asian female had been found undressed and
stabbed to death in her residence in Castro Valley, California. Detective Nice told Stahlman the victim had
been gagged and tied up with duct tape. There was no
DNA evidence, however. Detective Nice asked for a copy
of the drawing of the suspect in Amanda Carpova's case,
and Stahlman mailed him a copy.

In fact, by now, Stahlman was sending copies of the suspect's drawing to numerous law enforcement agencies,
from Kitsap County, Washington, to Santa Barbara County,
California. In that county, two Swedish hitchhiking females
had been found in a remote area in 1983, raped and
stabbed to death. A case also came to Stahlman's attention
about a woman in Seattle who had been tied up and raped
by a "Samoan."

A few days later, Detectives Stahlman and Bocciolatt
attended a meeting with the Portland Metro Area Sex
Crimes Investigators Unit in the Southeast Precinct and
shared information about their cases. Then they met with
PO Sandy Rorik, who worked with sex criminals in the
Portland area. They reviewed mug shots and client lists
to see if anyone matched the description given by
Amanda Carpova. They also met with detectives in coun-
ties that were adjacent to Portland, then talked to them
about the cases.

On November 21, 1997, ACSO detective Casey Nice
contacted Stahlman with a very important message. Nice
said that there was a possible suspect named Sebastian
Shaw, who might have been in Alameda County in the
spring of 1994. Shaw had stolen a car from neighboring
Contra Costa County, which was later recovered in Portland. Detective Nice said that when Shaw was arrested in
Portland in connection with the vehicle, he had a bag that
contained blindfolds, duct tape, pepper spray, ski masks,
flex ties and other items associated with burglary/rapes.

The most important part of Detective Nice's conversation was that Sebastian Shaw's physical description was similar to the suspect in Amanda Carpova's 1995 rape/attempted murder case.

Even though Detective Nice's conversation was very intriguing, other suspects could not be ruled out at that time. Detective Bocciolatt spoke with Detective Craig Stoelk about a Pacific Islander with the name of Lemsu. Terry Coons, at the OSP Lab, however, ran a DNA comparison and was able to rule out Lemsu as the contributor of sperm to both the Ferguson and Carpova cases.

On November 21, both Stahlman and Bocciolatt had a telephone conversation with Amanda Carpova and listened to her responses on speakers at a police precinct. The detectives explained that they were reinvestigating her rape, and they wanted to know why she was so sure she had been raped by someone who was "Japanese, Filipino, Japanese or half Japanese/half Caucasian." Carpova ruled out the suspect being Korean, because she had lived with a Korean woman for a couple of years, and she felt comfortable in describing the suspect with the ethnicities she had given. She added, "He was stocky, and not muscularly built. He was like a petite sumo wrestler." When asked about his speech patterns, she said, "He was very Caucasian in speech. He didn't have an accent."

Carpova said the suspect had worn sunglasses while coming into her apartment, and then he had taken them off. Asked whether the sunglasses could have been prescription, she answered that she she didn't know. Asked if he had any marks, scars or tattoos, she said that he never had his shirt off and she didn't know. Amanda added that since her rape she had become more familiar with firearms by going to a gun store to see what was there. She described the assailant's weapon as "charcoal gray in color, not small and not huge. The front end of the gun was approximately four inches long."

Asked if she noticed anything missing from her apartment after she had been attacked, Amanda said that during the assault, the suspect had asked her if she had any money. She told him where her wallet was, but he never took any money from her. When officers showed up at her apartment, they found her wallet, which still contained money in it.

Amanda added that when she was examined at the University Hospital, she spoke with a doctor about the assault, and the doctor indicated that some other woman had been raped about eleven days earlier by a man who had features like Amanda's rapist. The doctor seemed to feel that there was a similar MO involved.

A few minutes after the telephone call ended, Amanda called the detectives back and told them that she had been working at the Bread and Ink Cafe in her neighborhood at the time she was raped. She said that it was possible that the rapist had followed her from the Bread and Ink Cafe to find out where she lived.

The very next day, Detective Bocciolatt phoned Amanda again and asked her where she shopped while living on Harrison Street. Amanda said that she'd shopped at a Fred Meyer store on SE Thirty-ninth and Natures store on SE Division. Asked if she ever shopped at a Safeway grocery store, Amanda said that she shopped there occasionally, and when she did so, she used checks that had her address printed on them.

Because of his conversation with Detective Nice in Alameda County, Mike Stahlman started looking up information about Sebastian Shaw. He noted that Shaw had been arrested in Portland on various charges. The first arrest had occurred in 1994 in connection with the stolen car. In 1996, Shaw had been arrested for discharging a firearm in an unsafe manner in a residence, and another arrest had occurred when he threw an onion at his stepsister's head. Officers had checked on Shaw's place of employment then, and Stahlman noted that Shaw had worked at a Safeway store at SE Twenty-seventh and Hawthorne, not far from where Amanda Carpova lived at the time.

Three days later, Detective Stahlman contacted Armando Navarro, of Safeway Incorporated Security, and asked him to check on Sebastian Shaw's work record. Navarro told Stahlman that Shaw was employed by Safeway from February 4, 1995, until January 20, 1996, and had only worked at the store on SE Twenty-seventh and Hawthorne. Shaw was initially hired as a courtesy clerk, who would bag groceries, but he eventually worked his way up to checker. Navarro then faxed Stahlman job résumés Shaw had used when he applied for the Safeway job. These included references to jobs in Oregon and California, as well as the fact that Shaw had been in the Marine Corps.

Looking through other police reports, Stahlman noticed that Shaw had been working at a video store on the 4400 block of Sandy Boulevard in 1992, the same year as Donna Ferguson's murder. Looking into a Portland PD Pawn Unit report, Stahlman also noted that Shaw had sold or pawned camera equipment at the AAA Cash Now pawnshop on July 20, 1992. This was the same date that Todd Rudiger and Donna Ferguson's bodies were discovered in their mobile home. Todd's father had said in 1992 that some photo equipment of his son's was missing from the mobile home.

On November 25, 1997, Detectives Stahlman and Bocciolatt met with Probation Officer Terry Hanson, who confirmed that Sebastian Shaw was on probation with her office until 2001. Then Hanson and the detectives all reviewed Shaw's file. While this was going on, Detective Stahlman had Sergeant D. B. Falconer go to the AAA Cash Now pawnshop to see if the owner still had a pink copy of old purchases concerning a camera tripod. Falconer met with John Herman and showed him a pawn display ticket B142067 that was dated July 20, 1992. Amazingly, Herman said that he did keep all the old pink copies, even though he was only required by law to keep them one year. He let Falconer go through a shopping bag full of old pink copies, and Falconer found the one in question. Even more amazingly, Herman said he remembered the transaction that had occurred in 1992. The camera tripod had been brought in by an Asian male who was well-dressed, and had a stocky build. Herman remembered the tripod, because after he had given the Asian man money for it, Herman found out that the tripod had a piece missing, decreasing its value. He had been angry at himself for not checking that first.

On November 26, Detectives Stahlman and Bocciolatt met with Patrol Officer Wagenknecht to talk about Sebastian Shaw's arrest of a stolen car back in 1994. Wagenknecht told them he recalled Shaw having a backpack in the front seat of the vehicle, and the backpack contained clothing and an owner's manual for a pistol. Shaw acknowledged ownership of the backpack and a pistol found beneath the front seat of the vehicle. When Wagenknecht asked about who owned the vehicle, Shaw immediately asked for an attorney and declined to answer any further questions. Officer Wagenknecht said that Shaw spoke with a soft voice with no hint of an accent.

Because of all the interesting information that had come out of Alameda County, California, Detective Stahlman traveled down to the Alameda County Sheriff's Office in San Leandro and spoke in person with Detective Casey Nice. Detective Nice gave Stahlman all the items that had been found in the stolen vehicle from San Ramon, the same vehicle in which Shaw had been sleeping in, in Portland. Detective Nice said that no investigative testing had been done by his jurisdiction on the seized items.

The items were stored in three white cardboard boxes and were marked as evidence and sealed with evidence tape. In addition to these boxes, there was one blue nylon sports bag, which also had evidence tape on it. When Detective Stahlman flew back to Portland, he constantly kept the boxes and nylon bag in his possession.

Once he was back in Portland, Stahlman spoke by phone with Detective Doug Pendleton, of the San Ramon Police Department. Pendleton told him that the stolen vehicle had belonged to Dean Campbell, of San Ramon, who claimed that two .22-caliber rifles were also stolen from him, but none of the other evidence seized from the trunk was his.

Wanting to talk to possible witnesses to Amanda Carpova's rape, Detective Bocciolatt spoke with Amanda's friend Maya, who lived across the apartment complex. Maya was very concerned about her safety, and she initially didn't want to talk with Detective Bocciolatt at all. Eventually she did so, on the agreement that he would keep her telephone number and address out of the police reports. Initially Maya said that she couldn't recall anything more than what was already in the reports from 1995. After a while, however, Maya said she recalled that three or four days before Amanda was raped, someone rang her doorbell. She did not answer the door, but rather peeked out the window to see a stocky young Asian man heading across the apartment complex toward Amanda Carpova's door. Maya described the suspect as "East Indian, Hawaiian or Filipino, and he was about five feet seven inches tall. He had straight hair that was flat on his head." Then Maya added one more odd comment, she said that the suspect was "very Northwestern." By that, she might have meant the clothes he was wearing, which was casual attire. She said the man was "very, very average."

Asked once again what happened when Amanda came running to her apartment after being raped, Maya said, "Her face was blue and she had a scarf around her neck. She was naked and her wrists were scratched up and her hair was messy. She was extremely distraught and yelling, 'You have to do something! You have to do something!' Amanda kept on yelling and said that she had just been raped. I gave her a housecoat and called 911. I was told by the 911 operator that the incident had already been called in and the police were on their way."

Maya said that after the rape Amanda did not want to live in that apartment again. When she helped Amanda pack up her things, they found a black ski mask. Maya asked what had ever happened to this black ski mask, and Detective Bocciolatt told her that it was in evidence.

Just because Sebastian Shaw was coming more and more into focus as a suspect on the Donna Ferguson and Amanda Carpova cases, it didn't mean that detectives Stahlman and Bocciolatt could exclude all other suspects. On December 13, 1997, Bocciolatt received information that an Asian man, who was not Shaw, tried to make two underage girls get into his truck on NE 148th Avenue. He was driving a 1980s blue Toyota SUV and the man was described as stocky in build. He had ordered, "Get into my truck!" but they ran away.

Back to information concerning people who had lived in the same apartment complex as Amanda Carpova in 1995, the detectives spoke with various people who remembered events of May 1995. One of these was Eric Lindstedt, who had lived next door to Amanda's apartment. Lindstedt told the detectives that on the evening before the rape, he and his wife, Lisa Gabriel, were home at around eleven, along with Lisa's brother, Matthew Gabriel, and Matthew's girlfriend, Christina Nielson. The four of them were watching television in the apartment with the lights turned off. Matthew and Christina were sitting on a couch that could not be seen from the front window, and Lisa was sitting in a chair that could be seen from the front window.

Eric went into another room, when his wife suddenly called out, "Eric! Eric!" as if she was very startled by something. Eric walked back into the room and immediately saw a stranger standing at the front door. Eric told the detectives, "As I reached the front door, it was open, but the screen door was closed. The stranger came right to the door. I asked him what he wanted, and he replied he was looking for a family who once had lived in the apartments. He had a kind of sheepish grin on his face, and there just wasn't something right about him. His question didn't make sense, because the apartments were very small, and I wondered what a family was doing living in them. It was crowded for two people, much less a family."

The detectives asked Eric to describe the person and

he said that the man was Asian, in his mid-twenties to early thirties, five-seven or five-eight, stocky build, medium-length hair, no glasses, wearing a blue jacket or windbreaker and khaki pants. The suspect was soft-spoken with no trace of an accent. Eric had seen the drawing made of a suspect in 1995, and he said the depiction was "pretty accurate." Eric thought the man was Japanese, mixed Japanese and Caucasian, or Hawaiian.

Eric added that the next day he and Lisa slept in very late, and when they awoke, they heard about the rape of Amanda Carpova. Hearing about the description of that person, they believed it was the same man who came to their door at eleven P.M. on the previous night. After the rape Eric and his wife immediately thought of a nearby eatery named the Local Boyz Restaurant. It was a Hawaiian restaurant, and had Hawaiian employees. They even went there several times to see if they could spot the suspect, but they never did see him there.

Eric added that someone the detectives might want to talk to was named Dottie. She was an older woman who had lived in the apartment complex for years, and according to Eric, she "was very observant." At that point the detectives showed Eric the forensic drawing of the suspect made in 1995, and asked him on a scale of one to ten, to rate it for accuracy. Eric said, "It's about an eight. If I could just see him smile. He had a really eerie grin."

When the detectives spoke separately to Lisa Gabriel, she told them that she had been sitting in her living room that night, and because the room was dark—and her brother and girlfriend were sitting down low in the shadows—she believed she was the only one who could be seen from the front window. At some point Lisa became aware of a young man staring at her through the window-pane. She said, "He stared at me for like thirty or forty seconds with a weird, eerie look on his face. Like a schizophrenic staring at me. I finally called out, 'Eric!' and my husband walked to the front door and talked to him. The man told my husband that he was trying to find a family who had lived in the apartments. I thought, 'Yeah, right! At eleven at night!'

"The next day I heard about our neighbor being raped and realized that it could have been the same person. He'd had an ear-to-ear grin on his face. It was not a funny grin, but more like that of a maniac or schizophrenic. He was focused when he stared right at me. I didn't go to the door with my husband, because I was frightened of him, but I could see him through the screen door. He was Asian or Hawaiian. In his late twenties or early thirties, and about five-seven or five-eight. He weighed about one hundred fifty or one hundred sixty pounds, didn't have facial hair and didn't wear glasses. He wore some kind of jacket and khaki pants." She described him as being average in looks.

The detectives asked Lisa what kind of voice the person had. She said that it was mellow and soft and he didn't have an accent. She added that she saw a poster of the suspect in 1995, and didn't think the depiction looked like the person she had seen. The detectives showed Lisa the drawing again, and she said that it made him look too heavy, his hair wasn't right and he looked too young. Lisa said on a scale of ten, the depiction was about a five. Then she said he was not Caucasian, not Hispanic, not African-American and not Vietnamese. This last was an interesting comment, but Lisa's idea of Vietnamese men was that they were fairly short and usually thin in build. The man at her door had been stocky and had a round face. She thought he was Japanese, Polynesian or Pacific Islander.

Lisa told the detectives that she believed the man would have come in to rape her if no one else had been there at the time. Lisa added that she usually shopped at the Safeway on SE Twenty-seventh and Hawthorne and sometimes paid with a check, and that her name and address were on the checks.

Next the detectives contacted Mike Harpole by telephone. Harpole had originally spoken with Officer Chilen back in 1995 about visiting his friend Kim Gillespie at Amanda Carpova's apartment complex on the day of the rape. On the phone Harpole said that he and Kim had been at her apartment that day in 1995 to pick up something before going out again. Kim had turned on the music fairly loud, but even with the music on, they still heard loud noises coming from the adjacent apartment.

Harpole said that it sounded like an argument, and he turned the music down to hear what was going on. He said that he heard one shout, and then the noises got quiet. After a brief interval, he heard a female voice saying, "No, stop, stop, stop!" Harpole did not recall any banging noises or sounds of a struggle. After a while, he walked to a window in Kim's apartment and saw a young woman climb out a window in the neighboring apartment. The woman was naked, except for some clothing she held in front of her, and she was quite upset as she ran across the courtyard to another apartment. Harpole said he waited to see if anyone else came out of the woman's apartment, but no one did. At the same time, Harpole said, Kim Gillespie walked to her back window to see if anyone went out that way, but she didn't see anyone. Harpole thought the man had either already left the apartment or went out in a southward direction, which they could not see.

Detective Stahlman contacted Matthew Gabriel by phone. Matthew had been in the apartment with his sister, Lisa Gabriel, Eric Lindstedt and Christina Nielson on a night before the rape occurred. Matthew said that he never saw the person who had come to the door, nor could he see him from where he was sitting. Matthew also stated that the description of the suspect was not of anyone that he knew.

After talking to Matthew Gabriel, Stahlman spoke with Christina Nielson. Christina was sitting on the couch with boyfriend Matthew that night when she suddenly heard Lisa exclaim, "Eric, there's somebody out there, and he's coming to the door!" At that point Eric went to the door and talked with a man. Because of where Christina sat on the couch, she could see the person and hear him too. But she thought the person had said that he was looking for a yellow house in the neighborhood, where a family he once knew had lived. Christina added, "He looked really creepy, the way he looked at me."

Christina described the person as being an Asian male, approximately twenty-five to thirty years in age, with straight dark hair, with no glasses and smooth skin. She even remarked, "I was particularly struck by his smooth skin, and thought, 'Oh, what a waste! Lots of women would love to have skin like that.'" She added that the suspect was wearing jean shorts and a white T-shirt. (This was obviously different than Eric and Lisa recalling him wearing a jacket and khaki pants.)

Christina said that the man's face had been round, he was about Eric's height, and his looks were about a five on a scale of ten—in other words, just average. She had never seen him before and she thought the forensic drawing of the man "was not great." Christina said that she was an artist who took art classes in college, and the drawing of the suspect "had too full a jaw, and the eyes were too close together."

After speaking with Christina Nielson, Detective Stahl-man was able to contact Kim Gillespie by phone. Gillespie told him that on the morning of June 1, 1995, she had been with Mike Harpole, and they had stopped by her apartment to pick up some belongings before heading to a gym. As they walked up to her apartment door, she heard a woman in apartment 3 yelling something like, "No, leave me the fuck alone!" Then Gillespie heard a man's voice trying to quiet the woman down. He said something like, "Relax. Hey, baby, calm down." The man's voice was soft and low-key.

Once she and Harpole went into her apartment, Gillespie said the voices next door quieted down for a while, but then she heard noises start again, such as banging sounds, and the female being very loud again. Gillespie said, "The noises were like heavy thumping, as if someone was hitting the floor and wall." Gillespie thought the male might have been throwing the female around. Gillespie said she decided to call 911, whether it was a family quarrel or not. When she finally called 911, she believed that five to ten minutes had elapsed since the first noises in the apartment. This contrasted greatly with Amanda Carpova, who thought she had been struggling in the apartment with her attacker for over an hour.

While on the phone with the 911 operator, Gillespie told the detectives that she heard what sounded like a window opening next door, and she saw the female run naked, clutching some item of clothing in front of her. The woman ran to an apartment across the courtyard. Gillespie said that she was on the phone for about five minutes, and the police arrived within ten minutes of her call. Gillespie added that she thought the male probably left the apartment before she and Mike Harpole looked for him. Then Gillespie said, "I think someone had been prowling around the apartment complex two weeks previous to that. And I think the person might have tried turning my doorknob at least once, during that time, but I didn't see him."

As far as other residents of the apartment complex whom Detective Stahlman phoned, Christopher Tovell had only heard about the rape after it had happened, and when he looked at the sketch of the suspect later, it didn't bring anyone to mind. Sherry Carpenter, another tenant, said roughly the same thing, as did Linda Demary. Demary, however, said that a Caucasian young man who had lived in the apartment before Amanda Carpova did had an Asian friend who used to come to visit him. Whether that person matched the drawing of the suspect, she couldn't recall.

One very odd aspect of the case occurred because Amanda Carpova described her assailant as having a "penis so small, that it did not hang down, but only slightly poked out." Because of this statement, Detective Bocciolatt contacted Dr. Karen Gunson at the Oregon State Medical Examiner's Office and asked her about pathology pertaining to deformed penises and circumcision. Dr. Gunson told Bocciolatt that there were so many variables in regard to circumcision and possibly deformed penises, she couldn't render a professional opinion on that subject. But she did say that circumcisions were not necessarily related to culture as much as they were related to generation.

Meanwhile, Detective Stahlman received a message from Terry Coons that DNA connected to a man named Keith and a man named James could now be ruled out as having anything to do with the rapes of Donna Ferguson and Amanda Carpova. These two men had been convicted on different rape charges that were somewhat similar in type to those of Ferguson and Carpova. Detective Stahlman finished checking the names of Oregon State Penitentiary inmates who were Asian males between twenty-five and forty-two years of age, and he eliminated all the names except for two: John Pangelinan and Toby Botkin. These names he kept in a "persons of interest" folder.

Detective Linda Estes, of the Clackamas County Sheriff's Office Homicide Unit, spoke to Stahlman and told him about an Asian man named Linus Oey, who was caught attempting to break into an apartment where a young girl was home alone. Oey's mug shot photo and background info were also put into the "persons of interest" file.

One of the more interesting people to go into this file was an American Indian man with the name of Louis. Detective Bill Sawyer, of Clackamas County, told Detective Stahlman that this Louis had a small penis and was an "active sex offender."

Finally it was time for the detectives to go see Amanda Carpova in person, and to have her fill out an FBI sexual offender profile sheet with them. With this questionnaire the detectives hoped that Amanda would focus and be very specific about her attacker with information that would lead them one step closer to finding and arresting the man who had raped and nearly murdered her.

10

"We Thought He Was Weird"

On December 17, 1997, Detectives Stahlman and Bocciolatt met with Amanda Carpova in person and asked her to fill in an FBI Sexual Assault Victim's Questionnaire. A preamble to the questionnaire stated, *As you begin to answer the questionnaire, you will see that your careful thought and consideration is very important for each and every question. All the information obtained from your answers may further assist in the profiling of the offender, and may provide additional leads with which the investigators may continue this investigation to an arrest.*

The first part was about the offender's method of approach, with categories of *"Con, Surprise or Blitz"* that he might have used. Amanda wrote that it was a combination of surprise and blitz, because the attacker came right into her apartment with a handgun. The next set of questions concerned *"Offender's Control Over You."* It asked if the offender's mere presence was enough to control, and she answered yes, because of the handgun. As far as verbal threats went, she answered, *As soon as he walked in, he said, "Don't scream or I'll shoot you!"* She added that throughout the attack he kept repeating, *"Do what I say, or I'll kill you!"*

As to the *"Display of a Weapon,"* Amanda noted that her attacker from the very beginning kept pointing the gun at her. On *"Physical Force"* she wrote that he was rough with her during the rape, trying to strangle her. However, he had never hit her or used profanity. About injuries she stated that he had caused bruising on her body and especially around her neck when trying to choke her. On a section about *"Compromise/Negotiations,"* as to whether he allowed her to suggest alternatives during the rape, she answered no.

About *"Sexual Dysfunction,"* she wrote that he was never able to maintain a complete erection while raping her. Asked if he was only able to become erect when he forced her to have oral sex, or by manual stimulation, she answered yes. As to specific acts by the rapist, she wrote yes to kissing, fondling and manipulation of her vagina by the use of his fingers. About manipulation of her anus by use of his fingers, she wrote no, but added, *He later said too bad that he'd tied me up with my hands behind my back, or that would have been good too.*

On a list of other sexual questions: to fetishism, she wrote no; voyeurism, no; fellatio, yes; cunnilingus, no; anilingus, no; biting body parts, no; symbolic sadism, no. About verbal activity she wrote that he had carried on a conversation with her before raping her. About the context of this, she added that he had noticed she was wearing a knee support and asked if she played sports. When she told him no, he asked why she was wearing one, and she said that it was because she had hurt her knee. Her attacker then asked if she danced, and she said yes. When asked what kind, she told him ballet and modern dance. She added names like Cunningham and Graham. He didn't understand who those were, and he asked if that was related to jazz. Amanda said no, and because he didn't understand, it made him agitated and angry. Later he asked if anything such as this rape had happened to her before, and she answered, "No, never!" He replied, "Then you must have led a happy life so far." Amanda responded,

"Just because a person hasn't been raped, it doesn't mean they haven't had problems and pain!" Her attacker then asked, "So what has happened to you that was so bad?" When she didn't respond, he became very angry and put the gun against her again. Around this point was when he told her that he didn't feel bad about what he was doing, because "I've lost faith in man, God and myself."

Asked if the offender's attitude changed during the assault, Amanda said that his emotions and attitude changed very quickly. One moment his speech would be very angry, and the next moment it would be normal. A couple of lines in particular were noteworthy. She wrote, *He was sort of needy, as if he needed his Mommy. Frustrated and confused.*

As to concealing his identity, Amanda wrote her attacker wore sunglasses when coming into her apartment, then blindfolded her. On a question about whether she thought he had ever done this before, she said that he had tied her up very well and ordered her to shower afterward, which tended to show that he knew what he was doing and probably had done it before. Asked if her attacker had stolen any photos of her before leaving or stole her underwear, she responded no. About Peeping Toms and prowlers, Amanda was pretty sure that her attacker had come to her door asking about an apartment for rent three days prior to her attack. And despite Dorothy Connet's comments about seeing a young Asian man who followed Amanda and her boyfriend on the sidewalk before the attack, Amanda answered no to the question whether she felt like she had been watched or stalked prior to the assault.

She was asked to put in her own words how she thought others might describe her attacker. Amanda wrote that they would probably see him as slightly insecure, very needy and that he could become very angry at his job. (She was right on the mark about this last comment.) She also thought they would see him as unstable, seeming to care about people one minute and being very angry at them the next.

Asked if there was anything else that she thought was important, she wrote that he had wanted her to hold him while he put a gun up against her body. She also commented once again about his neediness. He seemed to be struggling with himself about this, wanting to give in to it, and also fighting it. His internal struggle was what made him change his emotions so rapidly, and this scared her.

Near the end of the questionnaire, Amanda was asked about places she frequented, such as buying clothes or jewelry, what restaurants she went to and any places where she had drinks. She was also asked what bus lines she took and at what grocery stores she shopped.

Because Amanda Carpova was a witness who had seen her attacker and lived to tell, Detectives Stahlman and Bocciolatt sought funding from the Portland PD for them to take her to visit internationally famous forensic sketch artist Jeanne Boylan in Bend, Oregon. Over the years Boylan was able to interview witnesses about crimes, and from their memories and descriptions, she rendered very accurate depictions of the perpetrators of the crimes. As *National Geographic* noted of Boylan: *She recovers fragmented impressions of shapes and textures etched deep in memory by trauma. The veteran forensic artist says her crucial skill is not drawing, but simply listening, often for hours.* Boylan added, "Witnesses surprise themselves with what they can remember."

On December 15, 1997, the detectives' wish was finally granted, and they and Amanda Carpova drove over a hundred miles to Bend, over the snowy Cascade Range. Boylan was able to take Carpova back to the day of her assault and listened for hours to Amanda's tale. By the time Boylan created a sketch of Amanda's attacker, it was very accurate. In fact, it looked very much the way Sebastian Shaw did on June 1, 1995.

Two days later, the detectives met with Amanda again, and they thoroughly went over everything she could remember about the day of her rape, the struggle to stay alive and her attacker. Most of the information was the same as before, but she added about her attacker's grin, "It was not a funny grin. It was more like, 'I'm in power! I know what I'm about to do, and you can't do anything about it.'" She also added that he wore his sunglasses into her bedroom, probably to try and disguise his face. As far as the gun he had used, Amanda looked at Detective Stahlman's weapon, which was a Glock 17, and said the attacker's gun was about the same size. She believed the assailant had carried the gun in his left hand. She added that he became very angry when he did not get fully erect in her mouth as he tried to get her to orally copulate him. He kept pushing the gun up against her neck, saying, "You have to do this! Try again!" Amanda kept repeating, "I can't!" He finally grew tired of the situation and had her lie down on the bed.

Once they lay down, side by side, he asked her if her knee hurt, and she said yes. He replied, "I'll try not to hurt it." As for the size of her attacker's penis, she said it was only about two or three inches in length, and "when he tried having intercourse with me, I could barely feel it inside of me." Amanda added that during the rape she never cried, because she did not want him to see her as vulnerable. As to the attacker's psychological problems, she said, "He was probably a psychopath or schizophrenic. He might have had a chemical imbalance. It was like he had different personalities that were very marked. He was like a child at times, the way he talked and acted. It was like there was a part of him that didn't want to be bad, but another part of him that was quite evil, and he couldn't quite figure it out. He'd snap back and forth between anger, confusion and needing his mother." Amanda added, "After he ejaculated, he shifted into a psycho/rapist mode and was never nice to me again."

Amanda once again went through all the events that had occurred while he made her wash up in the shower, the struggle for her life as he tried to strangle her and the fact that both she and her attacker thought that people outside her apartment had heard the struggle. Amanda once again answered the detective's questions about how she viewed the assailant. She said that he was probably a loner; she didn't notice odors of alcohol or tobacco on him, and no cologne or aftershave smell. He had worn Teva-brand sandals, which seemed to be expensive, and these had black soles and embroidered cloth straps, which she thought were pink and blue in color. His sunglasses could have been Ray-Bans or cheaper knockoffs. The sunglasses weren't the wraparound kind, but more like "Buddy Holly glasses," as she put it.

Getting back to the stocking cap that was found in her apartment after the rape, she said she had never seen it before the rape, but it could have come from her boyfriend. Amanda added that when the intruder had first brought her into the bedroom, he'd asked if she had any money. She said she had some under one of the cushions of her couch, but when she checked later, it was still there. Also she said, "At one point during the rape, my bedroom door rattled. He asked, 'What's that?' and I said, 'It's probably my cat, trying to get in.' He got very angry, and I begged him not to hurt my cat."

About her boyfriend at the time, she said, they often walked in the neighborhood and he had lived only a few blocks from where she did. Amanda didn't know of Dan having any Asian friends. The detectives and Amanda looked at crime scene photos from 1995, and she pointed out various things to them, especially about the cords she had been bound with. The detectives showed Amanda a list of names of everyone who had been interviewed on the Rudiger/Ferguson cases, and she recognized only one name, that of a man named Tony. The Tony she knew had the same last name, but she'd known him in junior high school, and doubted there was any connection to her rape.

Looking over the report that Amanda had originally given to Detective Carter in 1995, the detectives asked if she wanted to add or delete anything. She said she didn't want to delete anything, but she wanted to add that her attacker had "not been flabby, but not toned either. It didn't look like he exercised. He had a stocky build, but didn't have a noticeable stomach hanging over his belt." Once again, she said he was probably not "Vietnamese, Laotian or Cambodian." Her impression of these men, however, was that they were usually small in stature and wiry.

Amanda was shown a photo display approved by Deputy District Attorney (DDA) Helen Smith of persons who could have possibly attacked her. All of the men displayed were either Asian or part Asian. Detective Stahlman placed them in random order, and showed them to Amanda, one by one. Out of the twenty, she eliminated all of them except for a photo of Sebastian Shaw. Amanda said, "Except for the ears and glasses, he kind of looks like him." Amanda then went back through all the photos, eliminated them, but kept the one of Sebastian Shaw to the side. Looking at that photo once again, she declared, "He had that look."

Just because Sebastian Shaw appeared to "look" more and more like their suspect, it didn't mean that the detectives could eliminate other possibilities. As Detective Stahlman noted later, "One of the worst things you can do in [an] investigation is try and fit things to match your preconception of who the suspect might be." For this reason they checked out six other men of Asian descent who had sex crimes records, but these men's DNA profiles did not match that of Donna Ferguson or Amanda Carpova cases, and they were eliminated. Detective Stahlman also checked a list of suicides of former inmates, but none of them matched the DNA profile. On December 22, Detective Stahlman interviewed Dorothy Connet, who had seen Amanda, her boyfriend and the strange young Asian man all walking down the sidewalk not long before Amanda's rape. Connet told her story about the strange young man, and she said that he was between eighteen and twenty-five years of age, with a husky build. Connet saw the Boylan drawing and said, "That's the guy who was following her."

Stahlman phoned Amanda's then-boyfriend Dan, who said that he had last seen Amanda before the rape on a morning twenty-four hours previous to the attack. He did not remember anyone who matched the description of the suspect, but based on Amanda's description, he did not think the original forensic drawing looked correct. However, Dan added one important thing, the stocking cap found in Amanda's apartment did not belong to him.

The detectives contacted Bruce Fishback, owner of the Bread and Ink Cafe, where Amanda had worked in 1995. Looking at the forensic sketch, Fishback couldn't remember any customer who resembled the drawing, nor could he recall anyone loitering around the cafe who looked like that. Two employees who had worked with Amanda at the time, Hazel Laughlin and Baron Stevens, also drew a blank about anyone matching the sketch.

Just because it was the Christmas season didn't mean that all families in the Portland area were enjoying the holidays. Fifty people made their way to a home in northeastern Portland—all with one common denominator, they had lost a loved one to murder. Amidst the gathering was Debra Adams, whose daughter, Donna Ferguson, had been murdered in 1992. Debra was also there to remember Todd.

The people at the meeting of the Parents of Murdered Children ranged from those who were there to remember a four-year-old boy who had been strangled to death to those who were there to recall a seventeen-year-old killed by a shotgun blast. Terri Hanson, who was at the meeting, said of her twenty-four-year-old murdered daughter, "The deliberateness of the act is probably what's hardest to deal with. I could rationalize an accident or an illness. But murder is nothing but pure evil."

Debra Adams spoke to the others by saying, "I couldn't bring myself to cook a Thanksgiving dinner for more than five years because the thought of it was just too depressing. I was finally able to do that this year and it was great. But it's been five and a half years and I'm still going crazy."

The year 1997 rolled into 1998, and on January 15 of that year, Bocciolatt and Stahlman went to speak with Sebastian Shaw's probation officer and Sebastian Shaw himself. At 2:20 P.M., the detectives sat down with Shaw in PO Susan Rath's office in an interview room. The detectives told Shaw he wasn't under arrest, and he could leave at any time. Stahlman said that they were there to ask him some questions about an investigation they were working on, and Shaw said he would talk to them. Shaw confirmed that he had worked at a Safeway store on SE Twenty-seventh and Hawthorne in 1995, and Stahlman said that they were investigating a sexual assault on a woman who had lived in that neighborhood. Stahlman added that Shaw physically matched the suspect in the case. Then Stahlman said that they had DNA evidence in the case, and asked if Shaw would voluntarily submit to giving them an oral swab, which would be submitted to the OSP Lab.

Shaw told the detectives that he had no problem giving them an oral swab, but he wanted to talk to an attorney first. He said that he had talked to police in the past about other cases, and it had caused him problems. The detectives gave Shaw their business cards, and the meeting was over within five minutes. About an hour later, Detective Bocciolatt received a message on his voice mail from Shaw, stating that Shaw would not voluntarily submit to giving an oral swab.

Bocciolatt noted, "Because of the meeting, we felt that it would be important to background Sebastian Shaw in an effort to develop probable cause to obtain oral swabs

via a court order." For this reason, the detectives decided
to go and speak with Sebastian Shaw's stepmom and stepsisters. They contacted Lan Do at 5:00 P.M. on January 15.
Lan Do told the detectives about Shaw's early history,
about her father, Van Ho, who was also Shaw's father, and
about Shaw being in the Marine Corps. After the marines,
Lan Do said, Shaw had come to live with them on Thirty-
third Avenue in Portland. While living in the duplex next
door to them, he got a job with the Pinkerton Agency and
worked at a building downtown. In 1992, Shaw suddenly
left for southern California, but he was back up in Portland by 1994. He once again lived with them for a couple
of weeks before moving out. After returning to Portland,
he worked at a Safeway store, and was doing that in 1995.

Lan Do said that Shaw had assaulted her in 1996, and
had been arrested for it. Her mother, Ly Do, had a restraining order put out against Shaw, and she had not
seen him since. Detective Stahlman asked if Shaw had
ever sexually molested her sister, Khanh Do, and Lan Do
replied, "I wouldn't put it past him." She went on to say
that Khanh Do had told her that while she was going to
high school, Shaw had acted inappropriately toward her.
Khanh had said that while driving her to school, Shaw
would touch her thigh and make sexually suggestive
remarks. She even said that once he had offered her
money to have sex with him, but she declined.

Lan Do added that Shaw had touched her in ways that
made her feel uncomfortable as well. "He didn't grope
me or touch my privates," she said, "but what he did
made me uncomfortable. And he gave me dog kisses."
She explained that "dog kisses" were where Shaw would
kiss her on the cheek or toes with his tongue.

Lan Do said that Shaw had once dated a Vietnamese
girl and had become angry when she left him for another
Vietnamese boy. According to Lan Do, Shaw beat up this
boy pretty badly and threw him into a wall. Lan Do also
said that while in middle school, Shaw had become infat-
uated with a Caucasian girl named Sandy. Sandy didn't

like Shaw, but he became absolutely obsessed with her, and he still talked about her as an adult. Even when Sandy got married, Shaw would phone her on occasion.

Lan Do didn't know if Shaw had been circumcised or not, because she had never seen him naked. She asked her mother, Ly Do, about this, and she said that she didn't know either. Lan Do said that Shaw liked wearing sandals, would sometimes wear glasses and at other times contact lenses. He had worn black-framed sunglasses and she called them "Ray-Ban wannabees." Lan Do added that Shaw liked knives, and she remembered him showing her a big knife when he got back from the Marine Corps. Shaw often went to a knife store down at the Lloyd Center Mall and gazed at them in display cases. He would also comment to her while they walked around the mall, about girls who were fifteen and sixteen years of age. He would make comments like, "Oh, I'd want some of that if only she was older!"

The very next day, the detectives interviewed Lan Do again, and she said that Shaw didn't have Teva-brand sandals, but he might have had some that looked like Tevas. Asked if he wore any long shorts, she said that she remembered him wearing some that were khaki in color. Lan Do added that Shaw liked action movies and would go see them quite often. She didn't know about him patronizing nightclubs or taverns, but he did go to bookstores a lot. Then Lan Do added an interesting comment. She said that Shaw had told her, "I get girls to like me by being the perfect gentleman."

Turning to Dung Ho, Shaw's younger half sister, the detectives began asking her questions, and she gave them some information that was incredible. Dung Ho said while Shaw still lived with them, she had found a journal that he'd written. In the journal was a section he'd written about stalking a teenage girl, following her to her house and doing a Peeping Tom act. Dung Ho said the journal was in a bound-book cover and about four by six inches.

Then she added that Shaw had frequently touched her when she was growing up, and it made her uncomfortable.

The investigation about Shaw was spreading out in all directions by now. Detective Bocciolatt got some information that while working as a security guard at the Northwest Natural Gas (NNG) building in downtown Portland in 1992, Shaw would send flowers to a woman named Robin who worked in an adjacent building. When Bocciolatt contacted the Robin in question, she could not remember being sent flowers, but she did remember a guy who matched Shaw's description, who was a guard. She said of this person, "He was kind of odd. He always had a funny look on his face, a funny stare."

Contacting Christina Nielson once again, Detective Stahlman showed her the new sketch of the suspect created by Jeanne Boylan of the man who had attacked Amanda Carpova. Nielson said, "That's really close. It looks like him. That's a good drawing." She called the sketch significantly better than the original drawing. The detectives also showed the new sketch by Jeanne Boylan to Lisa Gabriel, who said, "It's really good. It looks a lot like him and it's better than the first drawing." Even Eric Lindstedt commented, "It's really close." Jeanne Boylan's drawing, of course, looked a lot like the way Shaw had looked in 1995.

The detectives contacted Brandon Sours, who had been a housemate of Shaw's in 1996 during the infamous shooting incident of Russ Sperou's room. Sours told them that Shaw pretty much kept to himself and was always studying technical books on science, math and history. Sours also noted that he never saw Shaw bring a girl or woman over to the house, and he didn't seem to date. During that period of time, Shaw had driven a gray- or silver-colored van. About the fight Sours repeated the comment Shaw had made to Russ Sperou when Sperou had him in a headlock: "You'd better kill me or I'll kill you!" Sours added a comment and said that Shaw had uttered, "You'd better kill me or I'll get my guns and blow

you away!" Of these guns, Sours said, one was probably a
.22, but he didn't know the caliber of the other one. Then
he added about Shaw's demeanor, "He could be nice to
you one second and wanting to cut your throat the next."

The detectives contacted Dung Ho at her high school
and reinterviewed her about Shaw's journal. She said
that she'd found it in a box, in the living room, where
Shaw had kept some of his belongings. She started reading the journal, and the part about stalking the teenage
girl was in the first third of the journal. Shaw had also
written about how he felt guilty about some of the things
he'd done to his sister, Khanh, though he was not specific about what those things were. She did recall that
he'd written, *Sometimes I feel real bad about how I treated her.*
Dung Ho thought that it might have been about his
sexual advances on Khanh.

The detectives went to see Ly Do once again, and took
along Doan Thaooanh, of the Community Policing Gang
Enforcement Team, to help them translate, because Doan
spoke fluent Vietnamese. Ly Do talked of raising Shaw in
Mt. Angel and Woodburn, and about Shaw returning to
Portland after the marines. Ly Do related that she did not
think that Shaw had sexually molested her daughters. She
said she was just being cautious, because she had seen such
situations on television, and wanted to be safe rather than
sorry when it came to those kinds of things. She said she
never saw Shaw with a knife, nor a gun. As far as Sandy
went, Ly Do told Shaw that he should forget about her. She
was white, and from a rich family, while he was Asian and
from a poor family. She told him, "She will never like you."
Ly Do added that Shaw once had an affair with a Chinese
woman, and this woman had three children. Shaw had
even lived with the woman for a while, but she couldn't
remember when.

Doan Thaooanh passed on some important information for the detectives, relating that Officer Preston Wong

knew Shaw personally from a prior incident. This had occurred because of the home invasion robbery of April 1995. When the detectives contacted Officer Wong, he told them that he'd spoken with Shaw at least ten times regarding that case. In fact, Shaw had been so helpful in that incident that it had helped to put away some of the home invaders, who were then part of the Original Gangster Boys (OGB). Even Wong related, "I think Sebastian Shaw is of mixed race. He doesn't look like he is from Vietnam." Detective Bocciolatt noted in a report, *This is important, as the original crime report by Amanda Carpova indicates that the suspect was of Asian and/or Asian/Caucasian descent.* Wong added that he knew that Shaw in 1995 lived in a house on the 1700 block of SE Thirtieth Avenue, not far from where Amanda Carpova was raped. The detectives went to the address where Shaw used to live, and found that by their car's odometer, it was five-tenths of a mile from that residence to Amanda Carpova's old apartment.

Traveling across the Columbia River to Vancouver, Washington, the detectives spoke with former employer Sue Tran, who had known Shaw by the name of Alex. (Perhaps he was using his middle name Alexander.) Tran said that Shaw had problems with his father, and was always talking about his father. Tran added that Shaw had once worked for her and her husband at their video store, USA Video, on Sandy Boulevard. She said that Shaw had been a video buff, and he always liked his surroundings to be clean. She thought at one time he might have been gay, because he never talked to girls who came into the store. She related, "He never took X-rated videos home, like other employees. He never had any friends come by the store, and he seemed a little effeminate."

Because of the movie angle, Detective Bocciolatt noted that Amanda Carpova spoke of liking to go to movies, and so had Donna Ferguson. Not only that, a few days before she was murdered in 1992, Donna Ferguson had indicated to her girlfriends Christi Hanner and Tessalie Brault that she had watched a video. Donna had probably obtained this video at a Blockbuster store, and the Trans had run a video store in the same strip mall.

Moving in a different direction, Detective Bocciolatt contacted Amanda Carpova once again and asked her if she ever went to a tavern called Claudia's on Hawthorne Avenue. Amanda said that she had gone there a few times in the spring of 1995 with two friends who had worked with her at the Bread and Ink Cafe. These people were Scott Kelley and Matt Kinney. Both Bocciolatt and Stahlman went to Claudia's and spoke with the owner, Martin Spathas. The detectives showed Spathas a photo of Shaw, but he did not remember anyone that looked like the person in the photo being at his tavern.

Christina Nielson came down to the Detective Division and looked at a photo lineup that included a photo of Shaw in position number three. Nielson gazed at the photos for two minutes, and said that numbers two, five and six were definitely not the person she had seen at the apartment who had peeked into the window and come to the door. Yet of the remaining photos, she said that number one looked most like him. The photo in the number one slot was not of Shaw.

Detective Bocciolatt was eventually able to find a Chinese woman who, others said, had been Shaw's roommate for a while. She spoke broken English and Doan Thaooanh had to help in translation some of the time. She had known Shaw by the first name of Alex, and she first met him at a sandwich shop where he worked on NE Eighty-second Avenue. Bocciolatt wanted to know why her name and Shaw's were both on a registration slip for a 1982 Mazda. She explained that she and Shaw both used to ride the bus and didn't have a car, so they decided to get one by pooling their money. They eventually purchased a used Mazda from Chinese people at a car dealership and shared use of the car, although Shaw seemed to have it most of the time.

Bocciolatt asked her if Shaw had been her boyfriend, and she said no. This contradicted what Shaw had indicated and Ly Do as well. The Chinese woman was even more adamant than her initial statement. She said that Shaw wanted to be her boyfriend, but "I said no. He was a fat pig and too ugly. He got mad at me for this and wouldn't talk to me anymore. He said he was going to move to California and become a doctor." Unlike others, she claimed that Shaw had never even lived with her as a roommate, much less as a boyfriend.

To get a better idea of how Sebastian Shaw acted at work when he was an employee at the Safeway store on Hawthorne, the detectives began interviewing coworkers who knew Shaw. They spoke with Korina Estes and she said that initially she'd been a bagger and Shaw was a checker. Korina said he was someone she could talk to, and that she was going through a breakup with a boyfriend at the time and Shaw treated her with respect. She didn't see Shaw very often outside of work, but they did go to the Oregon coast together on one occasion. During the trip he was courteous and acted normally, and she didn't have any problems with him. Korina added that he sometimes wore glasses and at other times he wore contact lenses.

Shaw had told Korina at one point that he liked her more than a friend, but she told him she wasn't interested in dating him. She said he enjoyed going to movies, reading books, and she often saw him reading a book in the break room. He asked her once if he could kiss her, but she declined and he didn't harass her about it. She added that she never saw him with any friends, but that he seemed to get along with other employees at the store.

The detectives next spoke with Kristi Benton, who told

them she used to babysit one of her fellow employees' kids, and the employee was named Anne Roland. Benton thought that Shaw and Roland might have dated. Shaw had told Benton at one point that he had feelings for Roland. She added that she'd seen Shaw wear Teva-type sandals on occasion. She also thought that Shaw and an employee named David Malone might have gotten into a fight over a girl named Nadia, who worked at the store. Shaw seemed to like Nadia, as well as Anne Roland.

Following up on the Roland lead, the detectives spoke with her, and she related that Shaw had been interested in having a relationship with her, but she did not want one with him. She said that he was a good worker, but "he went from woman to woman and tried dating them all. One would tell him she wasn't interested in him, and then he would move on to the next." She even found out that he'd told somebody at the store that they were dating, which wasn't true. When she confronted him about this, he moved on to Greta Matthews.

After the shooting incident, where Shaw shot up Russ Sperou's room, Roland heard that Matthews had received a letter from Shaw, who was in jail. Shaw wrote that he could still smell Greta's hair and feel her cheek. Roland described the letter as being "pillow talk." The letter scared Matthews, and both she and Roland went to their supervisor and expressed their concerns about Shaw. Both Roland and Matthews felt they had been followed by Shaw at different times as well. Roland said she would see him on a bus and in a library at odd times, and she felt as if he'd stalked her there.

One incident about Shaw working at the store stuck in Roland's mind. Shaw constantly had a battle with management, saying that the break room was too cold. As a "protest" to them, he hung up freezer bags around the break room, indicating how cold it was. They made him take the freezer bags down, and he would do so in a bad temper.

Roland added that she'd heard that Korina Estes had actually quit the Safeway because she was so uncomfortable working around Shaw (something Korina had not brought up with the detectives). Roland also said that Shaw had once told her that he'd been fired from a job for sexual harassment, denying that it had been harassment but rather just a joke that the woman took the wrong way. Roland did remember that around Memorial Day, 1995, Shaw seemed to be drinking more and would show up late for work. His uniforms, which had been spotless, would be dirtier then. He seemed to have an attitude that he just didn't care anymore. Then Roland added one more bit of interesting information: Shaw had told her about drinking at Claudia's. Roland ended by telling the detectives they should speak with Linda Yuckert.

Before speaking with Linda Yuckert, the detectives contacted Greta Matthews, who told them that she and Shaw had both been checkers at Safeway in 1995 and 1996. Matthews had gone to a restaurant with him at least a couple of times, but these were not dates. She also had a beer with him and some other employees at Claudia's. At a Safeway Christmas party, held at the Cascade Athletic Club, Shaw had danced with her one time. He wanted to dance with her more, but she wouldn't let him, since he was already very drunk. On New Year's Eve, 1995, Shaw, Matthews and other employees had a meal at the International House of Pancakes (IHOP), and he'd put his arm around her shoulder, which she didn't think was appropriate.

Matthews did remember the letter he sent her from jail. He'd written, *You are an orchid in life.* He also wrote about how it had felt to hold her while dancing. Matthews added that on occasion he would be sitting in his van out in the Safeway parking lot when she got off from work, as if he was watching her. She didn't see him after he was fired, but then in September 1997, he suddenly showed up at her checkout line at the Safeway store where she now worked on Woodstock Boulevard. She exclaimed, "Oh, I haven't seen you in ages!" He wanted to make small talk, but she was busy with other customers, so he left.

Next in line was Linda Yuckert, and she related that while Shaw worked at the Safeway store, she thought he was "weird." Yuckert said he asked her out on a date twice, and she turned him down both times. She thought he had asked every woman and girl in the store who wasn't married to go out with him, and they all turned him down.

Yuckert added, "He was stalking Greta Matthews for a while. He would call her house and talk to her daughter. Sometimes he would be waiting in the parking lot for Greta to get off work. I was so concerned for Greta's safety, I'd give her a ride home. Both I and Greta talked to management about Shaw harassing her. There were a lot of girls around there who thought he was weird." Yuckert said that Shaw used to drink a lot near the end of his time at Safeway, and he might have gone out drinking with a coworker named Josh Todd.

When the detectives talked to Josh, he told them that he and Shaw were not friends, and that Shaw had been "very antagonistic toward me." Josh related, "He would come to my check stand and yell at me and use profanity, even with customers around. He would bang his fist on the counter because he didn't feel I was getting things done quickly enough." Josh said he never went out drinking with Shaw, but he thought that a frozen-food worker named Bruce might have. Josh added, "Shaw had a small man's complex."

Once this Bruce was contacted, he said he never went out drinking with Sebastian Shaw, but he knew that coworkers Wade Lamb and Don Nees sometimes went to Claudia's. Then the detectives spoke with Nees, who said that he had been Shaw's supervisor at Safeway on Hawthorne, and that Shaw had done a good job while working there. Nees had heard a rumor that Shaw had dated Anne Roland but dismissed it, saying, "I don't think he got anywhere with her, and it was just his over-active imagination." Nees did remember Shaw at the Christmas party as Sebastian "checked out the girls." Nees added that he went to Claudia's once in a while, but he never recalled seeing Shaw there.

Nees admitted that near the end of Shaw's employment at Safeway, Anne Roland had come by to talk to him about Shaw stopping by her residence uninvited, and that she was concerned about this. Before anything was done about it, Shaw was arrested for the roommate incident, and that was the end of his employment at Safeway.

Wade Lamb told the detectives that Shaw was more of an acquaintance than a friend, and many people at the store thought he was kind of odd. Lamb said he saw Shaw at Claudia's a few times while Lamb was there with his wife. Shaw would say hello, but Lamb would start talking to his wife and tried to ignore Shaw, because he did not want him sitting down with them.

Looking into the Claudia's angle of the case, the detectives spoke with Matthew Kinney, who had worked with Amanda Carpova at the Bread and Ink Cafe. Kinney remembered going to Claudia's with Amanda on at least four occasions. They would go with fellow employee, Scott Kelley, to play pool because the pool table there was less expensive than other bars around the area. They always sat down near the video poker machine near the pool tables. They usually went to Claudia's between 11:00 P.M. and 2:00 A.M., and he didn't recall anyone else at the tavern talking to them.

Scott Kelley also recalled playing pool at Claudia's with a fellow employee from Bread and Ink, but he couldn't remember if it was Amanda. He did recall going out to have drinks with Amanda after work at the Horse Brass Bar, the Space Room and Sewickly's. Kelley added that he lived in the neighborhood where Amanda was raped, and he remembered the flyers. When he looked at them, however, he did not recognize anyone resembling the person depicted on the flyer.

Out of the blue, on February 6, 1998, Detective Bocciolatt received a phone call from Kristi Benton, who had worked with Shaw at the Safeway store in 1995 and 1996, and whom Bocciolatt had interviewed on February 3, 1998. Benton had not seen Shaw since he was arrested in 1996, and then suddenly in the previous few days, he had appeared out of nowhere, and she felt that he was stalking her. She told Detective Bocciolatt that she was downtown on the number 14 bus with her son when Shaw got on the bus, came over to her and said, "Hey, where are you going?" She told him that she was going to the Safeway Credit Union on SE Hawthorne, and he declared that was where he was going as well.

As they rode along, Shaw told Benton his version of why he had been fired from Safeway in 1996. Both Benton and Shaw did transactions at the credit union, and when she left, he was right behind her. Shaw asked her if she was going downtown, but she said no. She and her son went to a Subway sandwich shop, and within twenty minutes Shaw showed up. He pretended to act surprised and said, "Hi again, what a coincidence."

Benton then asked Detective Bocciolatt if she was purposefully being followed by Shaw and if she was going to have a problem with him. Bocciolatt said he didn't know, but he felt that it was more than just a coincidence. Detective Bocciolatt gave her his phone number and pager number and told her to call immediately if she had any problems with Shaw. Then Benton added that she had spoken to Carrie Hilliard, who worked in a Safeway store, and Hilliard had suddenly seen Shaw enter the store. Hilliard, as well, hadn't seen Sebastian Shaw in years.

Detective Bocciolatt wrote in a report, *It is important to note that Detective Stahlman and I originally interviewed*

Benton on February 3, 1998. Additionally we have interviewed several other people from the Safeway store in regards to this case.

Bit by bit, evidence pointed toward Sebastian Shaw as the person who had raped and killed Donna Ferguson, and the person who had raped and attempted to murder Amanda Carpova. Then at 12:47 P.M., on February 13, 1998, the detectives got a huge break that they'd been waiting for. Officer Wayne Baldassare, of the PPB Drugs and Vice Unit, was out keeping surveillance on Shaw. Officer Baldassare saw Shaw sitting on a step outside Cox Cleaners on SW Twelfth Avenue, where he was smoking a cigarette. Baldassare watched Shaw finish smoking the cigarette and flip the cigarette butt into the street. Then Shaw walked away. Baldassare immediately walked across the street and recovered the cigarette butt and put it in a Baggie.

Within a short time, Officer Baldassare turned the cigarette butt over to Detective Mike Stahlman, who placed it in a paper bag and hand-carried it to the crime lab on the twelfth floor of the Justice Center, submitting it to Terry Coons. Stahlman asked Coons to process the cigarette butt for DNA evidence ASAP.

Sebastian Shaw may not have voluntarily given an oral swab of DNA to the detectives on January 15, but once he threw the cigarette butt into the street, it was fair game for law enforcement. He had dodged and weaved and hidden undercover for years, but because of his anger and arrogance in shooting up Russ Sperou's room, back in 1996, his DNA profile was now in the criminal justice system. He was only one short step away from having that DNA profile compared to the person who had left semen at Donna Ferguson's crime scene and Amanda Carpova's crime scene. Many, many things were starting to come full circle.

11

"Those Are
Very Serious Charges"

Between the time Detective Stahlman handed over the cigarette butt that Shaw had discarded, and the time he got a report about a possible DNA match to the Rudiger/ Ferguson and Carpova crime scenes, he and Detective Bocciolatt were still busy talking to people about Shaw. On February 19, 1998, they spoke with Carrie Hilliard and she said that Shaw had come into the Safeway store at Hawthorne shortly before Christmas. She hadn't seen him in two years when he suddenly walked up to her check stand and said "Hi." Then he asked who was in charge of the store that night. Hilliard added that he gave her "the creeps."

Like many others, Hilliard thought that Shaw was pursuing Anne Roland back in 1995. He would come in on his days off and ask if she needed a ride home. According to Hilliard, Roland had been uncomfortable about this. What was interesting, as well, was that Hilliard recalled Shaw often carrying around a blue duffel bag, a description that matched the duffel bag found in Dean Campbell's stolen car from 1994.

The next day Stahlman and Bocciolatt went by Cox Cleaners, where Shaw worked, but they found out from the manager that Shaw had just quit. This set off alarm bells with the detectives. They had a hunch that Shaw was perhaps onto them and ready to leave town. They contacted the Danmore Hotel, where Shaw resided, and the desk clerk there said that Shaw was still registered.

At 10:00 A.M., February 20, 1998, the detectives got what they had been waiting for. Criminalist Donna Scarpone contacted Detective Stahlman and told him that she had completed a polymerase chain reaction (PCR)/DNA analysis of the cigarette butt he had submitted. (Stahlman had not told her who had been smoking the cigarette.) Scarpone told Stahlman she compared the DNA from the cigarette butt to that of a vaginal swab previously submitted to the lab—Case 95L-4431. Scarpone said, "The DNA recovered from the cigarette butt was consistent with having come from the same source as the DNA recovered from the vaginal swab." In other words, Sebastian Shaw was the same person who had smoked the cigarette and had left his semen at the Amanda Carpova crime scene of 1995.

Within an hour Detective Stahlman and Detective Bocciolatt met with Deputy District Attorneys Helen Smith and Bill Williams and discussed the case. A decision was made to locate Sebastian Shaw and arrest him based on probable cause. A list of charges were drawn up and included "Attempted Murder with a Firearm," "Rape 1 with a Firearm," "Sodomy 1 with a Firearm" and "Kidnap 1 with a Firearm."

Even before Detective Stahlman drew up a probable cause report, Detective Bocciolatt had gone to the Drug and Vice Division and spoke with Sergeant Ken Pacheco about creating a team to keep a round-the-clock surveillance on Sebastian Shaw while the probable cause report was being drawn up and submitted to a judge so that a search-and-seizure warrant could be implemented. During the meeting between the detectives and the district attorney, Sergeant Pacheco radioed in to Bocciolatt and said that his team had just witnessed Shaw entering the Portland Main Library. Unfortunately, they had lost him somewhere on the second floor. Pacheco, however, informed Bocciolatt that his team members were watching all the exits from the library.

Bocciolatt left the meeting at the DA's office and hurried to the main library, where he contacted Sergeant Pacheco and uniformed officer Ed Cummings. Soon thereafter, they were met by Mike Stahlman, Sergeant Van Stearns, Lieutenant Ron Schwartz and Lieutenant Larry Kochevar. It was determined the safest thing to do was wait until Shaw exited the library and then arrest him. It was February 21, 1998, and everything now was moving toward a resolution.

Bocciolatt and Kochevar took up position at the corner of SW Tenth and Taylor, while other team members watched different exits. A short time later, more team members made a sweep through the library, looking for Shaw. They were to spot him, but not arrest him, in the library. Then around 1:20 P.M., Shaw was seen exiting the library, northbound on SW Tenth and then onto SW Yamhill. Shaw was closely followed by team members. Once he got to Yamhill, members of the stakeout team confronted Sebastian Shaw and told him he was under arrest.

Officer Cummings and the others arrested Shaw, and Cummings placed him in the back of a patrol car. Shaw had a blue backpack, black fanny pack and three *Star Trek* paperback books from the library. On the way to the Justice Center, Shaw asked Cummings why he was under arrest. Cummings answered that he didn't know. All he knew was that plainclothes detectives had told him to arrest Shaw, and that's why Shaw was being transported to the Justice Center.

Shaw then asked if it was for a parole violation, and he

added that he had not paid $600, and thought he might have been arrested for that reason. (This may have been $600 of restitution.) Once they reached the garage at the Justice Center, Shaw asked Cummings, "Where are we going?" Cummings simply said, "Upstairs," and escorted him into an elevator. Cummings had Shaw face the wall of the elevator. On the ride up, Shaw sighed heavily and then muttered, "Shit!"

Cummings placed Shaw in a holding cell in the Detective Divison, and around 2:00 P.M., Detective Bocciolatt and Detective Wayne Svilar began talking to Shaw in an interview room. They sat down and Svilar took the handcuffs off Shaw. Bocciolatt told Shaw to keep an open mind about what he was going to hear. Then Bocciolatt added that if Shaw kept an open mind, "I'll make an attempt to help you out."

Shaw asked if he was going to be formally charged with anything, and Bocciolatt said that by the end of the day, that would probably happen. Then Detective Bocciolatt read Shaw his Miranda rights, which Shaw said he understood. After that, Bocciolatt said, "If you're one hundred percent honest with me, I'll make an effort to help you out in the future." Shaw replied, "I want a lawyer." After that, the interview was terminated.

From that point on, Detective Bocciolatt made comments, but he did not ask Shaw questions. Bocciolatt stated that he knew Shaw had a rough life because Shaw's mother died before he was one; he'd come to the United States under terrible conditions and his father didn't treat him well. Bocciolatt even repeated Shaw's own phrase about how he had lost his faith in God. Shaw replied, "You've done your homework."

Bocciolatt stated that after Shaw got an attorney, somewhere down the line, he might want to talk to him. Shaw asked what things he was being charged with, and Bocciolatt told him they would start with attempted murder, murder, rape sodomy and a host of other charges. Shaw

said in a calm voice, "Those are very serious charges."
Bocciolatt agreed that they were.

Bocciolatt declared once again that Shaw "should
keep an open mind," and down the road he might "want
to do something nice for the victims' families." Shaw
seemed surprised by that comment and asked, "You
mean I killed and raped more than one person?" Bocciolatt indicated that that was the case.

At around 2:08 P.M., Shaw was placed back in the holding
cell, and the detectives asked him if he wanted any water.
Shaw said that he did, and Detective Svilar went to get him
some. When Svilar handed the cup of water to Shaw, Shaw
uttered the phrase, "Today death, tomorrow life."

Since it was known that Sebastian Shaw had once tried
to commit suicide, Detective Bocciolatt did a body
search of Shaw. Bocciolatt took Shaw's sweatpants from
him, so he couldn't use the drawstring as a noose, and
Bocciolatt searched Shaw's underwear for weapons and
contraband. When he did so, Bocciolatt noted, "I noticed he had a very short penis that was somewhat pecu-
liar in shape and size." This was interesting to note,
because Amanda Carpova had spoken of her attacker's
short penis, which was unusual in shape and size.

Shaw was kept in the holding cell throughout the
evening hours while Detective Stahlman received a search
warrant. Shaw was checked twenty-seven times during the
night, and he asked for water and food. He was given a Big
Mac from McDonald's, as well as fries and a Coke. Shaw
asked for the three *Star Trek* books he'd obtained from the
library, and these were given to him. After that, he made
himself comfortable by lying on his back on the floor and
propping his feet up on a bench, so as to read his books.
At one point Shaw even got up and danced around the cell
and sang to himself. For someone who was facing very,
very serious charges, Sebastian Shaw seemed calm, cool
and collected. He was almost enjoying himself.

* * *

The charges were indeed serious, ranging from "Attempted Murder with a Firearm," to rape, kidnapping, sodomy, unlawful penetration and burglary with use of a firearm. While he was in custody, blood was drawn from Shaw, pubic and head hairs taken, and his penis was photographed—something he was not too happy about. The detectives then went with a search warrant to Shaw's room at the Danmore Hotel and began collecting evidence. Detective Stahlman and Sergeant Van Stearns collected the evidence, while Bocciolatt placed the items in bags at the middle of the room and noted each item seized. These ran to a wide range of items, such as a book review about teenage girls who had been gang-raped with foreign objects, a document about a restraining order, seven computer disks, a letter from Suzanne Garman, Shaw's sympathetic teacher, and a black-and-white diary. They also seized a copy of a police report from Contra Costa County, California, a box of .38-caliber bullets, 12-gauge shotgun shells, a short story called "The Crying Bells," a short story called "The Hunter" and a short story entitled "Who to Be Last." The detectives found and seized a blue stocking mask, pornographic videotapes entitled *Friends and Lovers, Gentlemen Prefer Ginger,* and others. Some of the most disturbing items included ropes; a graphic novel called *Lord Farris,* which depicted women being whipped, branded and raped; and pictures of dark-haired women tacked to the wall. Among the photos were those of Shania Twain and Kristi Yamaguchi, as well as photos of noncelebrities who had dark hair. Also seized were several cards with women's names and addresses.

The detectives spoke with various residents of the Danmore Hotel to see who might have had contact with Shaw while he lived there. A woman named Shirley Price told the detectives that Shaw had recently told her that he quit his job so that he could spend more time studying for college. Then on one recent afternoon, she saw Shaw in the hallway and he asked her if she wanted to go see the movie *Titanic.* Price said she didn't have enough money at the time, so he offered to pay for it. They went to the Broadway Theater and saw the four o'clock showing. She said during the movie Shaw continually leaned on her, and it made her feel uncomfortable. After the movie they went to a restaurant, where Shaw had a beer and she had tea. Once again, like others, Price thought that Shaw was part Hawaiian. She referred to him as "a nice college kid."

Looking into other aspects of the case, the detectives turned over the interviews of other tenants of the Danmore Hotel to Detective Sergeant W. S. Law. Over time he and Detective Sergeant Tom Nelson spoke with thirty-one people there. Some said they didn't know Shaw at all, others said he was quiet and kept to himself, and others had short conversations with him and nothing more. A few, however, had some important things to say. Arlan Meeks worked at the Danmore, and in the week before the detectives arrested Shaw, Shaw had told Meeks that he was leaving the area and moving up to Seattle. He told Meeks that he might just take off and leave all of his belongings at the hotel. Shaw added that he had already given notice at the place he worked.

Debra Omlor lived in a room directly below that of Shaw, and she would often hear him walking heavily on the floor above her, sometimes until 4:00 A.M. This annoyed her and she spoke to Shaw about it. It got better for a short while, but soon it was as bad as before. Omlor said that Shaw "lived in his own world."

James Patterson was one of the few people Shaw talked to in the Danmore, and he even drank some beers in Patterson's room. Shaw told Patterson of his experiences in Vietnam and being evacuated from Saigon. Ernest McCrae played some video games with Shaw, and he was one of the few people that Shaw told that he'd served some time in jail for an assault. Bridgette Rainier played poker with Shaw on a few occasions and he asked her to go to the movies with him, but she never did.

The person Shaw seemed to talk to the most at the

Danmore was Vanna Swiftcloud. She worked as a desk clerk until July 1997, and Shaw would stop by the desk and chat with her. He told her that he wanted to find "a desirable woman someday and start a family." He also said that he was going to anger management classes.

Another person who added some insight into Shaw's character was Stanley Hennon, who had lived next door to Shaw at the Danmore. Hennon told the detectives that Shaw was "spiritually confused." When they asked him what that meant, Hennon said, "He didn't know what he was going to do in life. Shaw told me he believed in God, but he doubted himself all the time."

There was one last person at the Danmore who also gave some useful information. Gloria Sawyer was one of the clerks at the front counter, and she said that Shaw never had any visitors come see him except for two people. On Shaw's birthday, on November 28, 1997, a man and a woman came by the hotel and dropped off a present for him. They did not want to stay there at the hotel, nor did they want to go to his room. Sawyer didn't know who they were, but later, after Shaw's arrest, a woman phoned and asked about Shaw. She gave her name as Suzanne Garman. She said she had a book of Shaw's and wanted to know what to do with it. Sawyer believed that this Suzanne Garman was the same woman who came by the hotel with the present for Shaw, along with an unnamed man.

The first newspaper articles about Shaw's arrest began showing up, including one in the *Oregonian* telling of the DNA links between the Todd Rudiger/Donna Ferguson cases and that of Amanda Carpova. It also spoke of Shaw's ties to a stolen car from California and all the disturbing items found in the trunk of the car. Donna Ferguson's mother was quoted as saying, "I'm just in a state of shock," regarding a suspect finally being named in the murder of her daughter after five and a half years. "I never gave up. I'm glad the monster is behind bars. It will never bring my daughter back, but it's good to know he won't hurt anyone else."

The detectives wanted to discover what might have occurred with Shaw at his Pinkerton security guard job in the weeks before the murders of Donna Ferguson and Todd Rudiger. They checked with John Breedlove, manager for Pinkerton Security, who told them that Shaw had worked in a building at One Pacific Square, from April 10 until July 19, 1992. This last date was significant—the detectives' theory was that Donna and Todd had been murdered on July 17, 1992. If Shaw had murdered them, it made sense that he would want to quit his job and move out of the area.

The detectives next contacted Douglas McIntosh, who had worked in the shift after Shaw at One Pacific Square. McIntosh said that Shaw generally worked until 8:00 P.M., and would work on weekends, as well as weekdays. Shaw would work both inside and outside the building and had keys to various offices within the complex. Then McIntosh added, "Sebastian Shaw was like a live round. We always wondered when he was going to go off." McIntosh had been in the tank corps in the army, and sometimes a loaded round would misfire. He said that when the round was taken out, it had to be handled carefully or it could explode. He said that Shaw was like that round. McIntosh recalled, "Shaw could be very charming and intelligent, but you always had the feeling he could get violent. I thought he had a chip on his shoulder."

McIntosh stated that he had only been working there about a month when he heard from female employees that they were uncomfortable working around Shaw. McIntosh related that there was a young cleaning woman who had come from Romania or Hungary, and she complained to her boss about Shaw following her around and bothering her. The girl's boyfriend had confronted Shaw about this, and Shaw got into a shouting match with him.

McIntosh said he didn't think it got physical, but "Shaw had a habit of getting in someone's face. He was right up in that guy's face and yelling. His face was contorted and twisted. He had a gut, but you knew he could do some damage."

McIntosh also said that Pinkerton was not happy with Shaw using his key to obtain access to a small convenience store on the premises on the weekends, taking some of their candy bars and Cokes, and then leaving them IOU notes. McIntosh believed that Shaw had been disciplined about this, but he had not been fired. And Shaw also did not leave the young cleaning woman alone. He kept following her around and, according to rumors, tried "pinching her behind."

McIntosh thought that the woman complained to a man named Charles Sellers, who was the chief building engineer, and Sellers went to Shaw's boss and told about the incidents. McIntosh also heard that Shaw had then been transferred away from the area; this way he couldn't bother the cleaning lady. One morning, about eight, according to McIntosh, Shaw came by the desk where he was stationed and told McIntosh, "I'm going to come back here and kill Sellers! He's such an asshole! I'm gonna come back here with my .38 and kill that bastard!" McIntosh took this seriously and wondered if he should write up an incident report about it. It was hard to know if Shaw was just blowing off steam or if he really would come back to the building with a .38 and kill Sellers.

McIntosh also recalled a woman who worked at a flower shop in the lobby of the Pacific One building. The woman told McIntosh that Shaw was "hitting on her" and acted like a "Vietnamese Casanova." The woman even related to McIntosh that Shaw had told her he once worked for Paragon Cable and had been fired for sexual harassment.

Then, oddly enough, McIntosh had seen Shaw on the streets of downtown Portland just before Shaw was arrested. McIntosh thought at the time, *Boy, this guy has really hit bottom.* McIntosh told Stahlman, "He looked like shit and was dirty." Asked by Detective Stahlman if it wouldn't surprise him to learn that Shaw had been arrested for murdering someone, McIntosh replied, "If you're talking about a scenario where he loses his temper and goes ballistic and kills somebody, absolutely! He had a thing about respect, and if he thought somebody dissed him, absolutely. I can see him saying, 'I'm going to get you!' and then waiting. He didn't know when to back off, especially where ladies were concerned. You could see he had problems with women not respecting him. If Shaw went off, I wouldn't want to be in his way."

Moving back to the Carpova case, Detective Stahlman interviewed Adam Smith, who had stayed over Amanda's apartment the night before she was raped. Adam said that after getting off work at a bar that night, he and Amanda had gone out to a restaurant and had something to eat. Then they had gone back to her place and listened to music before going to bed. Adam said that he and Amanda had been boyfriend and girlfriend at one time, but now they were just friends and were catching up on old times. He slept on the couch and she went into her bedroom and slept on her bed. On June 1, 1995, Adam woke up at about 10:20 A.M., saw that he was late for work, and went into her bedroom to tell her good-bye and that he'd call her later. Adam said that he didn't see anyone in the courtyard when he left that morning, nor anyone at the bus stop who matched the description of her assailant.

Stahlman next spoke with Mark Eklund, who had been Shaw's landlord in the spring of 1992. Eklund recalled that Shaw left in a hurry in 1992, and he still owed him $175 because a check Shaw had used to pay him bounced. When Eklund called Shaw's apartment, a woman named Barbara Phillips answered and said that she had given Shaw half the rent, but he had not passed it on, but rather kept it for himself. Phillips said that Shaw didn't tell her anything about leaving, but that he might have gone to California and she was angry about it.

Stahlman contacted Elaine Lees at Paragon Cable and interviewed her, and Lees told about Shaw's job duties at Paragon. She spoke about the harassment charges against Shaw, and she added one new angle. A woman named Kay contacted her after hearing about Shaw's recent arrest for rape and murder. Kay related that she had been raped in Salem, Oregon, in December 1992. In the weeks prior to her rape, she had been receiving anonymous harassing phone calls in which the caller would pretend to gag into the phone. On the night she was raped in her apartment, her attacker had tried to strangle her, and she gagged a lot, but she escaped. She had bruises around her neck, and the rape had never been solved by the Salem Police Department. Kay worked in a room adjacent to where Shaw worked at Paragon in 1992. Hearing this angle, Detective Stahlman contacted Detective Ron Sturdevant, of the Portland PD Sexual Assault Detail, to see if Kay's rape had any similarities to that of Amanda Carpova.

On March 5, 1998, Detective Sergeant Kris Ferrell and Detective Stahlman contacted Barbara Phillips, now Barbara Phillips-Crawford. She had been Shaw's roommate in the spring of that year. Crawford had originally met Shaw when she worked at the City Center Parking garage across the street from the Pacific One building, where Shaw worked for Pinkerton. They had become friends and went to a Cinco de Mayo festival together. There were also occasions where he said he missed his bus, and he would stay over her place and sleep on the couch. Since her bed was nearby, there was twice when he put his arm on her, but she told him, "Leave me alone!" and he did.

There came a time when Crawford needed a new place to live, and she asked Shaw if they could share the place where he was living next door to his stepmom on

SE Thirty-third. Shaw told her okay, but that he was going on vacation soon. In fact, it wasn't just vacation, he left her holding the bag on the rent. About two weeks after he left in late July 1992 (a few days after the murders of Todd Rudiger and Donna Ferguson), Shaw gave her a phone call from southern California and said that he'd gotten a job down there and that his aunt needed him. She replied, "You can't do this to me!"

A week or two after this conversation, Shaw came back for a short stay, grabbed his things from the apartment and left again. Crawford said that the things he took were mostly smaller items and he left his furniture. He seemed to have a car at the time, and she believed it was a relative's car. At least that's what he said. Sometime before he left for California for good, Shaw gave Crawford a knife "for protection." In fact, Crawford went out to her car and gave the detectives the knife Shaw had given her. It had a silver-colored blade and a black grip with grooves for the fingers.

Crawford said that Shaw had even given her instructions on how to use the knife, saying, "You should hold the knife like this." He demonstrated by holding it down from his palm. Then he instructed, "You should slash like this," and he demonstrated by making an X pattern, beginning with a downward slash from left to right, and then continuing with a downward slash from right to left. She asked him, "Should you stab them?" and Shaw replied, "No, they can grab your wrist." She said that Shaw had been in the Marine Corps and they had taught him how to fight with knives. She believed he knew what he was talking about. Crawford wondered why Shaw was giving this knife away, since he'd had it since he left the Marine Corps.

Crawford also recounted that before moving in with Shaw, he had told her that he'd killed someone in Los Angeles when he was young. He didn't give her any more details than that. Crawford also related an incident when she'd told Shaw that she was having trouble with a woman and "wished she was gone from the earth."

Crawford had just used that as an expression, but Shaw was serious when he told her that he would kill the woman for her. It scared her, and she told him, "No, please! I couldn't live with myself if you did that!"

Crawford related that Shaw had told her he was friends with the cops because he was a security guard. He even said he was going to apply to be a Portland police officer. She said that Shaw seemed to know a lot of women, but she told him, "'For a guy who knows so many women, you don't seem to be going out with anybody.' He got really defensive and said, 'Yeah, I've got a girlfriend.'" Crawford said she dropped it at that point because he was getting irritated.

Crawford added that without any warning Shaw showed back up at her door in the summer of 1994. She was still mad at him, however, for taking her half of the rent with him when he went to California. Crawford had a roommate at the time, but when this person moved out, she let Shaw stay with her for a couple of months, starting in September or October 1994. She also believed that during this time frame he told her about a gun he'd had in his car, but the police had taken it. She said, "This thing about the gun freaked me out." At one point she said Shaw may have threatened her, but it was vague. She was scared enough, however, that she told her father about it. Shaw moved out from the apartment soon after that.

Detective Stahlman spoke with Sergeant Robert Gebo, a Washington State detective, who was an expert on serial rapists and murderers. Looking at the information concerning Sebastian Shaw, Gebo told Stahlman that the kind of individuals who perpetrated those kinds of crimes generally came from a dysfunctional family, was not a stranger to home invasions and burglaries, at times stalked their victims, and sex was the primary motivation of their crimes. They also generally had explosive tempers, and some incident at work or in the family could trigger a new assault. All of these categories fit Sebastian Shaw.

Detective Bocciolatt contacted Khanh Do, who once again related that she was Shaw's stepsister. Bocciolatt told Khanh that they had arrested Shaw on sexual and murder charges, and that he thought Shaw was a dangerous person. Khanh agreed that Shaw was a "predator and dangerous."

Then Khanh said that from fifth grade through the eighth grade, Shaw was obsessed with a girl named Sandy. Khanh described Sandy as a white girl, with medium-brown hair, tall and skinny. She wore glasses but switched over to contact lenses. Shaw had called her "perfect."

Shown photos taken from Shaw's wall, Khanh was able to say that one of them was of Shaw's friend Jeff Krier, whom he had known in school, and another was probably Shaw's aunt Anna, who had raised him in Vietnam and Texas. Khanh said that Shaw was told by his father that he could not have a girlfriend while in school, because it would distract him from his studies.

While Shaw was in the marines, he contacted Khanh and did "weird things." Asked what these "weird things" were, she said that he claimed to have had sex with a woman on a stage. Then when he came back to Portland, he would tell her that he had "blow jobs" for $25 from the hookers on Eighty-second Avenue. And she also recounted an odd incident that supposedly happened to Shaw in 1988 or 1989. While waiting for a bus, Shaw got into an altercation with someone, and Shaw's neck was cut by a knife. This was odd in light of the fact that Shaw murdered his victims by slashing their throats. Khanh didn't know if this story was true or not, though the detectives were able to find a report that Shaw had checked into an emergency room at a hospital around that time.

Khanh related that Shaw always talked about guns and what a good shot he was. He said he could shoot someone from a great distance. Unlike others' revelations, however, she said he didn't talk about knives or show interest in them. Asked if Shaw had ever come on to her, she replied, "Oh, yes! I was a victim ever since I was in elementary school. But I couldn't say anything to my parents, because I was a female, and in that culture the female is secondary to the male. If I had reported anything to my mother, nothing would have happened." She then said that Shaw never had sexual intercourse with her, but he was always "groping" her. He had started doing this when she was only about eight years old. He had tried "doing the whole sexual intercourse thing," she added, but she prevented this from happening.

Bocciolatt asked when the last time was that he had tried having sex with her, and Khanh replied it was when he was driving her to school in his white Mercury Lynx. He had still been in the Marine Corps then, on leave, and he had begun by putting his hand on her thigh. He worked his hand up her leg to her vaginal area. Asked if he had penetrated her with his finger, she said no, because her panties had gotten in the way. Khahn added that that same day he groped her breast. She was able to thwart further groping because he was driving, so she scooted farther away from him.

Then Khanh added an incident from when they were living in Woodburn. Shaw sneaked into her bedroom, and she was still quite young then. He climbed on top of her and she thought he might have tried penetrating her with his penis. She told him to stop "because it hurts." He kept telling her, "Let me try again! Let me try again!" She wouldn't let him. He even tried having oral sex with her once, by putting his penis to her face, but she told him it was disgusting and refused.

Getting back to her mother, Khanh said that her mother knew something was not right between Shaw and her daughters, and that was why she changed the locks on the doors. It was not because of some program on television about stepbrothers and stepsisters. Khahn added that when she learned that Shaw was coming back to live with them after the marines, she packed her belongings in a backpack and immediately left to go live with some friends. After that, she never went home again, except to visit. She also said that when she left home, she told her mother not to let Shaw be around her sisters. Khanh added, "He was always talking about young females and how he would get young prostitutes to suck on his penis."

As far as the names and nicknames Shaw went by at times, Khanh said that he would sometimes go by "Joe," because it sounded like Chau, and he would also go by "Tony," because he was baptized or confirmed with the middle name Anthony, or so he claimed. Khanh confirmed that Shaw had relatives in Stockton and Alameda, California, and that he sometimes wore glasses and at other times contact lenses. Before Detective Bocciolatt left, Khanh cautioned him that in talking to Shaw's stepmom, Ly Do, that Ly Do still thought of Shaw as a child, and she would not say anything bad about him.

Detective Stahlman went by Shaw's creative writing class at Portland Community College and asked the instructor about Shaw and the stories he had written. The instructor told Stahlman the routine had been for students to hand in their stories, and then the stories would be passed around amongst the other students to be critiqued. The instructor also said that Shaw had been quiet in class, but "sharp." The instructor added that no one had ever complained to him about Shaw's behavior.

Detective G. H. Goodwin spoke with Son Nguyen, the owner of Portland's Lan Vin French Bakery. Nguyen told Goodwin that Shaw had worked for him in the bakery around the end of 1994. With his permission Shaw had taken Nguyen's two boys and two girls—five, six, seven and eight years old—to a park and also to a bowling alley. Nguyen didn't have any worries that Shaw would somehow harm his children. The last time Nguyen had seen Shaw was in December 1997, when Shaw had come by to play with his children.

Because of the search and seizure at the Danmore Hotel, the detectives recovered a voting pamphlet addressed to Michelle Lewis, of Redding, California. Detective Bocciolatt spoke with Investigator Fred Carrelli, of the DA's office in Redding, who told Bocciolatt that Lewis had reported a prowler near her residence on January 4, 1998. The theft of the voting pamphlet and other mail had probably occurred in the early months of summer 1994.

Michelle Lewis contacted Bocciolatt and said that while living with her parents in 1993 and 1994, she had started receiving harassing phone calls. At the beginning of the calls, the man would tell her what she was wearing and where she had been that day. These calls frightened her. This went on for months, until the last call she received, where the man said he was masturbating while talking to her. She changed her phone number after that. Bocciolatt asked Michelle what her hair color was. She said it was shoulder-length and light brown.

Deciding that it might be important to talk to Shaw's father, Van Ho, Detectives Bocciolatt and Van Stearns went down to San Bernardino, California, to interview him. Van Ho told them he had spoken to his son two months previous to his arrest. Then he indicated that he and Sebastian had not kept in contact very much over the years because of the tension between them. Van told the detectives about Shaw's younger years, and mainly addressed the same things that others had. He also kept repeating, "He was a good kid, but fucked up in the head!" When the detectives asked him what that meant, Van said that Shaw wanted to go into the military before finishing high school, and Van wanted him to finish high school first. He also said that Shaw would not obey his directives, and always argued with him. A lot of the problem, according to Van, was that Sebastian would tell him he was American, but Van would reply, "Don't forget you are Vietnamese too!" Part of the problem, as well, was that Van did not speak much English, while Sebastian did not speak much Vietnamese. There was a real language problem between father and son.

When it came to the suicide attempt, Van said that Shaw took too many sleeping pills. He added that he thought this occurred when Shaw had already left him and was in southern California. Everyone else said it occurred when Shaw was in Oregon with his father and stepmom. Khanh even said that it was Van Ho who had taken Shaw to the doctor after the incident.

Asked what kind of disciplinary problems Shaw had, Van replied, "He was lazy. He wouldn't do his homework and I would punish him." Asked what kind of punishment this was, Van said he would make Sebastian stand in the corner. He admitted that he'd spanked him until Sebastian had turned ten, but Van denied ever using his fists or boards on him. Once again, Van said that his son's "mind was fucked up," and added examples of Shaw going to school one day and not wanting to go the next. Or starting a job somewhere, and then soon quitting the job. Van did say that Shaw never hurt animals, started fires or wet the bed. He added that on some occasions Sebastian "would howl in his sleep."

Interestingly enough, Van said that Khanh was Ly Do's daughter, but not his daughter. Van added an interesting admission from Shaw. Shaw had told Van that he'd lost his faith in God sometime in the 1990s because "I have shamed myself." Shaw hadn't revealed what the shame was.

Van had not seen Shaw with knives or a gun, but he had seen him with nunchakus or, as Van put it, "sticks like Bruce Lee used." He said Shaw would drink beer as an adult, but he didn't think he took any illegal drugs or smoked marijuana. Van confirmed that Sebastian had relatives in Stockton, California. Asked if Shaw would have sex with his stepsisters, Van replied, "No way, sir!" Yet, once again, Van said that Shaw's mind was fucked up, and added, "He had a big problem with his mother's death."

The detectives discovered that Shaw had been enrolled at California State University in San Bernardino in 1993, and he had listed his major as biology. They also found out that Shaw had worked at the college bookstore for a while. In their investigation they were able to track down a person named Christina Portales. She'd had a license plate stolen off her car in 1994. When they spoke with Portales, she said that she'd been employed at the California State Board of Equalization in 1994, which had its office at Fourth and D Streets in San Bernardino. Portales didn't even know her front license plate had been stolen until a letter contacted her about this problem.

The investigators also discovered that Shaw had been a security guard at the nearby California State Court of Appeals in the spring of 1994, near where Portales had worked. Shown a photograph of Shaw, and asked if she'd ever seen him before, Portales said on a scale of one to ten, it was about a five that she had seen him. She added that she might have seen him during one of her daily walks at lunchtime. Asked if she had been stalked during that time frame, she answered that she wasn't aware of having been stalked.

Stearns next spoke with Teresa Battiste, who was the person who had actually noticed that Portales's front license plate was missing. Later, Battiste's husband got some mail saying that their vehicle had been parked illegally on Franklin Street in San Francisco in 1994. Since he'd not been there, he wondered what was going on, and discovered that the license plate to his car had been switched. His license plate was now missing, and Portales's license plate had been put on the front end of his car instead. Battiste reported this incident to the San Bernardino Police Department. Teresa Battiste was asked if she'd had any harassing phone calls, and she replied that she'd received some phone calls early in 1997 from a man asking "if she wanted to have some fun." The person who had made these calls was soft-spoken and had no accent.

The detectives next spoke with Glenda Eades, who had been Shaw's supervisor when he worked as a security guard for the Guardsmark Corporation in southern California. Eades had reassigned Shaw to the California State Court of Appeals in San Bernardino when it was found that he was stealing candy bars at the job site where he worked at a grocery warehouse. Eades added that Shaw "was a whiner, with always something to complain about." She said that lots of people didn't like working with him, and said "he had a creepy look."

When assigned to the court of appeals, Shaw had a stationary job sitting at a desk near the front entrance. He mainly worked evenings and would lock up after personnel left the building. Asked why Shaw had left Guardsmark, Eades said that Shaw had told her, "I want to travel around and see America." Other people thought Shaw had been fired.

Going to the court of appeals, the detectives spoke with Charlie Barth, who had been a coworker of Shaw's there. Barth described Shaw as a "jolly guy who was always smiling and laughing." The detectives next spoke with Henry Espinosa, chief clerk of the court, who said he knew why Shaw had been terminated. A female lawyer by the name of Letitia Pepper had been harassed by Shaw, according to Espinosa. Shaw had come to her office one day and out of the blue asked her if she wanted to make love with him. She was absolutely shocked by this.

Detective Bocciolatt spoke with Pepper and she described what had happened on that day in late spring 1994. Shaw had come to her office door. He was wearing bicycle shorts and he seemed to be squirming, as if wanting to ask her something. She thought he was going to ask about some legal advice. Instead, he blurted out, "I want to make love to you."

Letitia Pepper was absolutely shocked, and in an effort to take control of the situation, she told him that he'd never even asked her out and he didn't know anything about her. Shaw responded that he knew all about her, and it made her wonder if he'd been checking up on her. Shaw then said, "Are you going to tell anyone about this?" She replied that she would have to report it.

After Shaw left, Pepper was very scared, and she called a friend to come to the courthouse and be with her as she left the building. Pepper told Judge Timlin about the incident the next day, and Shaw was soon terminated from his job at Guardsmark. Then Pepper told Detective Bocciolatt that two other female employees at the court had been concerned about Shaw as well. One was named Jo Larick, and the other was Susan Streble. Streble was so scared, she quit coming in on Sundays to work because she knew that Shaw would be there in a fairly empty courthouse. Bocciolatt's conversation with Pepper was by telephone and he asked her what kind of hair she had. Pepper replied that her hair was medium-length and dark brown in color.

Contacting Jo Larick, she told Bocciolatt that while working at the courthouse, Shaw had come to her with a short story he'd written for a college class. When she looked at it, it was very sexual in nature, and it described one woman with "a 38D bra cup size." She thought a lot of the remarks in the story were inappropriate. Larick also had received harassing phone calls during the time Shaw worked at the court of appeals.

Speaking with Susan Streble next, Detective Bocciolatt learned that Streble indeed quit working on Sundays because of Shaw. He had asked "inappropriate" questions about her personal life, and those of another attorney named Anne Bittner. Bittner was going through a divorce at the time, and Shaw was particulary interested in her. Streble said, "He would sort of insinuate sexual things into the questions he asked."

While in the area, the detectives spoke with a cousin of Shaw's named Hung Tran. Tran said that Shaw had once showed her a large knife he'd obtained while in the marines. Asked what other relatives Shaw had in the state, she said that Shaw had some in Stockton, California.

Meanwhile, back in Oregon, Detective Stahlman was ascertaining how Shaw acted while at Paragon Cable. He spoke with Marcia Alex, who in 1991 had worked at the master control room at Paragon. Shaw would come in and watch pornographic movies on an overhead monitor. She said this made her uncomfortable, and no other employees besides Shaw did this. Shaw would say things like, "Hey, there's a hot movie on HBO, you should look!" She would answer, "I have work to do"; then she would try and get him to leave the control room. She said, "It was like I had to treat him like a little kid or something. I didn't feel threatened—it was just weird."

Stahlman next contacted Shirley Philip, the recipient of the satanic balloon, who had been a dispatcher at Paragon when Shaw was there. Philip said right off the bat she realized how uncomfortable Shaw made the women at Paragon, because he was always staring at them. "He made comments about sex, and was obsessive about sex. He was always talking about porn stars and about the prostitutes on Sandy Boulevard. One day he started talking to me about some porn star who was going to be signing autographs at the Fantasy Video Store next door. I told him I wasn't interested in that." According to Philip, however, Shaw kept on talking about it and the hookers on Sandy Boulevard.

Philip said that Shaw would come in almost every night and talk to her for ten to twenty minutes; it always made her uncomfortable. She would eventually tell him, "Don't you have work to do?" Philip added that Shaw never asked her out, nor talked about her sex life, but rather he talked about sex in a general way. Philip told Detective Stahlman about the satanic balloon incident, which had caused Shaw to be fired from Paragon Cable.

Because a woman named Kay, who had worked at Paragon, had been raped at her apartment in Salem, Detective Stahlman contacted her, and she said that she could never remember Shaw talking to her. When she had been assaulted, she described her attacker as wearing a black stocking cap and gray ski mask. Her attacker, however, was tall, which Shaw was not. She had received harassing telephone calls two weeks before the attack and the caller gagged into the telephone, and she added that her assailant had attempted to strangle her. In the end she didn't think it was Shaw, because she believed her attacker was about six feet to six-two.

Stahlman next contacted Linda Aday, who had been the human resources administrator at Paragon Cable when Shaw had worked there. Aday said that Shaw "seemed to be needy, and he would come into my office and talk about movies." Aday added that it was during this time period that Shaw changed his name from Chau Quang Ho to Sebastian Alexander Shaw. He came into her office and asked for a new name badge. She asked him how he had picked the name, and he replied Sebastian from Johann Sebastian Bach, and Shaw from the actor Robert Shaw, of *Jaws* fame. This was, of course, different than what other people said regarding how Shaw chose his name.

Aday had been the one who handled the sexual harassment charges against Shaw, and when she confronted him with these things, "he seemed incredulous and denied what he had done could have been interpreted in a sexual way." Aday said that she and other employees tried to get him to understand that what he was doing and saying was sexual harassment, "but he did not seem to understand." Aday didn't know if this was due to his culture or youth. Aday had even gone so far as to tell some female employees that if they felt threatened while leaving their jobs at night or in the early-morning hours, there was an escort service with employees who would escort them to their cars. On the day that Aday fired Shaw, she told a man named Mike to stand by, just in case. "I wanted him as backup in case anything happened," she said.

The next day Stahlman was contacted by Barbara Phillips-Crawford once again. She told him some new things that she'd recalled and thought might be important. Crawford remembered going to the movies with Shaw at the Lloyd Center Cinema. This was important to Stahlman, because someone had tried using Todd Rudiger's ATM card at the Lloyd Center on July 17, 1992, the day Rudiger was most likely murdered.

Stahlman then spoke with Lisa Bishop, who had taken the same creative-writing class that Shaw had, at Portland Community College. At the first class all the students were supposed to tell a little about themselves. Bishop told the others that she liked crocheting, and during the break Shaw had come up to her and asked if she would come to his residence and show him how to crochet. She declined, and two weeks later he asked the same thing, with the same result. Bishop told Stahlman that Shaw seemed to be very lonely.

Around this same time Detective Stahlman spoke with Charles Sellers, who had been chief building engineer for the Hellman Corporation. During 1992, one of his duties was to monitor the security guards and janitors who were under his supervision at the One Pacific Square building in downtown Portland. In the spring of 1992, Sellers recalled, some employee told him that Shaw was going over to the nearby Chamber of Commerce building and bothering a female janitor there. Around five-thirty the next evening, Sellers witnessed the female janitor's boyfriend get into a heated argument with Shaw. Sellers said, "Shaw and this guy got into each other's faces and words were exchanged. I think it would have come to blows, except the security manager came out and separated them. Shaw had told the other guy, 'You don't have any right to tell me not to talk to her! Only she can tell me that!'" Sellers added that this incident caused Shaw to be transferred from the Pacific One building to another job site. Sellers had not heard of the supposed threats Shaw made against him.

Going back to Paragon Cable, Stahlman spoke with Lisa Brooks, who had been a repair operator and dispatcher there. Brooks said that Shaw was always finding some kind of excuse to come into her room and talk to her. On some occasions he wanted to rub her shoulders and give her a neck massage. He would come up behind her chair, put his hands on her shoulders and give her a neck massage—despite the fact that she didn't want him touching her. She said that on one occasion she could sense his hips swaying, "as if he was trying to give himself a hard-on." He even put his hands lower one time and touched her breasts when she was on the phone, and she couldn't react right away.

Brooks said that Shaw would "peekaboo" around corners at her while she worked and it made her uncomfortable. He would go so far as to tell her, "You have nice breasts," and she'd tell him to get lost. He just would not give up wanting to touch her, and she told him, "Leave me alone! I don't want you touching me!" Brooks added that "sexual stuff was a big deal with him. He would come in and watch movies on the overhead screen when there were sex scenes." Then he'd ask what kind of positions she liked, as in "sexual positions." It got so bad that she did not want to work alone in her area if Shaw was around.

Brooks added, "Shaw was a spooky guy. He didn't know how to take no for an answer. He would ask me out every few weeks, and I always told him no." She was frightened of him and didn't want to upset him too much, because she was afraid of what he might do. Sometimes he would come in to work at night and seem "different" to her. She said he acted paranoid, as if he'd

Chau Quong Ho changed his name to Sebastian Shaw in honor of his hero, British actor Sebastian Lewis Shaw, who played Anakin Skywalker in *Star Wars: Return of the Jedi.* (Mug shot)

Shaw attended the Mount Angel, Oregon, Catholic church as a boy. He would soon take on devilish ways, however. (Mug shot)

Donna Ferguson was only eighteen years old when Shaw picked her out of a grocery store line and decided to rape and kill her.
(Yearbook photo)

In late July, 1992, Shaw forced his way at gunpoint into the mobile home shared by Todd Rudiger and Donna Ferguson.

Shaw tied up both Rudiger and Ferguson with telephone extension cords. Then he proceeded to rape Donna Ferguson.

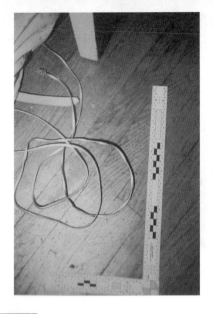

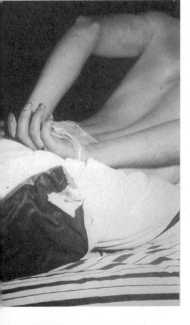

Todd Rudiger's hands were tied behind his back, and he could not help Donna during the sexual assault.

Todd suffered an epileptic episode during the assault and fell on the bedroom floor beneath some blankets.

Detectives arrived on scene two days later to discover the bodies of Todd Rudiger and Donna Ferguson. Both had died from severe wounds to their necks.

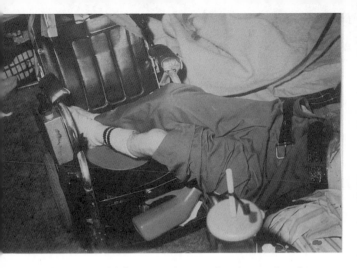

Only later would detectives discover that the murder of
Jay Rickbeil in 1991 had been perpetrated by the same person
who murdered Rudiger and Ferguson in 1992.

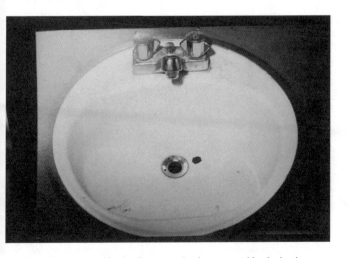

After murdering Rickbeil, Shaw washed up in Rickbiel's bathroom
sink. Shaw, however, left some of his victim's blood in the sink.

Shaw also splattered some of Rickbeil's blood onto a toilet paper roll.

Detectives didn't know it at the time, but a bloody piece of tissue left in the toilet would be incredibly important in solving the murder years later. On it was a mixture of Rickbeil's and Shaw's blood.

Fourteen-year-old Jenny Lin was murdered under mysterious circumstances in Castro Valley, California. Sebastian Shaw was in the area at the time. *(Yearbook photo)*

In August 1994, Sebastian Shaw was arrested in this car. The car had been stolen from San Ramon, California, not far from where Jenny Lin was murdered.

A Portland police officer listed all the items found in the stolen car, including a copy of *The Anarchist Cookbook*, which gave tips on how to make bombs and kill people.

Two stolen rifles were also found in the car. The guns' owner, who lived in San Ramon, California, recognized them as his.

Ammo for a handgun found in the stolen car would later match ammo found in Shaw's apartment. The ammo was significant because Shaw would use that same caliber handgun while tying up a young woman and raping her.

Duct tape was discovered among the items in the stolen car. Shaw liked to use duct tape on his female victims.

Other items in the stolen car trunk included a hammer, a ski mask, and a sock filled with a lead weight to make it into a weapon.

Officer Terry Long of the Portland Police Department later described many of the items in the stolen car as a "rape/murder kit."

While Sebastian Shaw looked at all the items in the trunk of the stolen car, a police officer snapped his photo.

Sebastian Shaw had a smug smile on his face when photographed by an officer. He was not prosecuted by either Contra Costa County, California or Multnomah County, Oregon on the stolen car/rifles incident.

In July 1995, Sebastian Shaw walked right into Amanda Carpova's apartment through an unlocked screen door, pointed a gun at her, and forced her into her bedroom.

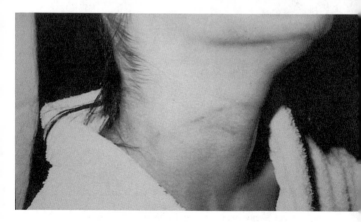

After raping Amanda, Shaw tried strangling her to death, but Amanda fought back hard to save her life. She suffered abrasions to her neck, back and legs.

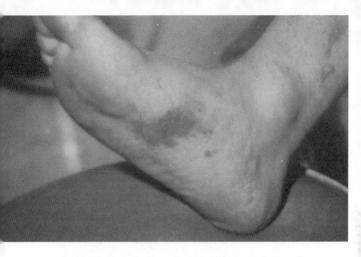

Amanda also suffered cuts to her feet when she stepped on broken glass that fell to the floor during the struggle.

After her rape, Amanda met a forensic sketch artist to describe how her attacker had looked. The sketch was close, but not quite accurate.

Later, world-famous forensic sketch artist Jeanne Boylan listened to Amanda describe her attacker, and came up with this representation that more closely matched the way Shaw looked at the time of the sexual assault.

A team of detectives searched for and arrested Sebastian Shaw right outside the Portland Main Library.
(Author photo)

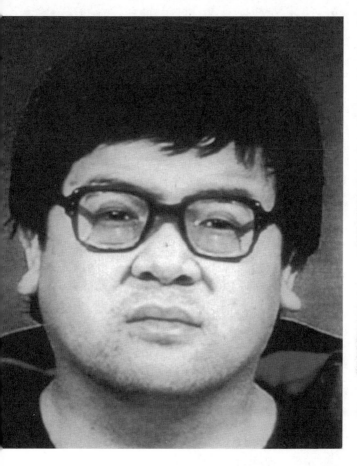

When Shaw was arrested, detectives would eventually find out
that he murdered Donna Ferguson, Todd Rudiger, and Jay
Rickbeil, and had attempted to murder Amanda Carpova.
(Mug shot)

Portland Police Department Commander Larry Findling and Detective Mike Stahlman were instrumental in the arrest and eventual conviction of Sebastian Shaw for various murders. They worked tirelessly on very difficult cases. *(Author photo)*

Sebastian Shaw received a life sentence without parole at the Multnomah County Court in downtown Portland, Oregon. *(Author photo)*

just done something bad. "His hair would be all messed up like he had just gotten out of a freak show."

Brooks related that she did get obscene phone calls at work, and she was sure that Shaw was the one who was calling, even though he tried to disguise his voice. The person on the line would say that he was masturbating while talking to her. She said that the call was coming from inside the building and it really freaked her out. The phone call that upset her the most was when he—and she was sure it was Shaw—said that he wanted to tear the buttons of her blouse with his teeth. She reported this incident to management and Shaw was disciplined about it.

Brooks also stated she was sure it was Shaw who had called her and made references to bondage. He would say things like, "Oh, I would like to tie you up!" and "Oh, I'd love to touch your breasts!"

The detectives had been all around Portland and San Bernardino tracking down leads about Shaw, but soon they would head to the San Francisco Bay Area as well, wondering if Sebastian Shaw was involved in the murder of another young woman who had dark brown hair— just the kind he liked.

12

"Too Bad No One
Would Listen to Me"

On April 2, 1998, Detective Stahlman, Detective Bocciolatt and Detective Monte De Coste, the latter of the Alameda County Sheriff's Office, met with the parents of Jennifer Lin, a fourteen-year-old dark-haired girl who had been murdered in Castro Valley in 1994. The parents told the detectives about Jenny's habits before and after school, and the fact that a bus let her off from school about a half block from her home. John Lin said that his daughter didn't know anyone in southern California, her movie attendance was very limited, and she only went to movies with her parents. Jenny may have bowled a couple of times in the past, but only when her father was with her.

Mei-Lian Lin, Jenny's mom, said her daughter would go to the library sometimes, but this had been when Mei-Lian was with her. Even though Jenny had taken some summer classes for gifted students at the University of California, Berkeley, she had never been to the University of California in San Bernardino. As far as Mei-Lian knew, Jenny had not received any hang-up calls or obscene phone calls, and she was sure Jenny would have told her if she had received anything like that.

Mei-Lian worked at a Mervyns department store, and about a month before Jenny was murdered, Mei-Lian took her to work with her. Mei-Lian said there were security guards at the store, but she hadn't had any problems with them. When they first moved into their home, it was in a new development, and the contractor had security guards around the area keeping an eye on the building material and development in general. At the time of Jenny's death, John was working at the Federal Reserve Bank in San Francisco, and that building also had security guards. Like Mei-Lian, however, he had never had any problems with any of them, and he didn't remember anyone who matched Sebastian Shaw's description.

John said that no license plates were stolen or switched on their cars in 1994, and they didn't know the Campbell family who lived in nearby San Ramon. The Lin family had never visited 29 Palms in southern California, nor had they been up to Portland, Oregon. John could think of no connection to Stockton, California, the court of appeals in San Bernardino, or any of the other places where Shaw had worked.

The Lins did say they shopped at a Safeway in Castro Valley, and Jenny would sometimes accompany them there. Detective Bocciolatt showed them photos taken from the wall of Shaw's room at the Danmore Hotel, and they couldn't identify anyone in those photos. But a photo taken from Shaw's wallet of an Asian girl did resemble Jenny somewhat. The Lins had no idea who the girl in the photo was.

John Lin related that someone might have stolen an AT&T phone card from them, because after Jenny's death, someone was using their phone card number to make calls. Even more interesting, on the day that Jenny was murdered, a woman in the neighborhood reported seeing a heavyset young Asian man in the area of the Lins' home. Not long after spotting this person, the woman may have heard glass breaking, as if a window had been smashed. A broken window on the ground floor was exactly how Jenny's assailant had entered the Lin residence. It was determined that this happened on the afternoon of May 27, 1994, a little before or after Jenny had come home from school. It could not be determined if the assailant was already waiting in the house for her, or if he had broken in while she was on the phone with a friend.

Moving on to the nearby city of Stockton, California, the detectives interviewed James Luu, who was a son of Son Ho, one of Shaw's aunts. James recalled that Shaw did visit them, about four years previously, which might have been around May or June 1994. At the time Shaw told James that he'd worked in security, and James related, "Shaw did not act like a normal person. He would drink a lot, and drink until he got drunk. He seemed depressed. When he saw a nice woman on television, he would say things like, 'She has a nice ass,' or 'She has nice tits.'"

The detectives next spoke with Shaw's aunt, Son Ho. She remembered Shaw driving a large American car when he stopped by, possibly in 1994, and he said he was going from southern California back to Portland. A large American car is exactly what had been stolen from the Campbells' home in San Ramon. Son Ho added that Shaw liked Anna Ho a lot, and called her "Mom." Son did not get along with Anna, and did not see her very often, nor had she seen Shaw very much over the years. Son Ho remembered Shaw talking to her children, and telling them to stay in school. She didn't think he was crazy or heard voices, and that he didn't seem to take drugs, although he drank alcohol to excess.

The detectives had more luck with Kim Luu Ho, one of Shaw's cousins, and she recalled that Shaw had come to Stockton in 1994 and might have stayed three or four days. She didn't feel comfortable around him and thought he had a "mental problem." One time he came into her bedroom, kneeled down, and placed his face very close to hers as she lay in bed. She woke up and said, "What the hell are you doing?" He answered that he was her cousin and was just being friendly. She told him to get out of her room, and he complied. A few days later she wondered if he tried coming into a bathroom when she was taking a shower. The more she thought about it, the more certain she was that Shaw had been there in May or June 1994. He said spooky things to her, "You have pretty toenails. The man who marries you will be very lucky."

In 1996, Kim got married and Shaw came to her wedding. At the wedding Shaw got drunk, and he touched Kim's sister on the neck in an inappropriate manner. Her sister got mad at Shaw and they started arguing. Kim said, "When you looked him in the eye, he did not seem normal."

Moving over to San Francisco, the detectives found that a car stolen from the San Bernardino area, with switched license plates, had been ticketed for parking illegally on Franklin Street in that city. This had occurred on June 6, 1994, six days after Jenny Lin had been murdered, about thirty miles away in Castro Valley. Just what Shaw might have been doing in San Francisco at that time, the detectives didn't know.

Moving back to Portland, Detective Stahlman once again started looking into what Shaw might have been up to in the days before the murders of Donna Ferguson and Todd Rudiger. Larry Bogan, who had worked with Shaw as a security guard for the Pinkerton Agency, recalled Shaw getting into a heated argument in 1992 with some guy who was a janitor. He believed that Shaw did threaten this person.

Checking further, Detective Stahlman was finally able to track down the female janitor that Shaw had been stalking in 1992. Her first name was Rita, and she had come to the United States from Eastern Europe. Rita vividly recalled being stalked by a young Asian man as she worked around One Pacific Square. The first time this occurred, she was cleaning on a floor with no one else around, and Shaw showed up. He asked her if she liked sex and if she had sex with her boyfriend. She told him it was none of his business. She told her boyfriend, Zoltan, about this, and he said, "Don't talk to him! There's something wrong with him!"

Shaw, however, kept stalking her, and Zoltan confronted Shaw about it. Shaw wanted to fight Zoltan right then and there, but Zoltan would not fight, even though he was bigger than Shaw. It may have been that Zoltan was worried about being fired if he got into a fight, since he was a new immigrant. Zoltan did not back down from Shaw's threats, but he would not get into a physical confrontation with him, only a verbal one, which other people saw.

Rita said that Shaw was "mean to me, and he would tell me that he was more important than my boyfriend. One time I was leaving the parking garage with my boyfriend, and Shaw dropped the security gate in front of us and stopped the car. He would not let us go, and Zoltan got out of the car and confronted him. Zoltan asked, 'Are you stupid? Are you crazy?' Shaw said he didn't see us, but I know he did it on purpose."

Rita added that one time Shaw showed her a large folding knife he carried in a pants pocket. She thought the knife was perhaps five inches in length. Shaw told her he had an even larger knife than that one. Rita related that on one occasion her boyfriend's car was vandalized, and he thought that Shaw had done it. Stahlman told Rita about Shaw's arrest for rape and murder, and she replied, "I believe it about him." She remembered his eyes being "crazy-looking," and her boyfriend had said, "He's sick! Stay away from him!"

Detectives Stahlman and Bocciolatt contacted Zoltan, and showed him a photo of Sebastian Shaw, whom Zoltan immediately remembered. Zoltan said that many times in the lunchroom Shaw would make comments about Rita and it made Zoltan angry. Zoltan could only recall one argument with Shaw. He said that Shaw had pulled his fist back as if to punch him. Zoltan would not fight him, however, and later his boss said that he had acted correctly. Zoltan recalled Shaw being gone for three days, but after that time he returned as a security guard to Pacific One. This made Zoltan very angry because he thought Shaw should have been fired. After Shaw came back, Zoltan's car was vandalized by someone who stuck a syringe in a door lock. Zoltan said, "He was very strange." When told that Shaw had been arrested for rape and murder, Zoltan replied, "Too bad no one would listen to me back then." In fact, Todd Rudiger and Donna Ferguson were murdered within days of Shaw leaving his job with the Pinkertons.

As if harassing Rita wasn't enough, Shaw apparently also harassed a young woman who worked at a flower shop at Pacific One. John Gregory contacted Stahlman once again and said that a woman who worked at the Luv and Stuff flower shop had once told him that Shaw was coming on to the young woman who worked there, and she didn't like it.

Stahlman was able to contact this woman, Sharon Paulsen, who said that Shaw had bothered her stepdaughter Jody. Stahlman asked her what Jody's age was and a lot of other questions about her. The woman had told Jody, "This guy's asking all sorts of questions about you and I don't like it."

Paulsen also told Detective Stahlman that Shaw came in more than once and bought flowers for a woman who worked in the One Pacific Square building. He would send the flowers to her anonymously, and the woman came in and complained to Paulsen about it. Paulsen told Stahlman, "The woman came in and told me she didn't want any more flowers coming to her." She was so upset, she told Paulsen, "Don't send me any more! Just throw them away!" Paulsen added that when that woman walked through the lobby, Shaw would ogle her and "act like he was drooling." Paulsen thought the woman Shaw had been sending flowers to was named Kathy. Stahlman was able to contact this Kathy, who had worked at the building, but she said that she'd never received any flowers from an anonymous source. She thought it might have been someone else there. In fact, another person named John Gregory, who had worked nearby, was able to give Stahlman more information about these flower incidents. He said, "Shaw was told to stay away from this woman and not send her any more flowers. But I had the feeling he was just laughing at the rest of us."

Around this same time the detectives spoke with David Malone, who had worked at the Safeway on Hawthorne with Shaw. Malone said that Shaw had been nice in the beginning, but he did have a temper. Sometime during the winter months, probably in 1995, Malone had been in the bathroom when Shaw paged him from the front of the store. Malone said he didn't hear the page, and Shaw came to the back of the store to confront him. Shaw told Malone, "When I call you, you come up there! I've killed bigger men than you!"

The investigation went one way for a while, then another, because Sebastian Shaw had obviously been involved in multiple crimes and moved around a lot. Looking at the Paragon Cable angle once again, Detective Stahlman spoke with Naomi Bledsoe, a woman who had worked there. She told him, "He was very creepy. He kind of looked through you." It was also discovered that Todd Rudiger had once received cable service through Paragon Cable, though any link to Shaw was very tenuous at best. Shaw had worked in the office, not at people's homes as an installer.

Stahlman was able to track down Rachelle Robbins, who was Donna Ferguson's cousin and lived in California. Robbins had traveled to Portland with her mother by train, and had a photograph dated 6/22/92. Robbins usually spent time with Delani Ferguson, Donna's sister, but Delani was gone then, so Robbins spent some time with Donna. Robbins recalled going to a movie theater one night with Donna and another girl. All she could remember about the movie theater was that it was inside a very large mall.

Robbins remembered going to a party in Beaverton with Donna, and they arrived there about 9:00 P.M. She could not remember anyone there who matched the description of Sebastian Shaw.

It took a while, but Detective Stahlman discovered a check written from Sebastian Shaw to Richard Riffle, dated May 15, 1992. Riffle had worked at the Northwest Natural Gas Company since 1979, and he sold guns on the side. Riffle said that everyone at NNG knew that he had this gun business. Shown the check made out to him from Sebastian Shaw, Riffle said, "I probably sold him a gun, though I don't remember him." Riffle then got his Federal Firearms Dealers Records from his closet and found a record that he'd sold a Jennings Firearms Model .38 to Sebastian Shaw. Because of the waiting period to receive a gun for background checks, Riffle did not give Shaw the gun until May 28, 1992. And since Shaw was not in the criminal system at the time, nothing came up as to why he should not have a firearm.

Stahlman noted that the .38 that was sold to Shaw had a two-inch barrel, was a semiautomatic and chrome in color. It matched fairly closely the firearm Amanda Carpova described that her assailant had at the time he assaulted her.

Every so often someone would call in out of the blue about the case, and this happened in regard to Tom Ierulli and his wife, Wendy Taylor. They said that they knew Ed Rudiger Sr., Todd's father. They were watching the television news one night in 1998 and saw Sebastian Shaw's photo and a story about the murder of Todd Rudiger and Donna Ferguson. It was then that they realized that Shaw had lived in back of their house during 1993 and 1994. Taylor told Stahlman that even then Shaw had seemed "weird" to her. Asked what that meant, Taylor said, "He was too chatty and outgoing with us. He would come over into our yard and start pulling weeds, even though I didn't ask him to. I thought he might be checking out our house. He came through a hole in the fence, and one time I spotted him carrying a hammer and wondered why he would have that in our yard. We had a female roommate in the house at the time as well, and we warned her about Shaw."

Asked how Shaw appeared then, Taylor said that he looked Hawaiian to her, not Vietnamese as she later learned that he was. "He looked like a Hawaiian-surfer type to me, with longish hair. He was kind of fat in the middle." Incredibly, there was a female police officer who lived nearby at the time. This officer had short dark hair, the kind of color that Shaw liked. Taylor wondered whether amongst all the other females that Shaw had stalked, if Shaw was stalking the female officer as well.

13

"Thank God for DNA"

The investigation by the Multnomah County District Attorney's Office spread out in many directions after Sebastian Shaw's arrest. Besides Commander Findling and Detective Stahlman's voluminous notes, they also began subpoenaing Shaw's school records to see what kind of disciplinary actions had been taken against him in school. These subpoenas went out to the Woodburn School District in Oregon and Narbonne High School in Harbor City, California. The Pinkerton Security and Investigation Services, where Shaw had been employed as a guard, and Guardsmark in southern California also received subpoenas.

Despite not knowing about Shaw's connection to the Rickbeil murder at that point, a Multnomah County grand jury brought back a bill of indictment against Sebastian Shaw in March 1998, and it was a very lengthy one, containing forty-two counts. The first counts were the most damaging to his cause—Count 1 being: *The said defendant, on or about July 17, 1992, did unlawfully and intentionally cause the death of another human being, to-wit: Donna Ferguson. Said defendant having unlawfully and intentionally, in the course of the same criminal episode, caused the death of an additional human being, to-wit: Todd Rudiger, contrary to the Statutes in such cases made and provided against the peace and dignity of the State of Oregon.*

Further counts of aggravated murder concerned his raping Donna Ferguson and robbing the mobile home. It wasn't until Count 18 that the rape and attempted murder of Amanda Carpova was addressed. There were also counts concerning Amanda that covered rape in the first degree, sodomy in the first degree, sexual abuse in the first degree with a firearm, and kidnapping in the first degree. The Honorable Joseph Ceniceros was assigned the case.

Shaw was assigned two defense attorneys, and right from the start they began looking into the arrest of Shaw, searching for technicalities of improper search and seizure by law enforcement authorities. After a great deal of investigation, Shaw's defense attorneys had enough to present a "Motion to Suppress Statements" to the judge.

The motion began by stating that forty minutes after Shaw was arrested and placed in a holding cell at the Detective Division, Detectives Svilar and Bocciolatt initiated an interview with Shaw. Bocciolatt even said, *"Keep an open mind that we have some things we want to discuss with you, and if you will listen to me, I will make an attempt to help you out."* It was only after this that Sebastian Shaw was read his Miranda rights, which he said he understood.

According to the motion, Detective Bocciolatt then kept talking to Shaw, saying, *"I then asked him if he would be one hundred percent honest with me that I would make an effort to help him out in the future."* Then, according to the same motion, *Shaw within seconds asked for counsel.* The motion stated that Bocciolatt, however, did not give up and continued to engage Shaw in conversation regarding his life in general and the case in particular. The motion stated exactly what Bocciolatt had said, even after Shaw had asked for counsel:

I told Shaw that I knew he had had a rough life by losing his mother in Vietnam at a young age and coming to the United States and being treated poorly by his father. I told him that I knew that he had lost his faith in God, and he interrupted me and said, "You've done your homework."

I told him that after he got an attorney and sometime down the line that he may want to get together and talk to me. Shaw asked me what the charges were going to be and I told him they were going to start with Attempted Murder, Murder, Rape, Sodomy and a host of other charges. He said, "Those are very serious charges." Shaw was very calm and collected throughout this conversation and almost matter of fact.

Again I told him that he may want to keep an open mind after he got his attorney, and in the future he might want to do something nice for the victims' families. He then said, "You mean I killed and raped more than one person?" And I nodded my head in the affirmative.

A few minutes after this conversation, Shaw had pronounced, "Today death, tomorrow life."

Not only was the defense contending that Sebastian Shaw had asked for counsel, but that Detective Bocciolatt kept "interviewing" him after he did so. They also had questions as to whether Shaw's denial of consent to provide saliva for a DNA test had been used for probable cause. One of the more bizarre notes of the motion to suppress was about the detectives' comment that Shaw had a "small and deformed penis." The defense contended this was way outside the limits of probable cause.

The legal matters bumped along during the rest of 1998 and into 1999, when the defense team had Detective Stahlman before a preliminary hearing to see if certain things Stahlman said and seized were going to be admitted into evidence when it came time for trial. The defense began by listing all the items noted in the stolen car in 1994, and they had a series of questions for Stahlman.

Q: *Going to the 1992 murders, as well as the 1995 rape, was there any duct tape associated with either of those events?*

A: *Not to my knowledge.*

Q: *Pepper spray?*

A: *No.*

Q: *Blindfold?*

A: *The '95 case, there was a blindfold.*

Q: *Flex ties?*

A: *No.*

Q: *You indicated that Mr. Shaw was working at a Safeway at the time of the rape, correct?*

A: *Yes.*

Q: *And we know pretty precisely when that rape occurred, is that correct?*

A: *That's correct.*

Q: *I think that the initial police officer on the scene said it had just been reported at around 11 in the morning. Does that sound right?*

A: *It was reported at 11:50 A.M.*

Q: *In fact, Ms. Carpova, the rape victim, indicated that she spent from two to two and a half hours with the suspect in her home?*

A: *Yes.*

Q: *So, presumably, this rape occurred sometime from 9 to 11 A.M., more or less?*

A: *Yes.*

Q: *So, in an effort to establish whether Mr. Shaw was working at that time, you went back to try to put together his work record at the Safeway store he was employed in at that time, correct?*

A: *That's correct.*

Q: *As I understand it, those records were destroyed, so you couldn't determine the exact hours he was working that day, is that correct?*

A: *That's correct.*

Q: *You interviewed a number of people why there would be a gap in the records, and there were various explanations provided, but no way to actually determine what hours he was working. Is that right?*

A: *That's right.*

Q: *In fact, a number of people you interviewed actually put Mr. Shaw working at different shifts then. Correct?*

A: *I remember that, yes.*

Q: *Do you remember a man named Bruce Wakely?*

A: *I remember his name.*

Q: *He was a store manager during the time that Mr. Shaw worked at that store, and he recalls that Shaw worked the day shift mostly.*

A: (No response. Stahlman couldn't remember).

Q: *I can show you the report?*

A: *Sure.* (Stahlman looks at the report.) *That's what he told me.*

Q: *If that was true, the day shift incorporated the hours of the rape, correct?*

A: *That's right.*

Q: *Again to the evidence, Mr. Shaw claimed the gun but not the contents of the trunk (of the stolen car), which were all the items you described previously—the duct tape and so forth, correct?*

A: *That's right.*

Q: *The gun (pistol) was actually in the glove compartment of the car, and not the trunk, correct?*

A: *That's right.*

Clearly, with all this, the defense was saying that Sebastian Shaw, by all probability, was working at Safeway on the morning that Amanda Carpova was raped, and that he never laid any claims to the items in the stolen car of 1994, except for a pistol and some library books. Shaw's attorneys wrote, *The information regarding the contents of the trunk of the vehicle add nothing to a finding of probable cause. Detective Stahlman states that based upon his training, he knows that certain of the items found in the trunk are sometimes associated with sexual assaults.* Shaw's attorneys claimed that just because those items were sometimes used in sexual assaults did not mean that Sebastian Shaw had ever used any of those items in a sexual assault. The attorneys further stated that each one of the items found in the trunk was legal and could be bought by anyone without breaking the law.

In a separate memo to the judge, the defense sought to throw out the seized cigarette butt that Shaw had thrown away. This was a crucial bit of evidence for the prosecution because it was the only link of Shaw's DNA to the DNA samples linking him to the rape of Donna Ferguson and the rape of Amanda Carpova. The defense claimed, *It is inconceivable that Mr. Shaw or any other individual would contemplate that the act of discarding a cigarette butt would reveal to the general public the most personal of the medical details of their lives. And it is inconceivable that any individual discarding a cigarette butt, a used tissue or straw would contemplate that another individual picking up that item would have at his or her disposal the immensely expensive and sophisticated technology to conduct DNA testing on a sample contained on any discarded item. An intrusion of such magnitude into an individual's privacy would offend social and legal norms of behavior.*

It was a good try by the defense, but luckily for the prosecution, the judge dismissed this motion and agreed that DNA extracted from the cigarette butt would be included into evidence, and everything that followed from that.

The defense tried one motion after another, trying to exclude various pieces of evidence. Their next foray into this area concerned Amanda Carpova's viewing of the photo lineup. In the photo lineup the defense contended that Amanda Carpova only thought that the photo of Sebastian Shaw looked "somewhat" like the person who had raped her. And as far as Christina Nielson went, she chose Shaw's photo third down the list from two others more likely as the man she had seen at the front door on the night before Carpova's rape.

Then there was the statement by Lisa Gabriel, who described the person as "definitely not Vietnamese." The motion even went further, stating that two people who had seen the original 1995 forensic sketch as "a good likeness" of the individual, while the second forensic sketch drawn by Jeanne Boylan looked so much different. Also included in the memo was a statement by Amanda Carpova when she had originally described the gun that the assailant had as silver, and later changed the coloration to gray.

In fact, the defense said that most of the so-called probable cause evidence used for an arrest wasn't probable at all. They declared that *the information is far too general to support a finding of probable cause.* Among their contentions of "generality" was the fact that over the years that Shaw had lived in the area, he had frequented Claudia's and so had Amanda Carpova, but there was no evidence that they had ever met there, or that he had even seen her there. Amanda occasionally shopped at the Safeway, where Shaw worked, but there was no evidence that she had ever been at his checkout counter. And they stated that Amanda had spoken of her attacker as wearing a white T-shirt, khaki shorts, Teva-style sandals and sunglasses, but those items were so common as to be meaningless. The defense wrote that all of these things presented by the prosecution were *consecutive inferential leaps,* and not allowed.

On January 10 through 12, 2000, the many issues brought up by Shaw's defense lawyers were finally debated before Judge Frank Bearden, and they all had huge ramifications as to whether key evidence was going to come into play during a jury trial. The judge heard arguments by both the defense and prosecution, and then addressed each issue, one by one. Judge Bearden noted that Detectives Stahlman and Bocciolatt had arranged a meeting with Sebastian Shaw at the office of his parole officer. The detectives asked Shaw to voluntarily give some saliva on an oral swab to assist them in eliminating suspects from a rape case. Shaw gave a "qualified" affirmative answer that he would, but first he wanted to talk to a lawyer. Then he said he had gotten into trouble once before by not talking to a lawyer first. The meeting was terminated, and Shaw did seek counsel. Within an hour he left a message on Detective Bocciolatt's voice mail saying he would not comply with their request.

The prosecution said of this matter that this interview should come in, because Shaw was not under arrest and free to leave at any time. The defense argued that Shaw was already a suspect at that point and he was asked to give incriminating evidence against himself because he had invoked a right to counsel. Judge Bearden agreed with the defense on this issue. "In my opinion, there can be no way to sanitize the statements made by Mr. Shaw since his initial aquiescence followed by his later decision not to comply can only be explained by the fact that his attorney advised against his cooperation, confirming his concerns about his DNA being used for purposes other than the present case."

Then the issue got into the matter of Shaw at the Detective Division reading and signing a Miranda warning, where he invoked his right to remain silent and seek counsel. The judge noted that Detective Bocciolatt began gathering up his materials and made further statements to Shaw—but Bocciolatt did not ask Shaw questions. The statements included what Shaw was being charged with, and statements about Shaw's personal life.

The prosecution argued that Detective Bocciolatt ceased asking questions of Shaw when Shaw invoked his right to silence and counsel. The defense argued that Bocciolatt's statements were "the functional equivalent of interrogation, since Detective Bocciolatt was using words and phrases that had emotional impact and would likely elicit incriminating response."

Judge Bearden responded, "The present situation is unique from any I have found in the case law. The brief conversation (with Bocciolatt) was matter-of-fact. Mr. Shaw did not appear to be overly nervous or under any emotional duress or strain. He clearly had previously shown a knowledge and very high level of sophistication about his rights and the consequences of proceeding without counsel, and he chose here to make certain statements. It is true that the statements made by Detective Bocciolatt were not in the form of questions, but it is also true that the law looks not to Detective Bocciolatt's intent, but to the effect on the focal suspect. With all this in mind, I am finding Detective Bocciolatt's statement regarding Mr. Shaw's early childhood was not the functional equivalent of a question and Mr. Shaw's response to that statement was voluntary and admissible. Mr. Shaw's response to Detective Bocciolatt's statement of the initial charges to be filed was also not in response to a question or the functional equivalent and was made voluntarily and is admissible. Mr. Shaw's statement at the end of the interaction after the detective brought him some water ('Today death, tomorrow life') was purely spontaneous and is admissible.

"A detective's statements that he might want to keep an open mind, 'and do something nice for the victims' families,' was the functional equivalent of a question. It is the first time Mr. Shaw knows that Detective Bocciolatt is talking about more than one victim. Mr. Shaw's response to this statement will be suppressed."

Then the judge addressed the defense's motion to controvert the probable cause, and the defense had even drawn up a chart to show several points they were addressing. They, in essence, were saying, "The affidavit presented by the prosecution was insufficient or defective and the arrest should be suppressed." The defense first argued that there were no ties between the victims and Shaw, and the fact that he lived in the neighborhood of Amanda Carpova, worked at a place where she sometimes shopped and went to a tavern that she sometimes frequented was not enough evidence for probable cause. The judge, however, noted, "While it is true that none of these items specifically tie Mr. Shaw to Ms. Carpova or the crime, they nevertheless combine to show that the defendant had proximity and opportunity, which makes up one building block of probable cause."

"Next, defense counsel argues that Mr. Shaw's denial of his consent to give a saliva swab should be deleted from the affidavit, and I agree."

Judge Bearden addressed the issue of the handgun seized in 1994 from the stolen car in which Sebastian Shaw was sleeping. Bearden ruled that an officer at that time noticed a handgun in the front passenger compartment. This was an observation before any seizure of the vehicle occurred. Then when Shaw was arrested in 1998 at the Danmore Hotel, the same handgun was found in his room. When officers showed Amanda Carpova a photo of this handgun, she said it was very similar to the one that the assailant had pointed at her when she was raped. As for the items found in the trunk of the stolen car, the judge agreed with the defense that those should be removed from the affidavit.

Judge Bearden noted that the defense stated that identifications of Shaw by various people were not definitive. But Bearden said that in general the people categorized the person they had seen correctly as to height, weight, age and racial background. Those comments and observations were allowed.

The defense contended that identifications by people that pointed to suspects other than Shaw were now being omitted by the prosecution. Judge Bearden, however, said that in the course of an investigation, police officers will look at certain people as possible suspects and then eliminate them. This was all part of the natural law enforcement process leading up to probable cause, and this case was no different. As a result, the information about other possible suspects did not have to be mentioned by the prosecution.

Finally, the defense argued that the DNA testing was "warrantless," because it occurred after a police officer had picked up a cigarette butt that Sebastian Shaw had thrown into the street. The defense argued that just because Shaw had thrown away the cigarette butt did not mean that police had the right to the DNA found on it without a warrant. And they also argued that Shaw never gave permission to anyone to extract DNA from an item that was in essence his personal property. Judge Bearden said, however, that while one's DNA is private, Shaw forfeited the privacy when he tossed the cigarette in the street. This ruling was a huge success for the prosecution. All of the DNA matching of Shaw to the murders of Todd Rudiger and Donna Ferguson, and rape and attempted murder of Amanda Carpova, stemmed from that cigarette butt.

The defense may have made a few points in Judge Bearden's decision, but the majority of decisions had gone the prosecutor's way. Perhaps Sebastian Shaw at that point saw the writing on the wall. A lot of the things he had done, and a lot of the evidence against him, would be presented to a jury. Sebastian Shaw had gambled on things before, but now he was gambling with his own life. And if he lost this gamble, he would lose his life.

Huddling with his attorneys, Shaw began to work out what kind of plea deal could be made with the prosecution. In a few weeks they had all come to an agreement, and Sebastian Shaw may have saved his life, but his days of life outside a prison wall were just about over.

On February 18, 2000, Sebastian Shaw, with his lawyers, Andrew Bates and Gwenn Butkovsky, entered the courtroom of Judge Frank Bearden, along with the prosecutors, Helen Smith and Bill Williams. The most serious

of the charges were addressed, those being Count 1—
"Aggravated Murder," Count 4—"Aggravated Murder"
and Count 19—"Attempted Aggravated Murder with a
Firearm." Counts 2, 3, 5 through 18, and 20 through 42,
were dismissed. For Counts 1 and 4, Sebastian Shaw
agreed that he would plead guilty, and his sentencing
on these counts would be "Life without the Possibility of
Parole." Added to the statement was: *The defendant may
not be considered by the executing or releasing authority for any
form of temporary leave from custody, reduction in sentence, work
release, or alternative incarceration program.* The sentencing
for Count 19 was basically pro forma, giving him 240
months of prison time. Since Shaw was going to serve a
life term without the possibility of parole on Counts 1
and 2, this really didn't make any difference.

Todd Rudiger's parents and Amanda Carpova had a
chance to speak at the sentencing hearing. Carpova told
Shaw, "You're a cancer! You're disgusting! I don't want
to tell you how much you screwed up my life! I don't
want to give you the pleasure."

Vicky Johnson, Todd's mom, told Shaw, "One day you
will have to come face-to-face with God."

Shaw was allowed to speak, and through tears he said,
"I will have to stand in front of Jesus on his white throne
and answer for what I did on this earth. I've already
asked for his forgiveness. I ask you to forgive me too."

There were many forms to sign, and all parties gave
their signatures to the documents. The only variance was
on line 15A, where in neat handwriting Sebastian Shaw
wrote the following: *I plead guilty that on or between
7/17/92 and 7/20/92, I intentionally caused the death of
Donna Ferguson and Todd Rudiger. On June 2, 1995, I intentionally attempted to cause the death of Amanda Carpova in the
furtherance of the commission of rape.* All of this was signed
and dated, February 14, 2000.

Outside the courtroom, after the sentencing phase,
Debra Adams, Donna Ferguson's mother, told reporters,
"Yesterday was Donna's birthday. And what a birthday

celebration!" Adams was obviously happy that at last Sebastian Shaw was going away to prison for the rest of his life.

Detective Stahlman also spoke to reporters and said, "Shaw was a hunter. He was a stalker. He followed women." And Larry Findling, who was Commander Findling by that time, added, "Thank God for DNA. Without it we wouldn't be here today."

Sebastian Shaw was indeed going to prison for the rest of his life. Yet, this did not mean that new information would not surface that he had killed other people besides Donna Ferguson and Todd Rudiger, or raped and attempted to murder Amanda Carpova.

14

"Dead Men Tell No Tales"

For someone who had gone to great pains to be kept from being captured, and picking his victims at random, Sebastian Shaw had one fatal flaw—he couldn't keep his mouth shut. Prone to bragging and exhibitions of being macho, Shaw apparently told a fellow Oregon State prisoner named Daniel that he had not only killed Donna Ferguson and Todd Rudiger, but had also killed several other people as well. Daniel was so shaken by what Shaw told him, that he couldn't keep it to himself. Eventually word got to prison authorities about what Daniel had heard.

On March 31, 2000, Oregon State Penitentiary staff contacted a guard about things that Daniel had been saying. At 9:10 A.M., the guard contacted Daniel and interviewed him in the "Parole and Probation" office at the penitentiary. No one else was present at the time. Daniel told the guard he was going to be released in four weeks and that he'd had conversations with a fellow inmate who had been talking about how it had felt to kill people. The inmate's descriptions had been so cold-blooded that it bothered Daniel a lot.

Daniel didn't know the inmate's name, but described

him as a guy with the nickname of "Ito," because he was
Asian and had looks somewhat similar to Judge Lance
Ito, of the O. J. Simpson trial. Daniel also said this
inmate was an ex marine. Daniel and this inmate had
played chess together on occasion, and it was during one
of these chess matches that Ito had told him how it felt
to kill. One comment by this person really struck Daniel:
"Once I started killing, I couldn't stop!"

Daniel said that the two Portland murders that Ito had
done were just the tip of the iceberg. Those murders had
happened about nine years ago (1991 or 1992 by his estimate) and the inmate said he was doing life without
parole. Daniel also indicated that this person had been
caught because of DNA coming from a cigarette butt he
had discarded. Daniel stated that Ito told him that he'd
committed his first murder when he was sixteen years
old, and the next one when he was eighteen years old.

Ito said to Daniel, "I got caught by the police because
I let the last girl live. Everybody knows you have to leave
the state when you kill somebody." Then Ito said he'd
done his first murder at sixteen because a friend of his
got beat up very badly. According to Ito, it had been hard
to kill the first time, but got easier every time after that.

The guard asked Daniel if Ito had mentioned any specific incidents, and Daniel replied, "He told me he killed
some guy in Nevada, maybe Las Vegas." Ito had said he
was driving to Las Vegas, passed a new car, and the guy
driving that car had looked at Ito's old car and laughed.
So Ito bumped the other guy's car on purpose, and
when they both pulled over, he shot the guy. Then Ito
pulled the body out of the car and out into the desert.
Ito hid the guy's car in an arroyo and then continued on
his way to Las Vegas as if nothing had happened.

Daniel said that Ito had told him he'd killed at least
ten people after he'd killed the two people in Portland
in 1992. Ito claimed to have committed one murder
each year while on the run. He also made comments
about killing girls, wherein he had killed two girls on

one occasion, and a single girl on another. He said he'd killed the single girl because she claimed he had sexually harassed her.

Daniel also said that Ito claimed to have killed a cop by using a .22 with hollow-point bullets. He'd shot the cop once in the neck and once in the head. Daniel added that he didn't know if this story was true or not, but the other stories sounded convincing.

The guard tried to discover who Ito was among the general population of the Oregon State Penitentiary, but he could not do so. He contacted Corporal Tagaloa Manu at the penitentiary, and Corporal Manu checked around and came up with two possible inmates, going by the information that Daniel had discussed.

Also an action was requested by the Oregon State Penitentiary to *review this case and attempt to determine if there is any information that correlates to any homicides in the HITS database, particularly with the Portland Police Department. Also check with any other western states with this information if possible.*

Because of the information finally making its way to Commander Larry Findling and Detective Mike Stahlman, they made their way to the Oregon State Penitentiary on June 13, 2000. They met Sebastian Shaw in the office of Brad Halvorson, Oregon State Corrections Intelligence Unit. Shaw remembered Detectives Findling and Stahlman, and they started off by telling him there were no more charges pending for the murders of Todd Rudiger, Donna Ferguson or the rape and attempted murder of Amanda Carpova. Stahlman told Shaw that they just wanted to ask him some unanswered questions about those cases, and they wouldn't ask him anything about any new cases. Stahlman said later, "I told him that both I and Commander Findling and various family members still had questions about how he had met Todd and Donna, and specifically what occurred on the day that they were killed. I told him that he did not have to talk to us."

Shaw did agree to talk to them, however, and the interview began. Shaw said that he didn't know Todd Rudiger or Donna Ferguson before he killed them. He had been mad about an incident that had occurred at work with two janitors in the previous week in 1992. He'd been accused of lowering a traffic control gate on their car, but he said he hadn't done that on purpose. Shaw stated that his anger got to him and he wanted to kill the janitors, but he realized that if he did, it might be too easy to track him down for the murders. People had seen him arguing with the janitors and could trace it back to him. Shaw added that he'd gone so far as to find out where the janitors lived, out on SE 131st and Division Street, in case he wanted to kill them later.

Shaw declared that he had first seen Donna Ferguson in a checkout line in a Fred Meyer store on the afternoon of July 17, 1992. He had never seen her before that time. A thought went through his head—*She's the one!*—and he followed her to her residence in a mobile home park. He also said he was driving a stolen car at the time. Shaw parked behind a chain-link fence and watched where Donna parked her car so he would know which mobile home she went into. He then parked his vehicle several blocks away and walked back to the mobile home park through the front gate.

Shaw knocked on the door of Donna's mobile home, and she answered the door. He made up a story that he was looking for someone who used to live in the mobile home park. As he talked, he suddenly pulled out a gun and forced his way inside. Shaw didn't know that Todd was in a back bedroom at the time, but neither Donna nor Todd screamed or made any noise as he held the gun on them. Shaw believed that both of them thought he was just there to rob them, so they cooperated with his demands. Shaw had Donna tie Todd up with telephone cord, and then Shaw placed him in a closet in the bedroom.

Stahlman recalled, "Shaw then sexually assaulted Donna Ferguson, and he said he knew he was going to kill them both soon after he entered the mobile home. Shaw actually said, 'I knew she was going to be worm food, anyway.'" According to Shaw, that's why he decided to rape her first.

After Shaw had raped Donna, he stabbed her in the neck, making sure she was dead. Commander Findling asked him why he chose the manner of killing that he did, and Shaw answered, "I didn't want her to suffer, and it was quick and quiet. If I cut the jugular vein, they would lose consciousness very quickly and bleed out." Then Shaw added, "She never said anything to me, never begged, and was very compliant the whole time."

Shaw went on to say that Todd had fallen out of the closet at some point and was lying on the floor while he was raping and killing Donna. Todd started having some kind of attack in which he was having trouble breathing, and Shaw initially thought Todd was just faking it. Later he knew that Todd wasn't faking it, and he was actually having some kind of "medical distress," as Shaw put it. After Shaw had killed Donna, he went over to Todd and stabbed him to death as well, then went to the bathroom and washed up. Shaw said, "I didn't get that messy, though."

Shaw left the mobile home, drove to a bridge in the Portland area and threw the knife into the water. Asked which bridge that was, Shaw said he couldn't remember. Shaw added that the only thing he took from the mobile home was Todd's debit card and he had tried using it at an ATM machine that didn't have a camera. Since he didn't have the pin number, however, the card was useless to him; he threw it away.

Stahlman asked how long he had assaulted Donna before killing her. Shaw answered that he was in the mobile home twenty minutes tops. He also said that Amanda Carpova's estimate that he was in her residence for two hours was wildly off the mark, and that he had only been in there for half an hour. Returning to the murders of Donna and Todd, Commander Findling asked Shaw if he had intended to kill someone that day, and Shaw replied, "Yes. I just saw her and it was approximately thirty minutes before I broke into her place. I killed them both because dead men tell no tales."

Then surprisingly, Shaw said he had a list of people he still wanted to kill, and he listed the two janitors from Northwest Natural Gas, some people at Paragon Cable and his ex-roommate Russ Sperou. Shaw said that if he wasn't in prison, he could find them on the Internet, track them down and kill them. Then he added, "If you guys hadn't got me when you did, I was planning to kill more people. I can wait twenty or thirty years. I'm very patient. If I went to kill those people (the ones on the list), I'd kill everyone in the house—the children, the pets, every person and animal there."

Then Shaw suddenly turned toward Mike Stahlman and said, "I have a question for you."

Stahlman replied, "I'll try to answer it for you."

Shaw continued, "If, hypothetically, I was to tell you about other murders—well, it's not hypothetical, it's a fact. Could I do fed time?"

Commander Findling and Stahlman both said they couldn't answer that, but they asked what he was proposing. Shaw replied, "I'd like to clear everything up at once, and make a package deal. That way families won't be wondering what had happened to their family members, and you guys can move on to better use of your time."

Shaw said he had killed twenty-eight people, and then laughed, saying, "No, the number is really about ten." Then Shaw added, "I know Hannibal Lecter is fiction, but I'd like to do time in federal prison. I'd like that so I could buy cigarettes." Shaw couldn't smoke in an Oregon prison, and that irritated him. He declared, "I'm doing life already, anyway."

Both Findling and Stahlman said they would talk to someone in authority to find out if such a deal was possible. Then Findling asked if Shaw wanted to discuss in detail any case he was hinting at. Shaw replied that he did not. He did say that he hated red tape and legal proceedings, and that he'd just like to tell someone what he'd done one time and clear it all up. At that point Findling told Shaw that he'd contact someone in the FBI and see what could be done. Findling asked what states Shaw had perpetrated his murders in, and Shaw replied, "Oregon and California at least." Findling and Stahlman told Shaw they'd be back to see him after talking to the FBI.

It was an intriguing offer, but one the detectives on their own could not fulfill. This had to be dealt with at a federal level, and those authorities were not willing to give Shaw a blanket deal about crimes "he may have committed."

In July 2000, Detective Lloyd Higgins, the lead investigator on the Jay Rickbeil case, resubmitted unidentified blood samples recovered from the hallway and bathroom of Rickbeil's apartment to the Oregon State Police Forensic Laboratory for reanalysis. One of the reasons Higgins wanted this done was that he was retiring soon and wanted to clear up his unsolved homicides before leaving the PD. Another reason was that he realized new advances were constantly being made in DNA testing. In 1991, the blood samples had been analyzed by restriction fragment length polymorphism (RFLP) technology. Higgins was aware that newer DNA technology could get results from smaller samples of blood and other bodily fluids, in 2000.

Incredibly, Detective Higgins put the blood samples from Jay Rickbeil's case in for reanalysis, not knowing of Findling and Stahlman's interview with Sebastian Shaw in June 2000. Even though the OSP Lab got the samples in July 2000, OSP criminalist Donna Scarpone didn't get around to reanalyzing the blood samples seized in the Rickbeil case until October 2000. She used a short tandem repeat (STR) DNA technique on the samples given to her—the blood from Rickbeil's hallway, bedroom wall, bathroom floor, tissue from the toilet roll and tissue found in the toilet bowl. After obtaining a profile for the unidentified blood samples, Scarpone tried getting a match to that from a convicted offenders list maintained in a Combined DNA Index System (CODIS) computer database that went back to 1991. Scarpone at first requested the computer make a comparison of subjects in the database having *both* STR and RFLP profiles. Because the CODIS database only contained Sebastian Shaw's STR DNA profile, and not his RFLP profile, she did not get a match. On the surface all of this would seem to be a matter of semantics, but computer programs are very specific, and if the exact words are not entered, there will be no DNA match. For that reason Scarpone did not get a match between Sebastian Shaw and the Jay Rickbeil crime scene.

In November 2000, while running a routine check of the DNA profiles of recently convicted offenders against the DNA profiles seized in unsolved cases, the administrator of the CODIS program obtained a positive match between Sebastian Shaw's DNA profile and the STR DNA profile of the unidentified blood samples recovered from the hallway and bathroom of Jay Rickbeil's apartment. In other words—this November check by the administrator used Donna Scarpone's *STR profile,* and it came back with a hit on Shaw.

In December 2000, Scarpone requested a new blood sample to be taken from Sebastian Shaw. Since Shaw was now an inmate, he could not refuse to give a blood sample, which he could have done if he was not incarcerated. These blood samples confirmed that Shaw's DNA profile matched the DNA profile of the blood drops recovered from the toilet tissue that he had not flushed down the toilet in Jay Rickbeil's apartment on July 2, 1991. The chances that the DNA profile did not come from Sebastian Shaw was less than one in 10 billion.

On January 4, 2001, Portland PD detectives Higgins and Mike Stahlman traveled to the Oregon State Penitentiary to talk with Shaw and wanted to know what he could tell them about Jay Rickbeil. Shaw would not admit that he had ever met Jay Rickbeil or that he'd been in his apartment, but Shaw did say that on July 2, 1991, he'd gone to a bar to get drunk because he'd just been fired from his job at Paragon Cable. When Detective Higgins informed Shaw that his blood had been found in Rickbeil's apartment, Shaw replied, "No shit!" Then he added, "I don't recall that, but then it was ten years ago."

For whatever reason, Shaw asked if Rickbeil was a drug dealer. Higgins replied he didn't think so. Then Higgins told Shaw about the new DNA testing, which allowed just a small sample of blood to come up with a match. To this, Shaw said only one word, "Damn!"

15

The Twisting Road to Trial

With all the new information coming in about Sebastian Shaw's alleged murder of Jay Rickbeil in 1991, a prosecution team of Mark McDonnell and Ethan Knight was put together by the Multnomah County District Attorney's Office. Once again, Sebastian Shaw was in the area's newspapers. Detective Mike Stahlman, speaking of the DNA link between Shaw and Jay Rickbeil, told a reporter, "Periodically the lab goes back on all of the unsolved cases and reexamines the evidence that's on file and compares it to the DNA from convicted persons. The crime lab was able to match the physical evidence from the old crime scene to Shaw's DNA. The technology is pretty powerful."

With all the evidence collected, the prosecution decided to go forward and ask for the death penalty to be imposed upon Sebastian Shaw. By 2001, Sebastian Shaw had a new set of defense lawyers, Richard Wolf and William David Falls, who generally went by the name David Falls. The defense team knew they had a real struggle on their hands, because of who the victim was. There could hardly be a more sympathetic victim than a man who was a paraplegic and had been murdered in his wheelchair in his own home by a man who barely knew him—if he knew him previously at all.

One of the first things the defense did was hire Lisa Deneen, a sociologist from Portland State University to compile a master list of possible jurors in Multnomah County, Oregon, as to their age, race and backgrounds. Deneen explained in her report, *Due to the nature of the case, I examined cognizable groups in relation to the death penalty. These groups include: race, age and education. In addition, the lists were examined for geographical representation.*

Deneen found that based on the 2000 census, Multnomah County was 5.3 percent black, 5.7 percent Asian, 1 percent Native American, 76.5 percent white, 7.5 percent Hispanic and 4 percent others, which included Pacific Islanders and Hawaiians. She noted of those who actually showed up for jury duty, only 2.5 percent of the Asians out of a 5.7 percent total did so, and thus underrepresented their community. Shaw, being Vietnamese, was, of course, a member of that community.

Deneen declared that there was a vast difference between the way whites and Asians of Multnomah County perceived the honesty of police, prosecutors and those who were alleged to have committed crimes. Minority individuals tended to distrust the police and law enforcement in general. Deneen also showed that the younger and older age groups of Multnomah citizens were underrepresented on actual juries. And people who made less money than others were more likely to be dismissed, because of hardship by not being able to work for the weeks in which the trial took place.

Despite these findings, it was ruled that the capital trial for Sebastian Shaw would stay in Multnomah County, and that Judge David Gernant would preside over the proceedings. This was the same Judge Gernant who had presided over the previous legal proceedings of Sebastian Shaw and the 1994 search and seizure of items from the Campbells' stolen car.

Even though Richard Wolf had been appointed as

Sebastian Shaw's attorney in March 2001, he was still trying to amass countless discovery documents by the summer of 2002. Wolf noted in a motion to "Continue Trial Date" that *we have received 616 pages of discovery in connection with this case, but only information contained in the discovery provided to me concerned the case of Amanda Carpova.* In essence, he and David Falls had nothing concerning Todd Rudiger and Donna Ferguson. Neither Wolf nor Falls had been Shaw's attorney on that case of 2000, and when Wolf contacted DDA Derek Ashton about the Rudiger/Ferguson case, he discovered that there were two thousand pages of documents concerning the case. Obviously, it was going to take Wolf and Falls a long time to wade through all this information. With a jury that was supposed to be selected in September 2002, Wolf said it would be impossible for a trial to go forward at that date.

Wolf went on to say that on June 12 he had asked the DA's office to send over specific information from the OSP Lab. Wolf wanted to send the defense investigator to the crime lab, but apparently Donna Scarpone objected to that person being there. Wolf noted in his motion, *I called Ms. Scarpone on June 13th, and she advised me that she intended to prepare a list of the things she would agree to provide us and also what items in our request she would allow our expert witness to access.*

Not only that, but the defense team's mitigation expert/investigator Jackie Page would be leaving them soon to take care of her ailing father in Nevada. Wolf noted that an immediate replacement for Page was impossible.

One of his more interesting subjects in the "Affidavit in Support of Motion to Continue Trial" was a section about Sebastian Shaw being a key witness for the prosecution on the home invasion of the elderly Vietnamese couple in 1995. Wolf wrote, *Approximately two weeks ago, I was having a telephone conversation with Senior Deputy District Attorney James McIntyre on an unrelated case, and I happened to mention Mr. Shaw. Mr. McIntyre responded, "Sebastian Shaw! He was a star witness in a home invasion robbery case!"*

Apparently, this came as a complete surprise to Wolf, and he wanted time to collect documents on that case. All the points that Richard Wolf made seemed valid to Judge Gernant, and he extended the time before a trial would commence.

Arguing back against the defendant's request about the exclusion of DNA evidence in a separate motion, Mark McDonnell said that Shaw didn't need to give consent about the DNA testing at the OSP Lab, because he'd already pled guilty to the murders of Donna Ferguson and Todd Rudiger, and the rape of Amanda Carpova—cases that used Shaw's DNA. McDonnell argued, "The prosecution has produced the certified reports of the Oregon State Police Forensic Laboratory confirming that the defendant's DNA profile does, in fact, match the blood recovered by the police at the murder scene of Jay Rickbeil." McDonnell said he'd already given the defense all the notes and reports on this, plus an offer to make available samples of Shaw's blood recovered from the Rickbeil murder scene for independent DNA testing.

McDonnell stated that the defense was now demanding the OSP Lab protocols, internal and external validations, copyrighted material by the DNA kit manufacturers and raw computer-generated data. Even Donna Scarpone had agreed to let the expert hired by the defense view most of the remaining material at the crime lab. What McDonnell argued was that some material at the crime lab was covered by copyright, and could not be revealed, and some material was prohibited to be seen by others outside the lab, by Oregon statute. McDonnell declared, "Put simply, the defendant is requesting the court permission to conduct a fishing expedition. While the defendant is entitled to a fair trial, he is not entitled to manufacture a defense out of thin air."

Donna Scarpone even weighed in on the issue, stating that "Dr. Libby (the defendant's expert) will be allowed to view the original QA (quality assurance) files at the OSP Forensic Laboratory. Copies of the lumirads and

photographs of postamplification yield gels will not be
provided by the Oregon State Police Lab." In particular,
the lab was not going to let the defense team go searching through its Combined DNA Index System. A lab
such as OSP had no right to be handing that information over to other parties outside of law enforcement.

Judge Gernant ruled on these and other issues, sometimes going for the defense and at other times for the prosecution. And as a trial date of August 2003 approached, a
new roadblock became evident in the spring of 2003.
David Falls, Shaw's co-counsel, learned that his seventeen-
year-old son had developed adrenocortical carcinoma, a
rare and aggressive form of cancer. Sebastian Shaw waived
his right to a speedy trial, and the prosecutors agreed that
things could wait until Falls was back on the case. Shaw had
a right to a new co-counsel, but he decided to stick with
Wolf and Falls. So the case, which had begun in 2001, now
looked as if it wouldn't begin until 2004.

In fact, by November 2003, Richard Wolf was trying to
have the initial search and seizure of Shaw's DNA from the
discarded cigarette butt declared illegal, just as Shaw's attorneys had tried in his 2000 case. This DNA evidence was
the cornerstone of the prosecution's case against Shaw.
McDonnell argued that if the cigarette butt DNA was
good enough in the year 2000, it was good enough now.
Not only that, but Shaw had pled guilty to the Rudiger/
Ferguson murders and the rape and attempted murder of
Amanda Carpova. McDonnell claimed that when Shaw
made that plea, he was, in essence, agreeing that evidence
found against him, including DNA from the cigarette butt,
was valid. In the end the prosecution won its argument,
once again, on this key issue.

During the course of the road to trial, there was everything, from "Motion to Require Prosecutor to Declare
and Elect Aggravating Evidence in Advance of Trial" to
"Motion to Prohibit/Limit Victim Impact Evidence as

Unconstitutional" to "State's Response to Defendant's Motion to Compel the Release of Juror Lists." Judge Gernant came back with key decisions on various motions, amongst which he found that the evidence about the Todd Rudiger/Donna Ferguson murder would be heard by a jury, but that testimony by Todd's parents and Donna's parents would be too prejudicial, and they were excluded.

Judge Gernant granted the state's motion to admit the circumstances of Shaw being fired at Paragon Cable on July 2, 1991, and Shaw's statements that he got drunk after being fired that day. Also in was Shaw giving Barbara Crawford a knife, along with some of his statements to her. Allowed was Shaw's comment "They'll never bother you again," and "No one will ever know," concerning getting rid of some person that was bothering Crawford. The statement that Shaw had told Barbara Crawford—that when he was young, he had killed someone—was denied.

Also denied was a statement that Shaw had written in his diary on February 10, 1990: *I've been thinking about murder lately.* The judge said this was not allowed because of its remoteness in time to July 1991. Also denied was a statement by Shaw in his diary from November 12, 1994:

> *No one knows my secret and it is to my eternal shame that I shall probably keep it until my grave. The blow to my self-worth seems continuous, one after the other, until there is nothing left but a nearly conscienceless time bomb. Once I wouldn't have harmed a rodent, but now I would nuke a city without blinking. Damn this creature I have become, for it is a dark beast just waiting for some unwitting fool to come and release it.*

Perhaps one of the most objectionable exclusions for the prosecution was that evidence of the rape and attempted murder of Amanda Carpova would be allowed, but Carpova herself was not going to be allowed to testify on the stand. Judge Gernant wrote in a statement, *The*

*court found that relevance of Ms. Carpova's personal testimony
is outweighed by the risk of unduly inflaming the jury.* The
prosecution would later press to have Amanda Carpova
on the stand, and in doing so, it unleashed something
that no one saw coming.

A jury trial for the murder of Jay Rickbeil looked as if
it would finally begin in April 2004, but the prosecution
asked for more time because they had found more witnesses to back up Amanda Carpova's story. Judge Gernant, however, had had enough by that point as far as
time extensions were concerned, and in a surprise move
he brought in both the defense and prosecution for a
hearing on April 21, 2004. What he had to say absolutely
stunned Mark McDonnell and Ethan Knight.

Two thousand five hundred summonses had already
been sent out to prospective jurors on Shaw's death
penalty case. Present on April 21 were DDA Mark Mc-
Donnell and DDA Kirsten Snowden for the prosecution,
and attorneys Richard Wolf and David Falls for Sebastian Shaw. Judge Gernant denied another request by the
prosecution to introduce more evidence that would
allow Amanda Carpova to speak before the jury, citing
once again that it would be too inflammatory and prejudicial. Gernant also declared, "Because of the lateness
of the filing of the 404 Motion, together with the immi-
nence of the scheduled assembly of the jurors in this
case, and because of the court's view that such an *in
limine* order denying the state the right to call a certain
witness is not an appealable order, the court denies the
state's request for a continuance."

With that ruling, the prosecution said they were unable
to proceed. The defense, possibly just going through the
motions, asked for a dismissal of the case. Judge Gernant,
beside himself about this latest delay, blasted the prosecution, saying, "Because of the state's inexcusable neglect in
its handling of this prosecution, culminating in its claim of

being unable to proceed less than forty-eight hours prior to the time of trial that had been scheduled for more than a year, because of the prejudice to this defendant of the difficulty of calling at some indefinite time in the future elderly or seriously ill witnesses who may not be alive at the time of trial at some future indefinite date, and to the people of Oregon, who are paying for his defense— because the defendant is already incarcerated on two true-life sentences, and his right to a speedy trial impinged by the state's neglect and the lengthy delay that the state invites—it is hereby ordered that the accusatory instrument is hereby dismissed! It is hereby further ordered that, pursuant to ORS 136.130, the court directs that this dismissal will be entered with prejudice, and thus will operate as a bar to another action for the same crime."

The prosecution was absolutely stunned. All the years of detective work, DNA testing, seeking out of witnesses in the Rickbeil case, were down the drain. The judge was not only denying the present trial, but declaring that Sebastian Shaw could never be tried again for the murder of Jay Rickbeil.

The *Oregonian* had an article titled "A double-murderer who boasted of other slayings won't face the possibility of Death Row." Richard Wolf applauded the judge's decision and told a reporter, "The outcome of this case is appropriate." The DA's office, on the other hand, blasted Judge Gernant and his decision. Chief Deputy DA Norm Frink said, "Every other delay in the past three years was caused by the defense. Why not wait and get it right?" Then he said that the DA's office was going to appeal Judge Gernant's decision.

James Reamsbottom, Jay Rickbeil's brother-in-law, told a reporter, "This man may think he's a judge, and he might have an education, but I don't think he has any common sense. When we've got DNA evidence proving the fact, and he's throwing the case out, that's not right." Jay Rickbeil's eldest sister, Cyrille LeBlanc, was also furious. She called Gernant "an activist judge," and added, "My brother had cerebral palsy and was in a wheelchair, and this madman slit his throat. My own sister had to clean up the murder scene!"

At the end of the article, the reporter wrote, *The sudden end of the case means significant questions remain about whether Shaw was telling the truth when he claimed he killed a dozen other people.*

The Multnomah County District Attorney's Office was so incensed by Judge Gernant's decision, DA Michael Schrunk declared that he would block Gernant from handling any more felony cases in that county. Schrunk said, "I don't make this decision lightly, but we represent the victims of crime. And if we feel we are unable to get a fair trial, this is a way we can put the case before a different judge. Disagreeing with a judge's rulings isn't sufficient reason to bump a judge off future cases. To do it, this office has to have a good faith belief that a judge cannot be impartial."

On the other hand, Richard Wolf believed that the DA's office was striking back at Judge Gernant exactly because of his unpopular ruling on the Sebastian Shaw case. Wolf stated, "The Multnomah County DA's office has never taken ownership for their own mistakes and always wants to blame the stupid jury, the stupid judge or the sleazy defense lawyer. Apparently, the DA's office is now only willing to appear before judges who grant their wishes—no matter how outrageous."

In the midst of this brewing storm, Judge Gernant would not comment on the tiff with the DA's office, but Nena Cook, president of the Oregon State Bar, said, "We should avoid the temptation to criticize a judge based on a single decision, even when that decision may be unpopular."

Just as planned, the DA's office did go ahead with an appeal on Judge Gernant's decision to acquit Sebastian Shaw, and they made it to the Oregon Supreme Court.

Richard Wolf was, of course, bent on the Oregon Supreme Court upholding Judge Gernant's decision, and he argued his case to them on several issues. He said, "It seems self-evident that the state's failure to be prepared for trial on April 21, 2004, was without sufficient cause. The state has never offered any sufficient cause for the untimely request to raise the other crimes' (Rudiger/Ferguson, Carpova cases) evidence. The state has not made sufficient showing as to why they should be able to appeal the ruling, much less prevail upon a claim that the court abused its discretion by not admitting such evidence."

Richard Wolf went on to point out that several witnesses for Sebastian Shaw were quite elderly, including his aunt Anna Ho and his stepmother, Ly Do. Another important witness for Shaw was Suzanne Garman, his sixth-grade teacher who had stayed friends with Shaw even while he was in prison—despite knowing what he had done. Currently Garman was battling cervical cancer and undergoing chemotherapy. Wolf declared, "Loss of the testimony of any one of these essential witnesses could make the difference between whether Mr. Shaw receives a death sentence or not. Most importantly, the state has never offered any source of evidence that is independent of the illegal June 13, 2000, interview of Mr. Shaw upon which to base even the theory of their indictment, much less a majority of the evidence they seek to introduce against him in a trial."

In fact, Shaw's defense lawyers challenged the state supreme court's jurisdiction to even hear an appeal of Judge Gernant's decision. This matter was ruled on by the Oregon Supreme Court, and in a unanimous decision it said that they did have jurisdiction to hear the district attorney's appeal of Gernant's ruling.

It was not a quick or an easy judgment by the Oregon Supreme Court as to whether Judge Gernant had erred in granting an acquittal to Sebastian Shaw for the murder of Jay Rickbeil. In fact, they didn't render a judgment until June of 2005, more than a year after the Rickbeil trial was supposed to have commenced. When the judgment came in, the Oregon Supreme Court jurists declared that the trial court (Judge Gernant) abused its discretion in excluding the testimony of the victim of one of the defendant's other crimes (Amanda Carpova).

Of the verdict, Chief Deputy DA Norm Frink said, "The ruling was a complete vindication of our position and an indication that the criticisms leveled at this office were unjustified." Richard Wolf, of course, was less pleased with the ruling and stated, "We've certainly lost the battle but haven't lost the war."

Since a judge in Oregon can be kept off a case at its beginning but not in the later stages, Judge David Gernant would be presiding over the Jay Rickbeil trial once it started. The ruling was a huge victory for the prosecution, because not only would they get another crack at Sebastian Shaw on the murder of Jay Rickbeil, but Amanda Carpova was going to be allowed to take the stand and tell the jury in very graphic terms how Sebastian Shaw had raped her and then attempted to murder her.

So now all the same players would be back for another jury trial: Judge Gernant, DDA Mark McDonnell, defense lawyers Richard Wolf and William Falls and, of course, Sebastian Shaw. Just how it would play out this time was anybody's guess.

16

In a Different Light

In the days leading up to Sebastian Shaw's second jury trial—for the murder of Jay Rickbeil—Shaw didn't help his cause any by getting into two fights in prison. Sergeant Beasley was assigned to the dining area of the Oregon State Penitentiary, and around 4:00 P.M., on June 29, 2005, he was the only guard watching over fifty inmates in the dining-room line. Beasley suddenly heard a loud argument between two inmates in the line, and discovered that the inmates were Sebastian Shaw and Clayton Lachman. Both inmates were standing about one foot from the other, yelling into each other's face. Beasley went to where they were yelling, and ordered, "Stop it, guys! Cool it! Break it up!" Both Shaw and Lachman ignored him and kept yelling at each other. And then Shaw spit on Lachman.

Seeing that, Beasley immediately called for backup, put his hand on Shaw's arm and ordered him several times to go to the dining-room exit. Only after about ten seconds, Shaw complied, reaching the door as other guards approached. Both inmates were handcuffed and taken toward DSU (the intensive security unit of the prison). All the while, Shaw kept yelling at Lachman such threats as,

"I'm going to kick your ass! I'm going to stab you in the neck with a pencil! I'm going to kill you!" For someone who had a death penalty case in the offing, it wasn't the smartest thing to say, especially since his previous method of murders had been by slashing people's throats.

In his report Beasley noted, *By spitting on another inmate, Sebastian Shaw committed Assault II. By failing to comply with my order to split up from Inmate Lachman, and to stop the confrontation, Inmate Shaw committed Disobedience of an Order I. By directing hostile and threatening language involving a physical threat to Inmate Lachman, Shaw committed Disrespect I.*

Sebastian Shaw wasn't through having confrontations at the penitentiary, however, and on October 1, 2005, at 6:34 A.M., prison guard Richard Miller looked over toward the chow line in the dining room and saw two inmates fighting. One of them was Lester Souza, and the other was Sebastian Shaw. According to Miller, "I immediately radioed for backup and proceeded to the fight. When I arrived in the area, both inmates were striking each other in the face and upper chest area with closed-fist punches. I gave several direct orders for both inmates to stop fighting and break it up, but both inmates ignored my orders and continued to fight. I was then able to grab the back of inmate Souza's T-shirt and pull him toward me, and by doing this, it separated both inmates. CO Cossavella and Corporal Warren arrived and placed wrist restraints on inmate Souza. I then observed Corporal Dewey and CO Maynard placing wrist restraints on inmate Shaw. Both inmates were escorted to DSU without further incident. There were no signs of visible injuries on either inmate."

It was bad enough that Shaw had been in another fight, but what was worse was the fact that it went on his record as "Disobedience of an Order." All of this could have serious ramifications for Shaw if he was found guilty in the upcoming Jay Rickbeil trial. If it ever got to the sentencing phase in a death penalty case, one of the questions the jurors would be faced with was whether they thought Shaw was a danger to others. If they thought so, they could vote yes on that issue, and it would be one step closer to a lethal injection for Shaw.

Even while this was going on, both the prosecution and defense were gearing up for round two of the Jay Rickbeil trial. Once again the defense attorneys were making motions to suppress a litany of evidence they said was improper. Wolf wrote, *Within six weeks of the illegal June 13, 2000, interview, Detective Lloyd Higgins resubmitted crime scene evidence from the July 2, 1991, Jay Rickbeil murder to the Oregon State Police Crime Lab for additional DNA analysis. Up until July 28, 2000, Detective Higgins had not done any follow-up investigation on the Rickbeil case for over eight and one half years.* Wolf found it hard to swallow that Detective Higgins had resubmitted blood samples from the Rickbeil case to the Oregon State Police Lab only because he was going to retire soon and wanted to clear up any unsolved cases he'd presided over. And Wolf, once again, wanted to know why Donna Scarpone did not come up with a match to Sebastian Shaw when she ran STR DNA tests on the blood evidence from the Rickbeil case. It was only after Daniel Peterson, the CODIS administrator, performed a search and got a match to Shaw that Scarpone ran another DNA test and got a match as well.

This issue was addressed in a hearing and Scarpone answered on the stand, "When I searched the data the first time, there are categories that you select of what you are going to search on. We came to the conclusion the categories I was selecting said PCR data, which STR is and RFLP. So when I searched it, knowing that we had additional data on this case, that's how I searched it. However, finding out later, because we had to do some homework, look into this and talk to the FBI . . . well, why did my search not hit? Uh, the normal way was our CODIS administrator would go through and evaluate data, the only thing they could come up with was because they did not have the RFLP profile in the computer. So my search said I needed both—but in reality they weren't both in there. I didn't know that at the time. But when the CODIS administrator did the search, he was only searching on the STR data, which is what hit. So the samples weren't rerun, it was simply a computer way of searching the data."

For the defense, this may not have been "manufacturing evidence," but it seemed like stretching the rules to the breaking point. For the prosecution it was as Scarpone had stated, the computer would not give out a match if the correct data was not entered. Entering for "RFLP and STR" was too much—entering only STR made the hit.

The defense lawyers were going down another avenue in the late months of 2005 and early months of 2006—seeing what information surfaced about Jay Rickbeil, people he knew and his habits. It was pretty well-known by this time that Jay had let many people into his apartment at all hours of the day and night, and that he never locked his door. Other information that the defense investigator came up with was intriguing and could cast doubt into jurors' minds about what really happened on July 2, 1991. They might not believe in the end that Sebastian Shaw wasn't the one who had killed Jay Rickbeil, but they might conclude that Shaw and Rickbeil did know each other before July 2, 1991. If the murder occurred between two people who knew each other, according to the defense, it may have happened in the heat of passion and not during a cold-blooded murder.

The defense investigator spoke with Pamela Hobson, who was an acquaintance of Jay Rickbeil's, and she said she'd been fifteen years old when she first met Jay. According to Hobson, she was introduced to Jay by Charles "Thrasher" Wilson, who helped Jay with chores around the apartment. Hobson also began to help Jay around his place, and said he was very eccentric and interested in taking photographs of nudes. Hobson added, "He asked if he could take nude photos of me to send places, but I said no." Then she added, "Jay was very sexually active, and he hired prostitutes at least weekly."

The investigator asked Hobson if Jay preferred teenagers, and Hobson said, "He didn't go for them too young." As for the other people who came around the place, she said they were "freaky, retarded and would grab me. They didn't have any boundaries."

Victoria Taylor had been introduced to Jay by a guy named Howard, her then-boyfriend. Howard was a volunteer for Meals on Wheels, and would take food over to Jay's apartment. Howard suggested to Victoria that she do chores around Jay's place in return for a salary, and she and Jay agreed to that. Taylor cleaned his apartment, did his laundry and bathed Jay on occasion because he had so much trouble doing it himself.

According to Victoria, Jay's apartment was "filthy" and he could be "difficult." He would try to interfere in her personal business, and at one point he wanted her to move in with him and be his girlfriend. She declined.

Taylor was aware of Jay's interest in photography, but she said that he didn't have much equipment. Supposedly, a roommate that Jay had in the past (not Sherman Polley) had run off with the photography equipment. Victoria described Sherman Polley, Jay's roommate, as a former veteran "who was trying to get off booze." Victoria also said that Polley was getting fed up with Jay, because he kept bringing street people over to the apartment. As far as the front door went, Taylor said, "Polley kept losing his keys and Jay was cagey about keeping the front door open."

Concerning the stream of visitors coming in, Victoria said the number started decreasing in the spring of 1991 because she warned Jay it wasn't a good neighborhood and he needed to be more careful. She described an incident where a homeless man wandered in one day, and Jay had to chase him out, using a cane. Even Jay thought the man was casing the apartment. Another odd thing concerning street people was that, according to Victoria, "Jay thought he was the master of the street, and he threw his weight around by breaking up street couples." In her words, by saying he was a photographer, Jay tried to lure underage girls away from their street boyfriends. She described Jay as "a desperately lonely guy."

Victoria spoke of one girl, Conni Ward, as Jay's "live-in" girlfriend, and Conni believed that Jay was going to support her. According to Victoria, Jay dumped Conni off in Las Vegas, essentially abandoning her there. "Conni wasn't used to the street life, and that's what Jay was all about." Victoria Taylor did admit that Jay had saved one girl named "Star" from the streets. He helped her find a job and get out of a desperate situation.

According to Victoria, Jay belonged to "some kind of coven, and participated in ceremonies." She remembered a pentagram being in his apartment and other symbols as well. She said Jay was really into it, and he would tell people that he was a priest. "He was always making up stories. He did it to get attention." In addition to this, Victoria introduced Jay to a friend of hers named Linda, and she thought that Jay and Linda may have had a sexual affair at one time. She said that Linda was loose, came from an alcoholic family, and this Linda was found murdered not long after Jay was murdered. After that occurred, Victoria went into hiding, and became very reclusive. She thought there might be some link between Jay and Linda's murders, and she was worried for her own safety.

Conni Ward was interviewed by the defense investigator in 2006, and she was developmentally disabled and living in subsidized housing in Salem, Oregon. Conni met Jay on a public bus in Portland on February 22, 1989. She remembered the date because it was the day before she turned eighteen years old. Conni was returning home from a job at Goodwill Industries when she heard Jay talking to someone and approached him. She couldn't remember exactly why, but she said she liked listening in on conversations. Conni started talking to Jay, and when he got off the bus, he was on his way to meet a female friend at a restaurant and asked Conni to come along. Conni couldn't remember who the woman was, but she hit it off with Jay and returned with him to his apartment. She ended up staying with him for the next several months.

Ward had been living in a group home prior to being with Jay. She described herself as not "retarded" but as "slow" when it came to learning. Conni considered Jay to be her boyfriend, and she said she was a virgin when she first met him. Jay talked a lot about photography, but she couldn't recall him actually taking any photos. He did, however, make some business cards saying he was a photographer. Ward continued working at Goodwill Industries and gave her paycheck to Jay, who then paid for rent, food, the phone bill and would buy her clothes if she needed any. She had no recollection of any satanic rituals that Jay was involved in or any covens. Like others, however, she did say that his front door was almost always unlocked.

Conni couldn't remember when, but she and Jay went to Las Vegas, and he left her there. In fact, Jay left her there and returned to Portland, and she had to call her mother for a ride home. She said of him, "Jay may not have been the best guy, but at least he wouldn't say things to make me feel bad."

Conni's mother, Kathy Owen, was less impressed by Jay's qualities, and she told the investigator she had met him on a couple of occasions, and she didn't like him very much. Owen said that Conni had an IQ of 78, and she thought that Jay took advantage of her.

A girl named Colleen didn't add any luster to Jay Rickbeil when she told the investigator that she'd met Jay when she was fifteen years old. Colleen and a friend were at a 7-Eleven store, asking patrons to buy them beer, when they met a girl named Rhonda, who was a friend of Jay's. According to Colleen, Rhonda took them to

Jay's apartment, where two other men were at the time. One of the men offered Colleen and her friend Rhonda beer in exchange for sex. Colleen said that she had never been asked to have sex for alcohol or money in her life and found this upsetting. According to Colleen, she returned home and told her mother, who was incensed and called the police. Soon thereafter, the police, her mother and Colleen went back to Jay's residence, where the police told the men not to contact underage girls again. As far as Colleen could recall, none of the men were arrested.

Colleen did go back a few more times to Jay's residence to get beer, and she recalled the door as being unlocked. Colleen added, "Another girl named Rhonda had lots of money, and when I asked her where it came from, she would just laugh and not answer." Colleen added, "I figured she was doing something for it." That Rhonda was only thirteen years old at the time. Colleen didn't know if Jay or his friends were paying Rhonda for sex, but she surmised that someone there was doing that.

All of these stories, supplied by people who knew Jay Rickbeil, placed him in a different light, according to Shaw's defense lawyers. It also painted a picture of Rickbeil as having a lot of street people over at his apartment, including underage girls. What was a constant was that he did not lock his front door, and any one of those street people could have come in and killed Jay. At least that was the theory the defense was starting to put together.

Co-counsel for the prosecution, Ethan Knight, sought to have none of these witnesses present testimony to jurors and he argued before Judge Gernant that Jay Rickbeil's personal habits had nothing to do with Sebastian Shaw murdering him. Knight argued, "With respect to the evidence regarding Mr. Rickbeil's associates and his sex life, none of this information is relevant to any fact of consequence. It violates the basic tenets of OEC 403, because it is highly prejudicial due to its salacious nature." Knight argued that all the defense wanted to do was blacken Jay Rickbeil's name to make the jurors believe that for some reason he had it coming to him when he was murdered.

As the date for a jury trial grew closer and closer, Sebastian Shaw had a new problem—he slipped and fell on the slick pavement while being escorted to court for a hearing, and he bumped his head and hurt his wrist. This particular hearing concerned whether Shaw should be shackled while sitting at the defense table during the trial. Shaw indicated to his lawyer that he really didn't need to be at the hearing the next day, because he didn't know how he could add anything to the discussion. Shaw asked to be excused from the hearing, and it was granted by Judge Gernant.

Mark McDonnell's argument to the judge that Sebastian Shaw be forced to wear handcuffs and leg restraints was compelling, to say the least. He brought up Shaw's two fights while in prison, and then ended by saying, "I have personally read the diaries and other personal papers seized from Sebastian Shaw by law enforcement officials. These documents, authored by the defendant, are filled with numerous references to killing in general and murder in particular. Based upon my twenty-six years as a prosecutor, I have never personally had contact with a defendant who is so fixated upon the killing of other human beings." Eventually Judge Gernant agreed that Sebastian Shaw did present a danger to court personnel and the jurors. The restraints, however, placed beneath his clothing, would not be visible to the jurors.

Finally it was time to bring in the prospective jurors, and it was going to be a long and tedious process seating a jury of twelve citizens and four alternates who had to keep their minds open about a death penalty conviction. Whether or not the prospective jurors wanted to speak up in front of others was beyond their control, since it was deemed it would be too lengthy a process for the defense and prosecutors to speak with each one individually. So groups of five were brought in and questions were posed to them by Richard Wolf and David Falls for the defense, and Mark McDonnell and Ethan Knight for the prosecution.

The questions ranged all over the board. David Falls started things off by saying, "Nobody is trying to change or criticize your views, we just want to see what you think about certain subjects. If you're excused, it doesn't mean you're a bad person or bad juror. But this is the most serious kind of case, and it's often hard to say openly what you believe in front of a group of people. But I want to encourage you to speak up when you don't know something. There couldn't be a bigger disaster than someone not knowing, but too afraid to speak up."

At that point Judge Gernant jumped in and told the jurors, "If there are some things you don't want to say in front of others, you can come back in front of just the attorneys and me later."

Falls began voir dire with one prospective juror who had a granddaughter suffering from leukemia. The girl, who was five years old, was in remission, but, of course, things could change. Since the prospective juror, the grandmother, was helping take care of the girl, things were very stressful for her. Falls asked, "How do you feel about having to spend time in court?"

The grandmother answered, "I worry about it. Court would change the normal routine for everybody. Whether I could sit in here and listen to a case with full attention, I don't know."

Falls said that he and the others would talk to her later.

David Falls asked the others if they had anything else of a similar nature, and one Vietnamese man said that he had memory problems. He had been born in Vietnam, in 1967, the same year as Shaw (Chau), and had lived for a while under Communist rule. He was eventually allowed to come to the United States, but he was still had family in Vietnam. His father had tried coming over to the United States, but was not allowed to come. In fact, his father had been put in prison for a while after the takeover, and would never speak about that time to his son.

Falls asked, "Is it part of Vietnamese culture not to share those kinds of things?"

The man answered yes.

Falls also wanted to know if in Vietnamese culture people were reluctant to seek mental-health treatment. The man agreed that was so.

"Culturally, are Vietnamese less likely to express their emotions in public?"

"Yes."

"Why do you think that is?"

"Because people don't share things like that."

It was very doubtful this man was going to be empaneled, because not only did he believe that a person was guilty before proven innocent—as it had been in Vietnam—but he also knew Officer Preston Wong, of the Portland PD, the same Officer Wong who had been in contact with Detective Stahlman about Shaw's activities in 1997.

Arguments by the prosecution and defense were still going on before Judge Gernant, right up to opening arguments in Shaw's trial on April 10, 2006. Falls wanted jurors to be able to ask questions during the trial, and Judge Gernant said that was okay if the juror wrote the question down on a slip of paper; then a clerk would pick up the question during a break and hand it on to the judge. Judge Gernant would then decide if the question was relevant or not, and needed further discussion.

The prosecution wanted to exclude certain defense witnesses, and they brought these concerns up, one by one. This was important because it would impact what Mark McDonnell said during his opening statement. Gernant found that defense witness Kathy Owen was conditionally relevant, because her daughter, Conni Ward, was developmentally disabled and had lived with

Jay Rickbeil at one time. Owen would be allowed to tell the jury about communicating with her daughter who had a low IQ.

The defense wanted some of Detective Higgins's statements to come in, that his investigation showed that some people related that Jay went to Eighty-second Avenue to seek out prostitutes, and that Jay wanted to photograph nude young women. There was even some reference that Jay would buy alcohol for underage girls if they would pose nude. Richard Wolf declared, "The police were summoned by Colleen's mother because he was furnishing alcohol to minors."

Knight responded, "There's no probative value there. It just maligns the character of the victim."

Judge Gernant wouldn't allow the comments about serving alcohol to minors, but he would allow the fact that it was known that a lot of people entered Jay Rickbeil's apartment, including many street people.

The defense especially wanted Victoria Taylor to testify. Wolf said, "She establishes about the photo business, and the fact that Jay Rickbeil was into Satanism and part of [a] coven. There is testimony that people in that coven would cut each other and there would be blood. That could be a reason why Sebastian Shaw's blood was found in Jay Rickbeil's apartment. We know that Mr. Shaw drew a satanic face on the balloon that he left at Paragon Cable."

Knight responded, "He's only trying to establish a link of what Victoria Taylor said to Satanism. It's a big leap as to why there is blood in that apartment."

The defense also wanted Pamela Hobson as a witness, saying that she knew Jay hired prostitutes on a weekly basis, and that area, when Jay lived there, had a high crime rate. The implication was that many people from the area could have killed Jay Rickbeil for any number of reasons—a robbery gone bad, Jay's interaction with erratic street people or the supposed satanic rituals.

Knight argued back, "No connection between Jay Rickbeil and prostitutes was ever found. It's all hearsay.

Prostitutes on Eighty-second Avenue have nothing to do with this case!"

Some of these motions, Judge Gernant left as undecided at the moment and they would be addressed during the trial. Finally with these things out of the way, it was time to bring in the jurors.

Fifteen years after Jay Rickbeil had been murdered, he was finally having his day in court. Sebastian Shaw and his defense lawyers had been able to stop one trial, but they weren't going to be able to stop this one. It was now a matter of life and death for Sebastian Alexander Shaw.

17

Witnesses

DDA Mark McDonnell began his opening argument by telling the jurors that this was a "cold case," but it was based on a positive match of DNA from Sebastian Shaw that was found at the Jay Rickbeil murder scene. Jay had been born with cerebral palsy, and he was strong in his mind and upper body, but his legs no longer worked. He was restricted to a motorized wheelchair, and by the use of this wheelchair, he would go out and shop and meet people on Eighty-second Avenue in Portland.

McDonnell stated that there was no evidence that Sebastian Shaw had ever met Jay Rickbeil prior to July 2, 1991. Shaw was fired from his job at Paragon Cable that morning, went out drinking, and by the late afternoon he was seething and ready to kill somebody—anybody. McDonnell contended that Shaw spotted Jay Rickbeil that afternoon and followed him home, knowing that Jay would be an easy victim because of his handicap.

McDonnell told the jurors about the helium balloon at the desk of Shirley Philip—the satanic drawing and threatening verse that Shaw had written—and Shaw blowing up in Linda Aday's office. Shaw had been so angry he had to be escorted off the property. It was 5:42 P.M. on that same day that Jay Rickbeil's body was discovered by his roommate, and the police were soon called to the scene. They found defensive wounds on Jay's hands and a large cut on his neck that severed the carotid artery and jugular vein. It took someone with a lot of upper-body strength, like Shaw, to have pushed Jay back onto the bed and cut his throat.

There was also evidence that there had been quite a struggle, and the killer had cast off blood droplets on the way to the bathroom to clean up. In fact, blood had been collected from the sink, bathroom floor and a tissue in a wastepaper basket. The most important blood of all that was collected was a piece of tissue that the killer had not flushed down the toilet.

McDonnell said that the identity of the killer remained a mystery for nine years, and during that time Sebastian Shaw pled guilty to the murders of Todd Rudiger and Donna Ferguson, and the rape and attempted murder of Amanda Carpova. It wasn't until Detective Higgins was going to retire that he resubmitted blood evidence from the Rickbeil case, and the Oregon State Police Forensic Lab was able to match that blood to the person who had committed the crimes against Todd, Donna and Amanda—in other words, Sebastian Shaw.

McDonnell also brought up the fact that Shaw was being charged with first-degree murder because he had done so in the act of committing burglary. McDonnell explained that in the state of Oregon an act of burglary commenced when someone simply entered another person's dwelling, uninvited. The intruder didn't even have to steal anything, he just had to have been there without the consent of the resident of that property. McDonnell said that there was no broken window at Jay's apartment, no smashed-in door, and everyone spoke of Jay keeping his front door unlocked. McDonnell declared it was common sense that Shaw came in uninvited, because Jay Rickbeil had been killed at his bed. "Common sense tells us that people don't invite a stranger to assault them. Defensive wounds show that Jay Rickbeil struggled with his attacker. Even if Sebastian Shaw had permission to enter the premises, it was revoked the instant he started his attack."

McDonnell brought up the fact that a year later, in 1992, Shaw was having trouble with people where he worked. And once again, instead of killing these people, just as at Paragon Cable, he took out his rage on complete strangers by murdering Donna Ferguson and Todd Rudiger. As with Jay Rickbeil's residence, there was no forced entry, no broken windows—and both Todd and Donna had been killed from their throats being slashed.

Then in 1995, Sebastian Shaw entered Amanda Carpova's apartment by pointing a gun at her and telling her to do everything he said, or he would kill her. No broken windows, no smashed doors. Amanda—just like the others—did not know Sebastian Shaw. The only connection she had to him was that she sometimes shopped at a Safeway store where he worked, and went to a tavern that he sometimes patronized. The crimes against Donna Ferguson, Todd Rudiger and Amanda Carpova were not guesswork or speculation. McDonnell said that these were crimes that Sebastian Shaw admitted to in 2000, and for which he was serving a life sentence.

McDonnell concluded, "After all the evidence has been presented, the state is confident that based upon the DNA evidence, you will find that Sebastian Shaw is responsible for the death of Jay Rickbeil. The evidence allows no other reasonable conclusion. The citizens of Multnomah County, in the state of Oregon, put their trust in you to render a true and just verdict of guilty."

David Falls began opening arguments for the defense and he admitted he had a head cold, which soon became evident to everyone as he constantly had to cough. Falls even joked, "I sound like an ol' frog." In fact, he sounded a bit like Andy Griffith in the television lawyer series

Matlock, or at least Matlock with a head cold. Falls said that the defense wasn't disputing there had been a homicide, but they wanted the jurors to look and see if there had been a burglary. One of the arguments Falls kept coming back to was that Shaw and Rickbeil did know each other before that day, and Shaw was not in the apartment to steal things, nor had he broken in. According to Falls, Shaw had merely come to see Jay Rickbeil, and something bad had happened. Jay Rickbeil wasn't a shut-in, he was constantly going up and down Eighty-second Avenue in Portland, and he knew a lot of people there.

Falls noted that the investigators seized a knife in 1991 in Jay Rickbeil's apartment, and the knife had an initial on it, the letter "J." The initial had nothing to do with SAS— Sebastian Alexander Shaw. A wallet with money inside was found in the apartment, no burglary there. There were no signs of a break-in, no cleanup in the hallway, no sexual activity. Sexual activity had definitely been part of the MO in the Rudiger/Ferguson and Carpova cases.

Falls pointed out that the state's theory rested on DNA evidence of a few drops of blood from a toilet tissue that held some blood. And from 1991 until 2001, not one match came back to Shaw. Then, not long after Sebastian Shaw confessed to the murders of Rudiger and Ferguson, and the rape and attempted murder of Carpova, this was why that tissue was retested, according to Falls. Falls contended that Stahlman paired up with Detective Higgins, even though they had never been partners, and on January 4, 2001, they went to interview Shaw at the penitentiary. Falls said, "The first thing Detective Higgins did was show Sebastian a photograph of Jay Rickbeil. And what did Sebastian say? 'Who is he? I've never seen him before.'"

Falls stated that the pivotal point in the case was not the DNA match, it was the illegal interview of June 13, 2000, when Detectives Findling and Stahlman decided to talk to Shaw on their own, without telling the DA's office, without reading Shaw his Miranda rights—they did it all under the guise of wanting to clear up a few things on the Rudiger/Ferguson case. And according to Falls—lo and behold—after they had done this "illegal" interview, Detective Higgins suddenly resubmitted DNA evidence on the Jay Rickbeil case, after years of nothing being done about it.

The first time a new DNA test was run by Donna Scarpone, there was no hit to Shaw. Then when it was retested by an administrator, there was suddenly a hit to Shaw. This was going to be a very big issue, whether the jurors believed that Detective Higgins, who was retiring in the summer of 2000, just happened to resubmit the Rickbeil blood evidence to clear up a cold case, or whether they believed that the DNA evidence was twisted around until it fit the mold the prosecution wanted it to fit—an indictment and arrest of Sebastian Shaw, no matter what.

Officer Marilyn Donner testified about her part in arriving as the first officer on the scene of the Jay Rickbeil murder scene. She also spoke of her interaction with the detectives, who arrived after she did.

On cross-examination, David Falls asked Donner, "Did you secure the crime scene?"

"Yes," Donner responded.

"Did you leave the apartment at some point?"

"No, I was inside the apartment, waiting for detectives to arrive."

"That wasn't technically sealing the crime scene, was it?"

"In my mind it was," Donner said.

At that point, outside the courtroom on the street below, there was a lot of chanting, yelling and some kind of demonstration going on. Judge Gernant wanted to know what was happening, and it turned out to be a rally about immigration laws and reform. There was so much noise from thousands of people in the street, and in the park beyond, that a recess was called by Judge Gernant until 1:00 P.M.

After the lunch break, the demonstrators in the park were gone, and Falls continued with his cross-examination of Donner. Falls asked, "What was there about the blanket under Mr. Rickbeil that caught your attention?"

Donner answered, "It had blood on it."

"Had that blanket been moved?"

"I don't know if rescue personnel had moved it."

Falls had Donner step down from the witness stand and point on a chart just how far she had gone into Rickbeil's apartment. Donner did so, and pointed to an area where she had stood and looked at the crime scene. Once again Falls wanted to know if she had actually sealed the scene by placing crime scene tape there. Donner replied that she hadn't done that, but personally protected the room and didn't let anyone in until detectives arrived.

When Ethan Knight asked on redirect if Donner had let anyone into the apartment at all, Donner said no.

"You had training in this, right?"

"Yes."

"You've done this at hundreds of crime scenes?"

"Yes."

Before Falls questioned Detective Bellah, he told Judge Gernant, "We have an issue I need to discuss." So the jury was told to take a break, and while they were gone from the courtroom, Falls said, "I need to ask Mr. Bellah questions you don't want to come in before a jury." So then Falls asked Bellah outside the presence of the jury about ads Jay Rickbeil had placed in a local newspaper concerning photography that had to do with nude modeling. Bellah said he had looked into that angle, but he hadn't had much luck with it. After that, Falls said to the judge, "Okay, that's all we wanted to do is make a record of it outside the presence of the jury. Is it still the court's ruling that we can't ask that question?"

Judge Gernant responded, "I don't remember making that ruling, but you've made your offer of proof."

* * *

Next on the stand was the criminalist Roger O'Brien, who told of his being at the crime scene and taking samples from the bedroom, hallway and bathroom. O'Brien had also been present at Jay Rickbeil's autopsy.

On cross, Falls queried, "Did you work with anyone else that afternoon except Detective Higgins?"

"I don't remember doing so," O'Brien responded.

"Take the jury through what Detective Higgins said to you."

This brought an immediate objection from Knight, who declared, "Hearsay!"

Judge Gernant responded, "No, he's going to recollect what he can of what Detective Higgins told him."

O'Brien then answered, "He met me at the front door, we walked through the apartment together and we looked for evidence that he might not have seen and noted. Detective Higgins pointed out blood on the floor, on the sink and the tissue in the toilet. In the bedroom the blood was very obvious. We were on the lookout for knives. He pointed at the windows and noted that the windows were locked."

"How many other officers were in there?" Falls asked, implying that the officers had contaminated the crime scene. O'Brien answered one officer and two detectives total.

"Did you look on the wheelchair for blood drops?"

"I did look there and didn't see any."

Falls then brought up a comment by Detective Bellah that every time anyone entered a crime scene, they took something from it and left something there as well. O'Brien responded, "That's possible."

"Detective Higgins never told you to look at the carpet to see if there was a blood trail from the bedroom to the bathroom, did he?"

"No, sir."

"Did you seize any items that Detective Higgins hadn't identified for you to seize?"

"I don't believe so."

Falls asked how the bathroom at Rickbeil's apartment had looked, and O'Brien said there were many blood smears in the sink, and all of them had been diluted to some extent. "It didn't look like someone had tried to wipe it up, but rather that they had washed their hands." Falls wondered if some of the blood could have come from roommate Sherman Polley cutting himself in the bathroom. O'Brien didn't think so.

Medical examiner Karen Gunson testified about doing the autopsy on Jay Rickbeil. On cross-examination, Falls, who had a bad cold, facetiously asked if she had anything to help him with his cold.

Gunson joked back, "See me at my office." (That was the morgue.)

Falls asked her if the stab wounds on Jay Rickbeil were from a single-edged knife or a double-edged. From the wounds Gunson couldn't tell, then added, "On the neck injury it had a scalloped appearance. Sometimes when you slice across, the skin can wrinkle up and cause scalloping."

Regarding the blood found on the wall, Gunson said it was not from the neck injury, but most likely cast off from the knife. Spurting blood from the neck injury would have left a finer spray pattern.

The next witness, Detective Findling, spoke of how he had been brought into the case and his earlier work on the Rudiger/Ferguson murders. During his questioning Falls wanted to know about the stolen ATM card from the Rudiger/Ferguson murders and wondered why Findling had gone that route.

Detective Findling answered that there had been some activity on Todd Rudiger's Visa card on the evening of July 17, 1992, and all indications were that Rudiger and Ferguson had been killed on July 17 *before* the card had been used. It was assumed that the suspect had tried to use it and was not successful.

Falls went into Findling's interview of Shaw on June 13, 2000, and wondered if that was the reason Detective Higgins resubmitted samples to the Oregon State Forensic Lab in July 2000. Findling said that those two situations were different, and one had nothing to do with the other.

On redirect Knight asked why he and Detective Stahlman had not read Sebastian Shaw his Miranda rights when meeting with him on June 13, 2000. Findling answered, "Because we weren't going to talk to him about a new crime. We just wanted to talk to him about Donna and Todd. Shaw had already pled guilty in that case, and we wanted to help the families with what Shaw's reasoning had been for killing them. Parents of murder victims, they always have questions about why it happened. And so we didn't have any clear picture of why Donna and Todd died. We didn't know if they had done anything that had contributed to their deaths. So that was the reason we wanted to talk to Shaw to see what made them victims."

The prosecution's theory in the Rickbeil case was that there was no connection between Jay and Shaw, just as there had been no connection between Donna and Todd and Shaw before he murdered them. Shaw picked his victims at random, after becoming very angry at other people.

Detective Stahlman, who was next on the stand, was now retired from the Portland PD, after thirty years, and taught at a community college in the area. Knight wanted to know at what point Stahlman had been assigned to the Jay Rickbeil case, since he had not been on it initially. Stahlman answered that he'd been assigned it in the fall of 2000.

Going back to the first time blood had been drawn

from Sebastian Shaw, Stahlman said he had been there on February 21, 1998, after Shaw was arrested for the murders of Donna Ferguson and Todd Rudiger, and the rape and attempted murder of Amanda Carpova. Stahlman had actually watched the blood being drawn from Shaw's arm at the Adventist Hospital in Portland. It was Detective Stahlman who personally took those vials of blood to the crime lab to compare them to evidence from the Ferguson/Rudiger case.

On cross-examination, Falls asked Stahlman why he had been assigned to the Jay Rickbeil case at all. Stahlman answered that Detective Van Stearns was supervisor of the Homicide Unit at that time, and he assigned him to work with Detective Higgins. Detective Bellah was retired by then, but Higgins and Stahlman didn't start all over on the case. Rather, they used what was already known and went from there.

Getting back to the Rudiger/Ferguson case, Falls asked him about that. Stahlman said, "We contacted two hundred thirty individuals from the phone books and talked to maybe one hundred in person. It was a complete whodunit in 1992. We couldn't find anything that panned out as a vendetta against Todd or Donna. We interviewed everyone in the trailer park. We interviewed all of Donna's high-school friends, all the people she worked with. Anonymous tips came in but didn't pan out. In March 1993, I talked with Larry Findling and we felt like we hadn't even come close to finding a suspect."

Asked about the Amanda Carpova case, Stahlman said that he had not initially been on that case. He didn't get involved until the crime lab told the Detective Division that they had a match between the contributor of the semen in the Carpova case and the contributor of the semen in the Donna Ferguson case. That had been in 1997. The lab didn't know who the contributor was—except that he was the same person. By that time, Commander Findling was a lieutenant in the Detective Division and didn't have time to work on the cases, so he asked Stahlman to do so. Even though Mike Stahlman wasn't in homicide at that point, he said he would do it.

From the fall of 1997, and on into 1998, Stahlman was teamed up with Detective Bocciolatt looking into the connection between the Carpova and Ferguson cases. Before Stahlman went very far down this timeline, Falls asked him if any work had been done on the Rickbeil case since 1993. Stahlman agreed that the investigation into Rickbeil's murder had petered out in 1993, and it hadn't resumed again until Detective Higgins asked for the blood samples from the crime scene to be checked again in the summer of 2000. Since it was getting late in the day, it was decided to quit for the evening and have Detective Stahlman back on the stand the following morning.

Stahlman was indeed back at 9:00 A.M., on April 11, 2006, with a few more statements. Then the defense turned toward Sebastian Shaw on the day of his being fired at Paragon Cable. Before this went too far, the jury was excused, and the lawyers and Judge Gernant discussed the matters in private. Falls wanted to get in a statement that Shaw had supposedly told Linda Aday before he was fired. According to Falls, Shaw had said that he wanted to be locked up by the Portland PD because he was so angry at the time from being accused of sexual harassment.

McDonnell said it shouldn't come in: "It's not relevant and it's hearsay." Falls, however, countered that he wanted it admitted because "the state is going to say in their closing argument the reason Sebastian Shaw killed Jay Rickbeil on July 2, 1991, is because he was fired from his job at Paragon Cable. This statement about being locked up was to the same person who did the balloon incident and sexual harassment incident. She knows about this."

McDonnell finally let this argument go and stated, "I don't have a problem with the June twenty-fifth statement coming in." (He referred to the statement about being locked up.) "I just don't want a bunch of other stuff coming in!"

Wolf and Falls, however, did want a "bunch of other stuff" to be heard by the jury. In fact, they wanted Shaw's whole personnel file at Paragon Cable to be available to them. McDonnell shot back, "We object to that! It's irrelevant."

Judge Gernant responded, "Well, I need to read all that."

Wolf chimed in, "It comes in under 803, records kept in the process of regular business activities. And Linda Aday kept records of a regular business."

Gernant asked, "This file . . . for what purpose? If it is to show that she kept records, that's fine. If it is to show the truth of the statement, that is something else."

Ethan Knight was soon adding his two cents' worth. "It's hearsay, and they are trying to get it in by the back door."

Judge Gernant finally stated, "I'm going to go through the file with a fine-tooth comb. You don't get to enter the file, just because parts of it are from a business record."

Donna Scarpone was called to the stand as a key witness for the prosecution and answered questions put to her by Ethan Knight. Scarpone had initially done RFLP testing of DNA in the 1990s, which took a large amount of DNA to work with and was time-consuming. PCR testing, which came along later, was faster and took less amounts of material to run a test. Scarpone said that she had first become involved with the Jay Rickbeil case in 1991, and she filed an original report on August 8 of that year. She did serology on it then, not DNA testing, because DNA testing was in its infancy, and only high-profile cases made it to the FBI facilities in Virginia. There was a large backlog of police cases all across the country in that era. From her serology tests of 1991, she tested a bloodstain from the hallway of Rickbeil's apartment, blood from the bathroom floor, a roll of toilet paper and toilet tissue found in the toilet. Each one of these contained human blood, and blood from the hallway and toilet tissue had characteristics that were foreign to Jay Rickbeil. Blood samples that had come from the bedroom wall above Jay's body were consistent with his blood.

Scarpone had tested items seized from Sherman Polley, Jay's roommate, such as a short-sleeved shirt, a pair of men's pants, a pair of black shoes, a small folding knife, a large folding knife—and all of these had no blood on them. At the time she could say that the blood from the hallway floor and part of the blood from the toilet tissue did not come from Jay Rickbeil or Sherman Polley, but she could not say exactly from whom that blood had come.

This didn't happen until the year 2000, when Donna Scarpone was asked to test the blood samples taken from the Jay Rickbeil murder scene once again. By then, she was doing STR testing, which was a type of PCR/DNA testing. The samples were submitted to her in July 2000, but she didn't get around to running the tests until October 2000. She ran some tests, and once again she proved that blood from the hallway, toilet roll and part of the tissue in the toilet bowl did not come from Jay Rickbeil. Since that was the case, she ran it against DNA profiles stored in a DNA database of convicted criminals. But because she had wanted to see the results of RFLP testing *and* STR testing, the computer sent her back no hits. It was because she had looked at RFLP *and* STR, the results came in that way. If she had only asked for results from STR, she would have had very different results— results that would have indicated that Sebastian Shaw was the blood donor.

That is exactly what happened two weeks later. A CODIS system, maintained by the FBI, was used by an administrator, using the same blood samples from Jay Rickbeil's hallway, toilet roll and toilet tissue found in the toilet bowl. This time it came back with a hit—the blood evidence positively came from Sebastian Alexander Shaw, who was serving a life sentence at the Oregon State Penitentiary.

Just to make sure, Donna Scarpone asked law enforcement to take a new blood sample from Shaw. Since Shaw was a convicted criminal, he couldn't refuse this blood sample being taken. In Donna Scarpone's new report of December 5, 2000, she noted there was a match between Sebastian Shaw's blood sample and blood from the evidence items taken from the Rickbeil crime scene. Blood from the bathroom floor, blood from the hallway, a blood droplet on the toilet tissue roll—all matched Shaw's samples. Even more important, the blood on the tissue in the toilet bowl had a mixture of Shaw and Jay Rickbeil's blood on it.

On cross-examination Falls wanted to know why Donna Scarpone had referred to certain blood evidence items as coming from cotton swabs. He asked, "Item 7a included a blood sample from the wall of the hallway. These were two paint chips from the wall. There was no swab, was there?"

Scarpone answered, "No."

"Another item, a small paint plaster chip. No swab?"

"No."

"Item 7c, a sample from the bedroom floor, it was a small bit of flooring. No swab?"

"No."

Falls wanted to know if there had been a different crime lab analyst on the Jay Rickbeil case at any time, and Scarpone answered that yes, Randy Wampler had done some work on it in 1993. Wampler had run an RFLP analysis on the blood items seized from the apartment. It was an RFLP technique that had created the analysis of items 7a, 7b and 7c.

Falls made Scarpone go through what she had learned, and Scarpone explained that she had learned things that

came from the medical fields that had created specific
DNA kits. This way she would know how to use the kit
and make an intelligent analysis. The kits she used came
from the Applied Biosystems company, and they contained reagents that needed to be added to samples. A
swab was taken from a crime scene, put into a tube and
buffers added to see if it contained human DNA. If it was
from a human, reagents were added to amplify the
sample, which was akin to Xeroxing it, and the process
took place by heating and cooling, very much like a body
would do. DNA typing was done through a machine, and
a computer would do the actual analysis of what was
found. It would show peaks and valleys on a chart, and
numbers were assigned to these.

Falls said, "We're dispelling television images, like on
CSI, aren't we? You don't go out and scrape up blood.
You depend on someone else to collect the samples?"

"Yes."

Scarpone testified that she was involved with the
Amanda Carpova case of 1995, and she had used PCR
technology on the cigarette butt that was given to her.
Scarpone had no idea at the time what person had
smoked the cigarette. PCR technology was good for the
time but only used six markers—as opposed to later
techniques that would use thirteen markers. PCR testing
was eventually phased out at her lab. In 1998, when she
started using STR technology, her lab started putting
that information into a database. She said that Randy
Wampler's findings from 1993 that were connected to
the Rickbeil case went into an unsolved-crimes database.
Kevin Humphreys had also done RFLP testing of the
Amanda Carpova case and put it into the same unsolved-
crimes database. Scarpone could not explain why a
match did not show up between the Rickbeil case and
Carpova case then—except that perhaps the computer
program didn't understand that there was a match.
Unless a person types in very explicit words for the computer to look for, it will not come back with a match. It

was much like going to a search engine on the Internet, and if a person doesn't type in certain keywords, you may not get the information that you're looking for.

Falls wanted to know if Donna Scarpone contacted Detective Lloyd Higgins in July 2000, but she said no, it was the other way around. Scarpone explained that she'd run into Higgins in a hallway, and he said he would be retiring from the force soon. He asked that evidence from an unsolved crime be resubmitted, and she agreed that she would do so.

Scarpone said, "The conclusion we came to was that the RFLP data from 1993 in the Rickbeil murder was not retained in the database when the system was upgraded. During upgrades information can become lost."

Falls was very dubious about this explanation, and he believed that Donna Scarpone and the detectives were in collusion in looking at Shaw in the year 2000. He insinuated that Scarpone and the detectives were basing their actions upon the "illegal interview of Sebastian Shaw in June 2000," as he put it. Falls contended that they bent the evidence to fit what they wanted to know. Falls asked, "Weren't you specifically looking for Sebastian Shaw in 2000?"

Scarpone replied, "No, I only knew it was an unsolved case. I entered the data from the tissue from the toilet bowl. I had no idea who it would lead to."

Since the questioning was ahead of schedule, the jury was let go for the rest of the day, and in the afternoon both the prosecution and defense brought up more issues with Judge Gernant. One person the prosecution did not want testifying on the stand was Rhonda, the thirteen-year-old who had gone to Rickbeil's apartment. According to a report, she had called Jay Rickbeil a "fucking pedophile!" In fact, Rhonda had been so angry at one point that she was looked upon as a suspect by the police in Rickbeil's murder. Her hair and blood had been tested to see if she had been responsible. That evidence showed that she had not stabbed Jay to death, but she did have an ax to grind with him over the subject of young girls and photography.

The prosecution did want the evidence from the Rudiger/Ferguson and Carpova cases to come in, and it was discussed between all parties just what the exact wording would be. Judge Gernant finally came up with this instruction to the jurors: *You are about to hear evidence of other crimes. The jury may not consider this evidence for the purpose of concluding that just because Mr. Shaw has committed other crimes, he is more likely to have committed the crime he is charged with in the present case.* Gernant went on to say that they could consider it if they thought it backed up the prosecution's theory of the Jay Rickbeil murder. They could also consider it if they thought it placed Shaw there to commit a burglary, and he ended up killing Jay Rickbeil, which supported the prosecution's theory that "Jay Rickbeil's death did not result from mistake or accident."

Richard Wolf still didn't like the wording because he thought it gave the impression that the prosecution was correct in its theory. So the lawyers went round and round on exact wording and phrases, finally coming up with one portion that stated, *If you consider it at all, for other purposes, such as to prove Mr. Shaw's motive, opportunity, intent, and preparation of a plan.* This phrase had the key element of "if you consider it at all." Both the prosecution and the defense said they could live with the new wording of the jurors' instructions.

There were other issues to take care of as well, and Judge Gernant spoke directly to Sebastian Shaw about these. Gernant said that it would solely be up to him if he wanted to testify, and not up to his attorneys. Shaw said that he understood, and Gernant warned him that whatever course he took, he could never bring it up on appeal later by saying that his attorneys were incompetent. Once Shaw made a decision, he would have to stand by it.

Another issue was that the prosecution argued that if the jury found Shaw guilty of murder, they didn't have to prove beyond a reasonable doubt about the burglary charge, which if tacked on could bring him the death penalty. The defense argued that the jurors did have to find a charge of burglary beyond a reasonable doubt, just like everything else. Semantics and the way instructions were going to be written had a huge impact down the line.

The defense also argued that the state had not put Detective Higgins on the stand because they were afraid if they did so, his testimony would be impeached, which was just a "lawyerly" way of saying that Higgins had been lying. The prosecution argued back that the reason they didn't bring Higgins in was a strategic move, and they could call or not call whomever they wanted. It wasn't up to the defense to say who should be called by the prosecution as their witnesses. One of the reasons they didn't bring in Higgins was that it would introduce some things that Shaw said—things that were self-serving and not true.

McDonnell opened up a can of worms, however, when he let it be known that Detective Higgins was starting to show signs of Alzheimer's, and Falls immediately wanted to know when Higgins had started suffering from this. Falls asked, "Did he have Alzheimer's when he testified on the stand in December 2003 in a hearing?" If Higgins did have Alzheimer's then, how reliable was his testimony?

McDonnell said that Detective Higgins had not been told he had Alzheimer's disease until February 2004. Falls, however, replied, "Well, that might show why we had such difficulty cross-examining him on a motion hearing."

In the end Judge Gernant agreed that it was the prosecution's business who it was they called as a witness.

Amanda Carpova took the stand, and her testimony was absolutely riveting. She took the jurors back, step by step, through her ordeal of June 1995. Carpova left out no details as she explained being forced into her bedroom at gunpoint, sexually assaulted, forced to take a shower afterward and her incredible struggle to stay alive. When her testimony was over, Judge Gernant made an extraordinary statement. "Sometimes I think it's an advantage to have an audio recording system instead of a court reporter. I think it was clear from what we just heard that the witness was not inflammatory. The jury was not inflamed. The witness told her story with dry eyes and composure. I think it's clear I should have had a 104 hearing [evidentiary hearing] a few years ago." Then Judge Gernant apologized directly to Amanda Carpova and the prosecution for denying Amanda Carpova the right to tell her story in the first attempt at a trial in 2004.

It was now time for the defense to make their case to the jurors, and before they could, the prosecution made motions to deny many witnesses that the defense wanted to put on the stand. The prosecution argued that many of these witnesses were only there to "blacken" Jay Rickbeil's reputation, and he wasn't there to defend himself. Wolf, however, replied that the witnesses would show that Jay had had "inappropriate contact" with some young women, and that could have been his prior connection to Sebastian Shaw. "Both men may have known each other from this area," Wolf said. In fact, Wolf stated that Jay Rickbeil may have let Shaw into his apartment on the afternoon of July 2, 1991. In that case, according to Wolf, there was no breaking and entering—and no burglary. The state, Wolf argued, never showed that Shaw took anything from Jay's apartment, and they had only tacked on a burglary charge to try and get a death penalty imposed against Shaw.

Judge Gernant asked what Detective Stahlman would say, as to this matter, since the defense intended to call Stahlman to the stand. Gernant then brought Stahlman in on a 104 hearing to see if there was indeed a prior connection between Sebastian Shaw and Jay Rickbeil.

Falls said to Stahlman on the stand, that during the January 4, 2001, interview, Detective Higgins had said to Shaw, "'Both you and Mr. Rickbeil solicited prostitutes on Eighty-second Avenue.' Do you remember that statement?"

Stahlman said that he did remember the statement. "I've got the report right here." Stahlman took a moment to look at Higgins's statement and added, "Higgins asked if he got hookers on Eighty-second Avenue. Shaw looked at Higgins, laughed and said yes. Then Detective Higgins informed Shaw that Jay Rickbeil had solicited hookers on Eighty-second Avenue. Shaw then asked, 'Did he sell pot or something?'"

After hearing that from the report, the judge said, "There's still no connection established." Then Judge Gernant turned directly to Stahlman and asked, "Did you have any belief that Mr. Rickbeil and Mr. Shaw knew each other?"

Stahlman replied, "No, none at all. There was no information that they both went out at the same time. Detective Higgins might have been trying to establish that Rickbeil and Shaw knew each other from that area, but we never made any connection."

Judge Gernant responded, "Well, it was wonderful detective work, but it didn't work." Then turning to Falls, Gernant asked, "What's the relevance of all this?"

Falls answered, "Because the state's theory is that Rudiger, Ferguson and Carpova were strangers to Sebastian Shaw."

Gernant asked, "And what's your theory?"

Both Falls and Wolf answered simultaneously, "We don't need a theory."

Then Falls added, "Mr. Gerhardt, a probation officer, can show that Jay Rickbeil had a thing for young women. And we can show that Sebastian Shaw had a thing for young women. There is a good chance the two knew each other. There is a reasonable inference that Shaw was at Rickbeil's apartment because of Mr. Rickbeil's activities."

Going to another area of how they might have known each other, Falls said that Detective Stahlman had asked Officer McDonald, of the Portland PD, to look into covens and satanic cult practices concerning Jay Rickbeil. "Some of these witnesses say that is true. And Mr. Shaw had a balloon with a devil's face on it."

Ethan Knight came back with "the only bit of evidence is Shaw and the balloon, but he never made any comments about Satanism or being part of [a] satanic cult. Let's say that Rickbeil and Shaw were baseball fans. That doesn't mean that Mr. Shaw was over at Mr. Rickbeil's apartment to talk about baseball."

The same issues between the defense and prosecution came up about the girl named Colleen, concerning Jay Rickbeil's sexual activities out on Eighty-second Avenue, and Satanism. Also there was a report about Rickbeil offering alcohol to young girls in exchange for sex, but Judge Gernant sustained the prosecution's objection to these issues as well.

When it came to Pamela Hobson, she was going to say, "Lots of people were coming and going from Jay's place. His friends were freaky, and they grabbed me." The prosecution, however, only wanted her to be able to testify about the physical condition of Jay Rickbeil's apartment, and the judge agreed.

Getting back to the interview of Shaw by Stahlman and Higgins, Knight said, "We were surprised when the defense mentioned Stahlman and Higgins, and if the defense opens that door, we're going to drive a Mack truck through it," implying that they were going to talk about things mentioned at that interview that the defense did not want jurors to hear, such as Shaw's comment that he'd murdered more people than the detectives knew about. Falls replied, "We're not going to ask any questions about what was said at the interview, just dates and times."

Judge Gernant, however, said that it sounded like they were going to get into more than just dates and times, and if they did that, then the prosecution was going to be able to speak about what Shaw had said, including his comment that he'd killed ten more people than the detectives knew about at the time.

Judge: *How does that undercut the fact that there was a DNA match?*

Wolf: *It doesn't undercut that. It undercuts what the witnesses have already said. To say we can't do this seems to undercut Mr. Shaw's right to due process. The court has ruled that interview (by Higgins and Stahlman) was illegal.*

Knight: *To interject the defense's conspiracy theory at this point in the trial is not relevant to the jury.*

Wolf: *We are entitled to impeach the state's entire theory. And this evidence does that.*

Judge: *How?*

Wolf: *The jury doesn't have to believe that the match was made on a random basis.*

Judge: *If you impeach the credibility of the detectives, how does that change any of the things the crime lab did?*

Wolf: *Because if the jury believes our version, they don't have to believe anything the crime lab has testified to. We've been denied access to the DNA database. We want to show that everything that was done is suspect.*

Judge: *The detectives are not relevant to the DNA evidence. I've ruled on this. It's not a jury question.*

Richard Wolf, however, was not giving up on this important point, and around and around it went. He was really starting to get wound up, and said, "No, Your Honor! We're not limited to impeach the state's theory of the case by the witnesses they proffer. We're entitled to all the witnesses whose testimony calls into question the testimony of other witnesses!"

Knight argued, "They have an insinuation that there was

some insidious conduct by Detectives Stahlman, Higgins and Scarpone about going after Mr. Shaw. And if they go down that road, it opens the door on all of the June 13, 2000, interview."

Judge Gernant said that this issue was still irrelevant, but he would not stop Wolf and Falls from questioning Detective Stahlman. Then Gernant added, "But if you open the door about the interview, then the prosecution can come back on this issue."

This was a big gamble on the defense's part, and they took five minutes, huddled together, to discuss it. Wolf then spoke up and said, "If we put Detective Stahlman on the stand, and if we establish that Stahlman went to the penitentiary that day and made a conscious decision not to Mirandize Mr. Shaw, told Mr. Shaw that he was not a suspect in a different case—when, in fact, he was—does that somehow open the door on what Mr. Shaw said?"

Mark McDonnell piped up and said, "The detectives didn't ever ask him information on other cases. It was Shaw who brought that up. And then the detectives said, 'We're outta here.'"

Judge Gernant replied, "I'm not going to make rulings in a vacuum."

Wolf said, "We're not going to put Stahlman up there, if out comes the content of ten or twelve other murders. In light of the inclination of the court, we are not going to call Detective Stahlman. We cannot simply take the risk of exposing to the jury what has already been ruled illegal. I'm not sure how clear Detective Stahlman would be about the parameters of his testimony. Unless the court would declare a mistrial at that point, I don't think we can run the risk."

So after all the debates between defense, prosecution and judge, Detective Stahlman was not called to the stand by Wolf or Falls. As Wolf noted, it was too big a risk that something would be said regarding how Shaw had claimed to kill ten other people.

* * *

A person who was called to the stand, however, was Victoria Taylor, and she explained to the jurors that she had been Jay Rickbeil's housekeeper in 1991. She had tidied up the place, cooked meals for him and even helped him bathe on occasion. Falls asked her if she knew a person named Sebastian Shaw back in 1991, and she answered that she knew his face, and that's all.

"Why did you recognize his face?" Falls asked.

"In 1991, Jay was changing his rules in his household and turning people away that he'd talked to before. He had too many people at his place, and I was dismissing them at the door."

"Did you come into contact with Mr. Shaw in 1991?"

"I remember his face."

"How do you remember his face?"

"Well, there was some discussion after I told him Jay was not having company. He got all upset."

"Was he at the door with anyone?"

"Yes, a blond female."

"Why do you recall it was the spring of 1991?"

"Because that was the last time I was there."

Knight, on cross-examination, asked Victoria Taylor, "Back in 1991, you talked to Detective Bellah about this case?"

"I talked to two detectives," Victoria answered. "One brought me down to the Justice Center and took a snippet of my hair." (She was obviously being checked to see if it was her hair found on Jay's body.)

Knight once again asked, "Did you talk to a detective in 1991?"

"Yes."

"Did you make some statements to a detective then?"

"Yes."

"The detective asked specifically if Mr. Rickbeil knew any Asians?"

"I don't remember that."

Knight read from what she had said: *He knew some Vietnamese or Chinese person. Someone real nice to him in a restaurant. I think it was there on 82nd Avenue.*

"I don't remember that."

"But you have a good recollection from 1991?"

"I have a good memory of faces."

"You talked to a defense investigator this year?" Knight queried.

"Yeah. I talked to him a lot."

"There was no mention to the investigator about Mr. Shaw coming to the door."

"I didn't recognize him until I was subpoenaed."

"You came in a couple of weeks ago, and you say you recognized Shaw then? But you didn't tell anyone at that time?"

"It took me a while to recall him."

"You said there were a lot of folks who came to the door that year?" Knight asked.

"There was this street kid who came in, and she was kind of a misfit in the house. She let the key out, and when she left, all hell broke loose."

"Can you describe some others who came by Jay Rick-beil's apartment?"

"Oh, people wearing chains, black, leather."

"Can you describe their faces?"

"Well, some just came off the street. They looked exhausted."

"But you remember specifically what Mr. Shaw said?" Knight asked.

"No, just that he raised his voice, and was gruff. He took protest that he wasn't allowed inside."

Falls began to recross Victoria Taylor, but after his first question, he quickly stopped. Falls had begun to ask Taylor, "When you talked to Mr. Wolf . . ."

Taylor asked who Wolf was, and Falls had to point him out as the man sitting next to Sebastian Shaw. After that exchange it became apparent that Victoria Taylor might not recall faces and names so well after all. At that point the defense decided to rest its case.

On April 17, 2006, Judge Gernant began giving the jurors instructions. One of Gernant's key admonitions was that they had to reach a decision based upon his instructions throughout the case, and he gave the analogy of "a river that must run through a concrete conduit." They could not take into account anything outside the conduit.

Judge Gernant said, "The lawyers' statements are not evidence. You cannot allow bias or sympathy to cloud your judgment, and you cannot think about what sentencing might be during the penalty phase. You can take into account the perceived bias, motives or interest of a witness. Also you may take into account whether a witness correctly remembered what Mr. Shaw said in previous years."

Judge Gernant told them to use their common sense in deliberations, and to decide whether a burglary had been committed during the course of the murder. All of this had to be beyond a reasonable doubt. They could not take into account that Mr. Shaw had not spoken in his own defense, and they were not to imply anything by that fact.

Then it was time for closing arguments. Mark McDonnell told the jurors that in the beginning he had said the evidence would prove three things: DNA evidence would prove that Sebastian Shaw killed Jay Rickbeil; Sebastian Shaw intentionally killed Jay Rickbeil; Sebastian Shaw murdered Jay Rickbeil in the furtherance of a burglary.

McDonnell went over once again where DNA from Shaw showed up on blood samples taken from the murder scene. The most telling one of these was the toilet tissue Shaw had failed to flush down the toilet, which contained his blood and that of the victim Jay

Rickbeil. DNA evidence proved that the chances it was not Shaw's blood were one in 10 billion.

McDonnell addressed why there hadn't been a DNA match earlier to Shaw, and he said that because the database system had been upgraded several times since 1991, some of the information may have become lost. The original had been stored on a 5½-inch floppy disk, something that modern computers didn't use. McDonnell noted, "Anybody who has tried to upgrade from one computer system to another knows that there can be problems, and information can be lost. Also, everybody knows that if the exact words are not typed on a search, you will not get the information you are looking for."

McDonnell stated that evidence showed that Sebastian Shaw had intentionally killed Jay Rickbeil, because there were numerous defensive wounds on Jay's hands. If it wasn't intentional, Shaw would have stopped after he inflicted the first defensive wound. Shaw, however, kept going until he had inflicted the fatal wound to Jay's neck, which severed the carotid artery. "This was intentional," McDonnell declared. "It was no accident."

As for the burglary charges, McDonnell said that by law any person entering another person's residence, without being invited in by that person, is committing burglary under Oregon law. It didn't have to be to commit a theft, rape or assault. Just the fact of being there without permission was enough. McDonnell said, "Common sense shows that Jay Rickbeil did not invite Sebastian Shaw in to murder him. And evidence shows that Jay Rickbeil resisted the attack with every bit of his strength. Even if Shaw had permission to enter Jay's apartment, that permission ended the moment when Jay resisted his attack. At that point Shaw's right to be there was revoked."

McDonnell declared they knew how Shaw committed crimes by the evidence at the Todd Rudiger/Donna Ferguson murder scene. Shaw had entered a dwelling without permission to commit a crime. Both Rudiger and

Ferguson died of stab wounds to the neck, just as Jay Rickbeil had. And McDonnell added, "I doubt if any of us have ever heard testimony as compelling as that of Amanda Carpova. Because of her strength and courage, we got an insight into the motivation and intent of Sebastian Shaw. After her testimony it's understandable why there was no broken door or window at Jay Rickbeil's apartment. That didn't happen at Amanda Carpova's apartment as well."

McDonnell declared that Sebastian Shaw picked his victims with little or no prior contact. When he was fired from Paragon Cable on July 2, 1991, he flew into a rage and decided to kill someone. He knew that if he killed anyone at Paragon Cable, it would be easy for the police to find him. So he decided to kill someone who had nothing to do with Paragon Cable, and that person was Jay Rickbeil.

McDonnell ended by saying, "Sebastian Shaw told Amanda Carpova, 'I don't care if I screw up your life, as long as my needs are satisfied.' But the citizens of Multnomah County do care. They put their trust in you to render justice in this case."

At least by closing arguments, David Falls's voice was better, and he wasn't coughing as much. Falls told the jurors that the state tried to prove there were connections between the Todd Rudiger/Donna Ferguson murders, the Amanda Carpova case and the Jay Rickbeil murder. Rudiger, Ferguson and Carpova, however, had all been tied up with telephone cords or stereo speaker wire before being assaulted. That had not been the case with Jay Rickbeil. Sebastian Shaw had pled guilty to the former cases, but not the Jay Rickbeil murder. Falls added, "It's okay to be mad at Sebastian Shaw for the things he did to Todd Rudiger, Donna Ferguson and Amanda Carpova. The terror and horror that she went through. And we have to assume that Rudiger and Ferguson went through the same thing. Now tell me, what do these pictures (evidence photos of Rudiger, Ferguson and Carpova) have to do with July 2, 1991? The prosecution is saying, 'Hey, this guy must be a monster!' So that way you'll convict him of anything."

Falls showed the jurors documents that stated that Sebastian Shaw would spend the rest of his life, without possibility of parole, in prison for the murders of Rudiger and Ferguson, and the rape and attempted murder of Carpova. Falls asked if that was payment enough, and he answered his own question by saying that for many people, it probably wasn't. "For most of us we'd probably like to drag him through the gravel for the vengeance we feel. But even as Mr. McDonnell said, we are a civilized society. Because of the law, Todd Rudiger, Donna Ferguson and Amanda Carpova have had their day in court. That has nothing to do with July 2, 1991."

Falls declared that evidence is only as good as the people who collect it and process it. He asked rhetorically if there was a swab containing blood in the evidence bag there in court, and then he answered the question by saying no. They heard from criminalist O'Brien in the trial, but the prosecution wouldn't even put on their lead detective in the Rickbeil case, Lloyd Higgins.

As far as burglary went, Falls said McDonnell was stretching the truth to the breaking point. Everyone knew that burglary was an attempt to steal something, and there was no proof that Sebastian Shaw was in Jay Rickbeil's apartment to steal anything on July 2, 1991, or at any other time. Then Falls added, "It doesn't make sense to say he went in there to kill somebody, and in the furtherance of killing somebody, you kill somebody. That's nonsensical."

Falls declared that the detectives thought that both the Donna Ferguson murder and attempted murder of Amanda Carpova were sexually motivated. That was Sebastian Shaw's MO. So where was the sexual intent in the Jay Rickbeil murder? Falls asked. There wasn't any, he responded. He said that the state never proved any motive at all in this case. Everything they had came from blood

spots on the bathroom floor and on a toilet tissue, something that Shaw could have done at any time, and not
during the course of a murder. Falls added that Shaw
and Rickbeil most likely did know each other, and there
was good reason to believe that Rickbeil let Shaw into his
apartment. There was no breaking and entering.

Falls even admitted that the testimony by Victoria
Taylor caught him by surprise. Then he added that she
had actually seen Sebastian Shaw at Jay Rickbeil's door,
sometime before the murder, "and he acted like he was
supposed to be there."

Falls told the jurors that they heard evidence that Jay
Rickbeil was trying to start a photography business, where
young women would be photographed nude. He also
noted that a lot of people were coming and going through
Jay Rickbeil's unlocked front door. Falls declared, "You
can't look at Sebastian Shaw and say, 'You didn't prove to
us that you didn't commit a murder.' Under the law you
can't do that. Even if you go back there and are all con-
vinced that Sebastian Shaw got into a struggle and Shaw
killed Jay, that's the most the evidence will show. Nothing
shows he went there to commit burglary and murdered Jay
Rickbeil in the course of it. There is no prior intent. He's
admitted his guilt in the other cases, but it doesn't change
one fact in this case. I'll submit to you that the reason the
prosecution tacked on the burglary charge is because they
want the chance to kill Sebastian Shaw."

Ethan Knight delivered the prosecution's rebuttal,
and said, "The only reason you're sitting here today is
because an individual who had a chilling disregard for
human life wandered into the apartment of a paraplegic
man, who he had virtually no connection with, slashed
his throat several times and almost severed his head. And
all that because he lost his job at a cable company."

Knight stated that the law about burglary in Oregon
didn't ask them if it made sense or not, that was up to the

voters and legislature to decide. What the jurors needed to
decide upon was whether first-degree murder had been
committed upon Jay Rickbeil on July 2, 1991. Their job at
the present time was not to decide whether or not to put
Shaw to death, it was to decide if he was guilty. Knight said
that they could consider the Ferguson/Rudiger case and
the Carpova case, as well, in their decision. The prosecution didn't bring those cases up "just to make you mad.
What does Sebastian Shaw do when he goes into people's
apartments uninvited? He kills or attempts to kill."

As far as binding went, Shaw didn't need to bind Jay
Rickbeil because the man couldn't walk. And Shaw left
his DNA in blood in Jay Rickbeil's bathroom. Two scien-
tists confirmed that fact independently of each other.
Knight also explained that on their verdict form there
was no box that had to be checked about motive. They
might never know what Sebastian Shaw's motive was for
killing Jay Rickbeil. That part didn't matter in the case
at hand—what did matter was simply the fact that Shaw
had committed the murder.

Like McDonnell, Knight declared that common sense
showed that people didn't invite other people into their
dwellings to kill them. And Knight added that even Victoria Taylor said that Shaw had not been invited into
Rickbeil's apartment but was turned away, perhaps further inflaming Shaw to future murder. "You have a job
to do, and that's applying the facts to the law. When you
do that in this case, you can come to only one conclusion, and that is this defendant, on July 2, 1991, committed the crime of aggravated murder."

After the prosecution and defense were done giving
closing arguments, Judge Gernant instructed the jurors
that they would be polled by number, not by name, when
they came back with a decision. Then he added, "I always
tell a jury there is no right or wrong time for a length of

jury deliberation." At 10:50 A.M., the jurors filed out of the courtroom and went to a deliberation room.

It did not take them long to come to a decision. By 1:44 P.M., they were back in the courtroom and seated. Judge Gernant read their form and said, "The jury finds Sebastian Shaw guilty of felony aggravated murder." Gernant then asked the jury foreman if this was correct, and he said that it was. Judge Gernant polled each juror by number; and one by one, they said yes to the question of guilt.

There was only one more legal process now between Sebastian Shaw and the death penalty—a sentencing phase, where he would get his final chance to speak to the jurors in a gamble to save his life.

18

Life or Death

If jury instructions were important in the penalty phase, they were absolutely crucial in the sentencing phase. The defense in particular had points about mitigating circumstances that they wanted to get into the instructions, but they were not going to be able to get in some things without a fight. Even on the topic of "reasonable doubt," Judge Gernant told Wolf and Falls that their proposed instructions were "incredibly unclear" and needed to be worked on.

The defense wanted jurors to be able to say that if Sebastian Shaw did not have adequate mental capability, that could be a mitigating circumstance to keep him from receiving the death penalty. And they declared that even if the state argued a point about aggravation that was beyond a reasonable doubt, and a juror agreed that it was—but still wanted to vote no for death—that could be mitigation and would automatically mean life without parole for Shaw. McDonnell, however, stated that if a juror agreed a point was beyond a reasonable doubt, they had no option but to vote yes on the form. They just couldn't ignore the law. The one great hurdle the prosecution faced in this phase was that they had to have all twelve jurors vote yes on all four questions.

One important area where Judge Gernant agreed with the defense was that mitigating circumstances about mental capacity, age, prior criminal conduct, plus *anything else* the jurors thought was mitigating, were all valid. It was, in essence, up to each juror to decide on his or her own if something was a mitigating circumstance, and not one other juror had to agree with that person on that point. As Wolf noted in his arguments, "There is no burden of proof in mitigating circumstances."

It took Judge Gernant and the various lawyers an hour and a half just to reach an agreement on how the jury instructions would be worded. The next area of debate was who was going to be able to be called as a witness in this phase, and what they would be able to say. Wolf, for instance, wanted a woman named Rhonda to testify about Jay Rickbeil being into "Devil worship," as he put it, but Knight argued it was no more relevant now than it had been during the penalty phase. Wolf went so far as to say, "The jury is entitled to know if Sebastian Shaw may have gotten fired from his job because Jay Rickbeil suggested to him that he leave a balloon with a devil's face on it at Paragon Cable."

Judge Gernant was incredulous, and asked, "Where did you get that?"

Wolf answered that there could have been a connection, and he was free to ask the jurors to ponder that possibility.

Judge Gernant, however, replied that they were not going back to the guilt phase on this matter.

Wolf still argued, "It doesn't question the verdict in the penalty phase. Shaw could have killed him in the course of a burglary, but it could have the jury think about provocation."

Knight replied, "It goes right back to the guilt phase. The jury shouldn't have this kind of stuff, because it is so tenuous. There never was any connection between the two men!"

Judge Gernant agreed with Knight and there wasn't going to be any mention about Jay Rickbeil suggesting that Shaw leave a devil-faced balloon at work.

Wolf wanted to bring back Detective Stahlman during the sentencing phase, in effect to say that he and Detective Findling had tried badgering Shaw into a confession. "Their supposed purpose was to say that he was already doing life, it would give closure to the victims' families, and they weren't going to ask him about any other crimes, which, of course, Jay Rickbeil's case was."

Knight responded that comments made then were hearsay and also that it would open the door to the rest of the interview, where Shaw claimed to have killed ten other people. Besides, Knight declared that the state back in 2000 had offered Shaw a chance to talk about the other people that he had supposedly killed in exchange for no death penalty, and Shaw had declined to do so. Now it was too late.

Judge Gernant agreed that it would open the door to all the interview statements of June 2000 that were coming in, and he added, "If you only give one instance from that interview, it paints an unfair picture for the jury."

Wolf, however, responded, "No, the one who has an unfair picture painted about him is Mr. Shaw, because of activity by the detectives that the court found to be illegal."

Knight replied, "Even if the conduct was illegal, it would still open the door," and the judge agreed once more about this. This was just too big a risk for the defense to take, so they dropped it.

The next issue was an interesting gambit by the defense and Sebastian Shaw. His lawyers said Shaw was willing to waive all appeals to the penalty phase if the jurors did not give him a death sentence but rather life without the possibility of parole. In essence, Shaw would not make any appeals from here on out as to whether he was guilty or not for the death of Jay Rickbeil. Wolf said this would save the state taxpayers four times as much money than if a death penalty process went forward.

Judge Gernant asked how any of that was relevant to the jurors and what they must decide now.

Wolf replied, "It shows a reflection of Mr. Shaw's character. It shows his willingness to save the state money."

Knight countered that "the cost is not relevant, and Shaw is already serving a life term. So what money would it save?"

Wolf argued, "It is important! It will save the state hundreds of thousands of dollars."

"All it shows is he is willing to do what he is already compelled to do. It doesn't show his character. And the court says the cost of an execution shall not be taken into account. That will be part of the instructions," Gernant stated.

"It is important as to character," Wolf countered, and then Wolf spoke of someone doing a cost analysis.

Gernant replied, "At some point you got an okay from the treasurer in Salem to pay for an expert to produce a report about waiver in a death penalty case? I am astonished, and I will be in touch with the proper authorities in Salem. This is a real misuse of public funds in my view! It had no chance of coming into court."

The defense next cited potential prosecution witnesses and they wanted a 104 hearing on these outside the presence of the jurors. These included Debra and Ray Adams, the mother and stepfather of Donna Ferguson; Lucille Campbell, whose husband's vehicle had been stolen in San Ramon in 1994; and John Lin, father of murdered Jennifer Lin in 1994. Falls said they had no relevance to the case at hand.

McDonnell, however, stated, "Debra Adams can testify

to circumstances to which her daughter's knife wound was inflicted. It goes to future dangerousness of Mr. Shaw. The Campbells' car was stolen in 1994, and the defendant was found sleeping in their car in Portland. That car had a 'rape/killer' kit inside its trunk, stolen firearms, a book of anatomy and mail from a young woman who lived in Redding, California. Like the others, she had no prior contact with Mr. Shaw."

Falls replied, "The only thing brought forth in trial was a weapon, and you (Judge Gernant) ruled the firearm was illegally seized by police."

McDonnell went on, however: "All of this is to show future dangerousness by the defendant. Those can be uncharged acts, such as the stolen rifles in the trunk."

Falls disagreed, saying, "There has been no establishment of any wrongdoing on that. They had the ability to prosecute those things, and they didn't."

McDonnell replied, "We're not offering the gun under the seat (the pistol). We're offering the stolen rifles in the trunk. I have a witness who will say those guns were stolen."

Judge Gernant asked if Falls wanted to hear this witness in a 104 hearing, and Falls replied that he did. Gernant responded, "That's easily enough done."

Then Falls had another objection. "They want to bring in photos about Rudiger and Ferguson. I don't see how that is relevant now."

McDonnell replied, "The state was very careful the way we brought in this evidence. There was no mention of sexual assaults, until brought up by the defense. This also goes to future dangerousness."

Judge Gernant turned to David Falls and asked, "Why do you say the state can't bring that in at this point?"

"The state of Oregon has already entered into a contract with Mr. Shaw that was based on that homicide, and they did not seek the death penalty," Falls said.

As far as John and Jenny Lin went, McDonnell said, "The state doesn't intend to offer evidence about Lin at this time. But if the door opens . . . Jennifer was bound with duct tape and rope tied around her."

"We've received minimal discovery on this. I believe Mr. McDonnell knows more about this case than he's told us," Falls stated.

Eventually there was a hearing on Bruce Campbell, the son of Dean Campbell, whose car had been stolen in August 1994. Before this went very far, however, Wolf made a motion to suppress, because the judge from a November 22, 1994, hearing had said that this evidence was not admissible. Wolf stated, "The state already had a chance to litigate this issue, and cannot now come in and offer the evidence. He was arrested for a stolen firearm."

Judge Gernant, however, replied, "Now they are calling the son of the owner of the car, not a police officer."

McDonnell chimed in, saying, "Mr. Shaw was also arrested for being in a car that did not belong to him and was stolen. That charge was not taken up at the time. There were decisions made then that it wasn't worth the time and money to have people come up from California. But there are different parts to this now. The items found in the trunk were not suppressed. Officer Long got permission from Mr. Campbell to search the car the following day. Looking into the trunk, he found a ski mask, throwing knives, flex cuffs, a book on how to make keys, manuals on anatomy, a chemistry book, surgical gloves— and, in essence, a murder kit. The decision to suppress evidence on the handgun does not go to the other material."

"What is relevant about bringing it up today?" Judge Gernant asked.

"Uncharged acts are admissible," McDonnell answered.

"Isn't this hearsay, because Dean Campbell is no longer alive?"

McDonnell responded, "The consent to search isn't hearsay. It's a matter of record."

Wolf did not want the jurors hearing anything about a

stolen car that Shaw was in, or the things found in its trunk. He said, "There is a matter of timeliness on this. We were not told about this by the prosecution until yesterday. Those items were observed by officers in 1994. We cannot now cross-examine Dean Campbell. This is double jeopardy."

Judge Gernant thought about it, then replied, "If they were charging Mr. Shaw with those crimes, I'd agree with you. But the decision made by a judge in 1994 is not relevant to this issue. I reject your argument."

So, one by one, the prosecution presented photos of items seized from the trunk of the Campbells' stolen car that they wanted the jurors to see. Zip flex ties, two ski masks, Mace, *The Anarchist Cookbook*, Michelle Lewis's stolen voter booklet and nunchakus. The judge agreed that all of these would come in as evidence.

When the jury was brought in to start the sentencing phase, McDonnell went over the four questions they would have to answer to impose the death penalty, and asked, "What possible provocation is there that a paraplegic in his own bed would do to lead to his own murder? You know it was a deliberate act on Sebastian Shaw's part. He had time to deliberate, and he knew right from wrong." McDonnell also said that the prosecution was going to introduce more evidence that the jurors hadn't heard during the penalty phase that was "downright chilling."

And then he got into the 1996 arrest of Shaw for the illegal use of a weapon against Russ Sperou, which had started out over something so minor as "washing the dishes." McDonnell spoke of Sperou putting Shaw in a headlock during a scuffle, and Shaw kept yelling, "As soon as you let me go, I'm going to kill you!" In fact, when Sperou let him go, Shaw went and retrieved two pistols and, in a hail of bullets, shot up Sperou's room.

McDonnell also spoke of the detectives who, in 1998, found in Shaw's room at the Danmore Hotel, a ski mask, items from women he had sexually harassed in the past, addresses of women he didn't even know and pornographic material about rape and torture.

Then McDonnell said that the defense would offer as mitigating evidence that Shaw's mother had died before he was one year old, he barely knew his father growing up, he had been helicoptered from the American Embassy in Saigon in the last days of the war and that his father abused him when they lived together in Oregon. McDonnell said, "I have no doubt all that is true, but that does not change the fact or excuse Sebastian Shaw's conduct in killing three people. It doesn't change who he is. He's a cold-blooded murderer who picked his victims at random. We all know, if given a chance, he will kill again. Sebastian Shaw deserves to be executed. Not for vengeance, not for 'an eye for an eye,' but because he deserves it."

Richard Wolf began his opening argument by saying he had an awesome responsibility and that the people in the jury box had the most serious matter on which any juror could make a decision. He said he respected their decision in the guilt phase but that the sentencing phase "was a different animal."

Then Wolf opened a dictionary and looked up the word "justify." He wrote the word down on a piece of paper, ripped up the paper and told them they were not here to justify Sebastian Shaw's actions. He did the same with the word "excuse," written on a piece of paper, telling the jurors they were not there to excuse Shaw. He told them that this part of the case only had to do with mitigating circumstances, adding that those included, but were not limited to, age, severity of prior criminal conduct, mental factors, background and character.

Wolf said that everyone was worth more than the worst acts they had ever done. And he declared that try as he might, Sebastian Shaw never fit in anywhere, not in civilian life, not in the marines, not in Vietnam and not in the United States. His life now was behind bars and "that is punishment every single day until he dies." And Wolf added that the jurors were going to hear things by the state about Todd Rudiger, Donna Ferguson and Amanda Carpova, but all those things had been dealt with in an agreement signed by all parties in 2000. Wolf declared that the state back then could have rejected a deal and gone for the death penalty on those same charges, but they didn't. And now they were trying to get the death penalty enforced for those same crimes, via the back door, by tagging them onto the killing of Jay Rickbeil.

Wolf acknowledged that Shaw had been in two altercations with fellow inmates since he had been incarcerated, but it was, according to Wolf, the other inmates who had started the fights by taunting and abusing Shaw. "He hasn't attacked a guard in prison, he hasn't killed someone since he has been in prison. We want you to realize the harsh life he has to look forward to, day in and day out, for the rest of his life. We're going to ask you for life."

Trying to prove that Sebastian Shaw had done many more dangerous and illegal things than the jurors had heard during the penalty phase, the prosecution called Bruce Campbell to the stand to talk about the burglary to his parents' home and the stealing of their car, a 1978 Pontiac Bonneville. Campbell was mainly there to establish a foundation about the stolen car and stolen rifles from his parents' home. It was the next witness, Officer Matthew Wagenknecht, who placed Shaw in that stolen car in Portland, Oregon, in August 1994. Officer Wagenknecht stated that he had been dispatched to recover a stolen vehicle on August 30, 1994, at the corner of Fifty-first Avenue and Klickitat. When he got there, he found Sebastian Shaw sleeping in the stolen car. Shaw was taken into custody, and the car was taken to the impound lot. Once it was in the impound lot, the VIN numbers matched, but it was obvious that someone had removed the original license plates and placed other stolen plates on the car.

On cross-examination, Wolf wanted to know, "Did Mr. Shaw comply with your demands?"

Wagenknecht answered, "Yes."

"Was he polite?"

"Yes."

"What did you inventory?"

"The front seat, the backseat and the trunk."

This bit of information was very important, and a break was taken. It concerned the items in the trunk that Officer Terry Long had described as a "rape/murder kit." While the jury was out, Wolf renewed his objection that all the items in the trunk of that car should not be brought in as evidence. Supposedly, these items were inventoried by Officer Wagenknecht before Dean Campbell gave him a right to do so, and that constituted an illegal search and seizure.

McDonnell responded, "We're not here to offer the guns seized from the interior of the car. We're just here to make a record."

Judge Gernant looked at what evidence he had excluded in 1994, and he noted that he had only excluded as evidence the things found in the interior of the car, which only concerned the pistol found in the interior of the car—and not the items in the car's trunk. Those items would now be heard as evidence by a jury.

Officer Terry Long next took the stand, testifying about all the things he had discovered in the trunk of the stolen car and listed them, one by one. As Long noted, these were items that he considered to be a "rape/murder" kit.

Wolf asked Long if he had a copy of Officer Wagenknecht's report, and Long said that he did. Wolf then asked, "Had that property been inventoried already?" This

was important, because if Wagenknecht had inventoried
the items, he had done so before Campbell had given
consent for a search of the vehicle. Long, however, said
that he didn't think those things had been inventoried by
Wagenknecht.

Wolf wondered if anyone else had gone through the car
before Long did, and Long answered that two rifles had
been removed prior to his being there. "I don't know if
they went through the rest of the stuff."

"Did you put in your report that you returned some
property to Mr. Shaw?" Wolf asked.

"No. But Shaw claimed everything that was there, including the rifles. I told him that some stuff had been
sent to another police agency," Long replied.

Moving on to photos the prosecution wanted to present
to the jurors, there was one of the body of Donna Ferguson, lying nude on a bed; another of her face with a gag
in her mouth; a photo of Todd Rudiger on the floor; and
one of Todd's hands tied behind his back. Wolf stated
once again, "Those photos are inflammatory and prejudicial." Knight argued, "The photos accurately depict the
crime scene. We didn't offer them during the guilt phase.
They go to Mr. Shaw's future dangerousness."

"If they were crime scene photos of this crime scene
(Jay Rickbeil), they would have relevance. But Mr. Shaw
has already been prosecuted on those other cases and
entered into a deal," Wolf declared.

Then Wolf wanted the prior bad acts of inmates with
whom Shaw had been in altercations submitted to the
jurors. "We don't think it can come in until a door is
opened," Knight responded.

Wolf replied, "We have disciplinary records of these inmates. Inmate Lachman has three prior conduct reports,
and Souza has been disciplined for twelve rules violations.
One of these was just a few months prior to getting into a
fight with Mr. Shaw. In that one, Mr. Souza assaulted

a Native American in a chow line. This is relevant. The state is introducing these altercations to show that Shaw is a threat. We have a right to show these inmates had a record of unprovoked aggression. Mr. Shaw was not the aggressor in these incidents, he was the victim."

"Then the defendant, Mr. Shaw, would have to come on the stand to talk about those fights. Mr. Wolf is just trying to say that these guys get into a lot of fights," Knight responded.

"Is Mr. Shaw claiming self-defense in these fights?" Judge Gernant asked.

"The reports are not specific as to who started the fights. We do have a video of Mr. Shaw just standing in line with a food tray when he was assaulted by Souza. Another incident with Souza was with an inmate in a security threat group. We think this is relevant to show motive for the attack on Mr. Shaw. The attacks were on a Native American and an Asian, Mr. Shaw," Wolf answered.

After these arguments Judge Gernant allowed Wolf to bring up the prior bad acts of the other inmates.

Captain Dean Harlow came on the stand and told jurors that by 2006 he had worked for the Oregon State Penitentiary for sixteen years. He had prepared a video for them to see of the Oregon State Penitentiary, and it showed the sally port, where visitors came in; and a receiving and discharge area, where all inmates were brought, strip-searched and put into restraints before being transported outside the prison walls. The jurors were shown a special management unit, which had forty-three beds, and was used for inmates with mental problems. These inmates were watched twenty-four hours a day, and they did not mix with the general population.

The main part of the prison had separate "blocks," each one holding up to 550 inmates of the general population, of which Sebastian Shaw was one. D Block housed older inmates, and A Block was the preferred area, and housed

222 inmates who had shown they could behave themselves while in prison. There was a long waiting list for this area. A Block had more privileges than the other blocks, with a televison room and library, and the inmates were allowed to stay up until midnight. There was a legal library within the complex, an education room and chapel.

C Block, in which Shaw was housed, was a little newer than the others, and had double bunks in each cell. An inmate could go to the canteen once a week for snacks, personal items, such as combs, and sodas. The dining room served three buffet-style meals a day, with its own bake shop and culinary department. There was a metal detector for inmates going to and from the metal shop area; the automotive shop and the laundry room area were also screened by guards. The laundry facility was one of the largest on the West Coast, and an inmate had to be in the penitentiary at least four years to even get on the waiting list for working in there.

The Intensive Management Area was separate from the general population and had its own laundry area, medical facility and counselors. This area was for those who had broken the rules and misbehaved. Death row housing was a part of the Intensive Management Area. The inmates there had their own recreation yard and legal computer room; everything was the same for them there except it was more secure than in general population.

The video was stopped at that point, and Knight asked Harlow what would happen in this case if Shaw got life without possibility of parole, instead of death. Harlow said that Shaw would be in the general population, where less than one hundred staff guarded 2,465 inmates. No guards carried weapons, because it was feared that inmates could overpower them and take their weapons. There were often tours of the penitentiary, consisting of attorneys, students and court-ordered tours, and each visitor was advised that there would be no hostage negotiations if they were ever taken hostage.

Knight asked about the inmate pecking order, and

Harlow answered that robbery was high on the list, while those who committed rape were down near the bottom. He also said that "lifers" often did more misconduct because they felt like they had nothing to lose. Nothing could be done by the guards about an inmate if they were "just perceived to be a threat." They had to actually break the rules *before* any actions could be taken by guards.

"There have been inmates who murder other inmates. They are in and out of their cells all day long. The supervision of the general population is limited all day. For instance, there would be one staffer in the card room, while up to two hundred inmates could be in there. Some areas, like hallways and stairways, might not have any staffers. Assaults do happen there. Tools have been taken from the industrial area, despite the metal detectors," Harlow said.

> Knight: *Have you seen weapons in the general population, not allowed in there?*
> Harlow: *Yes.*
> Knight: *What is a weapon in there?*
> Harlow: *It can be as little as a pencil or piece of metal or altered toothbrush.*
> Knight: *Where do these weapons turn up?*
> Harlow: *In all areas.*
> Knight: *Despite misconduct reports, do you still find weapons?*
> Harlow: *All the time.*
> Knight: *Does contraband cause problems in the institution?*
> Harlow: *Yes, when inmates can't pay for drugs, it causes fights.*
> Knight: *Are there assaults between inmates and staff?*
> Harlow: *Yes.*

Harlow noted that not all assaults got reported and that the last murder within an Oregon State Penitentiary happened in an activity room. As far as escape attempts went, several times a week guards confiscated maps, altered sheets, self-made grappling hooks and other escape items. During the year 2000, some inmates had started digging a tunnel from the culinary area of the penitentiary and extended it thirty feet, before getting caught.

Knight asked, "Do you do everything you can to prevent assaults and homicides in prison?"

"Yes," Harlow answered.

Knight added, "Is there a term in the pen, 'Where there's a will, there's a way'?"

"Yes."

On cross-examination Wolf got Harlow to admit that it was actually the defense who had requested the video be made at the Oregon State Penitentiary, and what the jurors hadn't seen were the numerous areas where hidden cameras were installed that monitored the various areas. His purpose was to show how secure the prison was. Wolf also got Harlow to admit that even though the guards did not carry weapons, there were eight guard towers surrounding the Oregon State Penitentiary at Salem, and all the guards there had rifles, pistols and shotguns. All of these guards were authorized to use "deadly force" if necessary.

Wolf had Harlow note that all incoming mail was searched—except for legal mail from attorneys—and even that mail envelopes were opened and shaken out in the presence of guards. Searches of inmates could come at any time, and privileges to certain areas could be taken away for misconduct. Good conduct was rewarded by the hope that one day an inmate could move into A Block. There was an education area, industrial-arts training and other activities to keep the inmates busy and out of trouble.

Specifically concerning Shaw, Wolf had Harlow testify that when Shaw first went into the penitentiary system, he was sent to an intake center and evaluated for an incarceration plan. There he had psychiatric testing, a medical evaluation and a "look at the big picture" about him. Based upon that evaluation he was sent to the penitentiary on March 14, 2000. Shaw had no fights at all until 2005, when he had been in prison for five years, and his photo had recently shown up in a Portland newspaper. Shaw was not in a gang, never found with any drugs, and had never threatened a guard. Shaw had played volleyball in the pen, trained to barber inmates' hair, and worked in the culinary department and laundry room.

Wolf brought up the two fights in 2005, and he asked if that was a high number for someone who had been in prison for five years. Harlow answered, "I'd say they were unusual for being so close together in time."

"Have you seen guys who have twenty or thirty misconducts in a year?"

"Oh, yeah."

"There are no records of Sebastian Shaw ever trying to escape?"

"No."

On redirect Knight asked, "Are you able to search inmates all the time?"

"No, it's a hit-and-miss thing."

When the jurors came back in after a break, they listened to Corporal Steven Panther describe a fight that Sebastian Shaw had been part of on July 29, 2005. Corporal Panther witnessed an altercation between inmate Clayton Lachman and Sebastian Shaw at 4:50 P.M. in the dining-room area. There were about fifty other inmates around them at the time, and both Shaw and Lachman were yelling at each other at the top of their voices. Panther was about twenty-five feet away, and he gave them orders to "cool it!" Neither inmate lowered his voice, and though

no punches had yet been thrown, Panther heard Shaw
spit on Lachman. In the prison system this was considered
an assault.

Panther got on his radio; then he put his hand on
Shaw's arm, and at that point Shaw complied. While
Panther restrained Lachman, other deputies arrived, re-
strained Shaw and led him away to DSU.

Wolf, on cross, asked Panther if he heard Lachman
start the altercation by calling Shaw a "rapo [rapist] and
a freak." Panther answered that he hadn't heard that.
Wolf next wanted to know if inmates received the *Oregonian* newspaper. Panther replied that they did. Wolf then
handed Panther a copy of the June 17, 2005, *Oregonian*,
which depicted a photo of Sebastian Shaw on the front
page, and also had an article about him. In one of the
paragraphs, it mentioned him raping two victims.

The next witness was Charles Zeigler, who also worked
as a guard at the Oregon State Penitentiary. He was working on the yard on July 29, 2005, when he got a call to
help Officer Panther in the dining room. When he entered the area, he saw Panther standing next to Shaw, and
it was Zeigler who actually cuffed Shaw and led him to
DSU. Zeigler said that all the way down the hallway, Shaw
would not stop yelling, even though he was ordered to do
so. Shaw shouted at Lachman, "I'm gonna kick your ass!
I'm gonna stab you in the neck with a pencil and kill you!"

Next it was Officer Richard Miller, who worked as a corrections officer at the Oregon State Penitentiary. He told
the jurors that on October 1, 2005, he witnessed a fight between Sebastian Shaw and Lester Souza. He didn't see the
beginning of the fight, or know why it started, but he did
give several direct orders to both inmates to stop fighting

immediately. Neither one of them obeyed his orders, and four guards eventually had to break up the fight, taking both inmates to DSU.

Since all of that altercation had been taped, McDonnell showed the jurors a videotape of the actual fight. It depicted inmates going past a beverage area, the initial altercation between Souza and Shaw, CO Miller trying to break up the fight and both inmates being led away in restraints.

On cross-examination Wolf asked Miller if Shaw was compliant after being placed in restraints, and Miller said that he was. He also asked if Shaw had a hearing on this, and Miller agreed that he had. The final report about Shaw was that Shaw was not found in violation of a disobedience order and that he had only one major rule violation in the last four years.

Russ Sperou took the stand, and for the first time jurors heard about the incident in 1996 when Shaw had shot up Sperou's room and said that he was going to kill Sperou. Sperou told of all his actions that day, and Wolf, on cross, went in another direction with Sperou. Since Sperou had been a prison inmate for many years, Wolf wanted to know how other inmates viewed someone who had been convicted of rape. Wolf's line of reasoning was to show the jurors just how tough a time Shaw was going to have in prison if they voted for life without the possibility of parole, instead of death.

Sperou admitted that many inmates hated rapists, and many of these rapists could not be housed in the general population, because they were targets for other inmates. Sperou said that rapists were called "PCs" by the other inmates, because many of them were in Protective Custody. "When they're in the compound, they're called all sorts of derogatory names. Bush jumper, rapo, things like that."

Wolf asked how other inmates found out that a person had been convicted of rape. Sperou said that in the past other inmates had access to that person's criminal record, but that was starting to change. Sperou added, "Lots of times, when someone new comes into a penitentiary, other inmates will ask for their paperwork. And also, high-profile cases will be in the newspapers they read."

Wolf questioned, "What kind of things can happen to those who have raped?"

"They are warned about it," Sperou answered.

"Assaults on them?"

"All the time."

"Is it important in prison to watch your back?"

"Absolutely!"

"Let's say you're in a dining hall where someone with rape charges came to sit down?"

Sperou said, "A certain person in a prison gang would make sure they didn't sit there. Younger inmates, trying to get credibility, will attack a rapo. Once someone went into protective custody and came back out, it would be constant beatings. Whatever it took."

"When somebody who did that (the rape) was at a workshop, would things happen in their cell?" Wolf asked.

"Oh, yeah. Somebody might urinate on their mattress or light it on fire."

"What do you expect life is like for Mr. Shaw in prison?"

An objection immediately came from the prosecution.

Perhaps knowing this was speculation, Wolf changed his question. "If an article appears in the *Oregonian* that Mr. Shaw was convicted of rape and murder with sexual assault, what might happen to him?"

"When I was in there, he would have had to go into protective custody. It would have been pretty rough on him," Sperou answered.

Wolf said, "People in prison congregate according to race. What if Mr. Shaw testified against some Asian gang members, what would happen to him?" (Wolf was probably alluding to the time Shaw fingered the gang members who had done the home invasion of the elderly Vietnamese couple when Shaw lived in their residence.)

"It would bring on anger. They wouldn't want to include him in their group."

On redirect Knight asked Sperou, "What is the status of a lifer?"

Sperou replied, "They would be pretty heavy. They would be looked up to by some people. A lot of inmates would stay clear of them and leave them alone."

The next witness was Officer Paul Kennard, who had responded to the shooting at Russ Sperou's residence in 1996. He said that Sperou was pretty shook up and still scared hours after the incident. Kennard had looked at Sperou's room and noted that "the television, AM/FM radio, cassette player and JVC audio cabinet were all shot with two different guns. I was surprised that none of the bullets came through the wall. I had no contact with Mr. Shaw that night, but later he was arrested the next morning. I found in a stolen van, in his possession, a pistol. The pistol was forwarded to the ID section for fingerprints. He said the van was his sister's, but it was a stolen van."

If the defense did not particulary want to call to the stand Detective Mike Stahlman, because of what doors might be opened, the prosecution did want him to testify. And before the jurors heard what Stahlman was going to say, the defense asked for a 104 hearing, and it was granted by Judge Gernant. Outside the presence of the jury, Stahlman told McDonnell about the items seized from Shaw's room at the Danmore Hotel when he was arrested in 1998. Among the items were stories written by Shaw, a list of people's addresses who had installation by Paragon Cable, two ski masks, Remington buckshot, a classified advertisement about how to create false identifications, a box of cartridges and a copy of a Contra Costa County police report on Shaw, concerning the Campbells' stolen vehicle. In addition to these were comic books about branding naked women with hot irons, anal intercourse with them and vaginal intercourse as well.

Mark McDonnell said of these last items, "Shaw fantasized about rape and murder. He has tied up women in the past, and it all goes to show what he thinks about and who he is. He had a book about Ted Bundy, and Bundy talks about his tactics of not being apprehended. There are photos of women with long brown hair, similar to Amanda Carpova and Donna Ferguson. There is even a story by Mr. Shaw about stalking a woman who goes into a Safeway store. This was done for his writing class."

This last part drew an objection by Richard Wolf. He said, "There is no way of knowing if that story was written by Shaw. The teacher of that class was Mr. Staley, and we contacted him. The stories in his class did not have names on them, only numbers, and then students critiqued the stories, not knowing who wrote them. Anyone could have written that story."

McDonnell retorted, "It doesn't matter who wrote that story. Mr. Shaw was in possession of it. He definitely wrote something called 'The Time Is Right.' It's about a hunter stalking someone."

The judge agreed that two stories written by Shaw would come in as evidence, but not the one about a person stalking a woman who had gone to a Safeway store. It was impossible to tell who had written it.

An important item that the prosecution definitely wanted included were excerpts from Shaw's diaries. In one section he had written, *No one knows my secrets, and to my eternal shame I will probably keep them until my grave. . . . I am a nearly consciousless time bomb. Once I wouldn't have harmed a rodent, but now I would nuke a city.*

Mike Stahlman was eventually allowed by the judge to take the stand to talk about one very specific event—the search and seizure of items at Sebastian Shaw's room after he was arrested. Neither the prosecution nor the defense wanted to get into other areas with Detective Stahlman, because it was all murky ground that could either lead to a mistrial or let a lot of new information out of the bag, as far as the defense was concerned.

After Detective Stahlman, the area of testimony went into the psychology of Sebastian Shaw and the safety issues of prisons. Chase Riveland had a degree in psychology and sociology and he had been an executive director of the Colorado Department of Corrections for four years. He had also been the warden of a prison in Wisconsin, and a warden in Washington State as well. Currently he was in private practice, teaching and working in settlement agreements with courts as a mediator. A federal judge had once appointed him as a "special master" in a mediation concerning a case in California. Riveland had been an expert witness for both the prosecution and defense in fifty cases around the nation. While a warden in Washington, he had presided over two executions.

The defense wanted to know, "How do you manage someone serving life without parole?"

Riveland answered, "Classification is a very important thing. You must have classification that you trust so you can place them where everybody is safe. The first couple of weeks in an introduction to the system is very important. It is based on past behavior and the seriousness of the crime. A review every six months is also critical, and you can move the person up or down the list. A person serving life without the possibility of parole has to be in a medium security prison or above, and mental and medical services have to be available to the inmate within the prison. An inmate's age, typically when they are younger—well, there are more problems then. They are generally safer risks as they age. The older ones tend to try and find their own space and not bother anyone or be bothered. If someone performed well in the military, they generally do well in prison. I think that anything positive we can find in the inmate's past history, we have to look at, and service in the military can be one of those."

Since the prison that Shaw was in had television and video game consoles for those who behaved themselves, Wolf asked what the point of that was. Riveland said, "When they are imprisoned, the fact they don't have those items is a great punishment in and of itself. The value of television is that when they are watching that, they aren't getting into more devious behavior. Those who aren't engaged somehow are going to get into trouble. I've seen it time and time again."

Wolf wanted to know how the security was at the Oregon State Penitentiary. "It is surrounded by nine towers, and it's probably as secure as any facility around the nation. When I was there, the mood at OSP seemed positive between the staff and inmates. Generally there was a mutual respect, and that enhances security," Riveland answered.

Wolf next wanted to know how other inmates would view a person who had committed rape. Riveland said, "Sex offenders are at the bottom of the hierarchy, especially if they raped a child. Assaults against them are high on the list."

"What happens if they don't respond to a challenge?" Wolf asked.

"In the inmate culture, if you fail to defend yourself, you will probably be challenged again. It can go from verbal taunts about weakness to taunts about ethnicity. It can also include extorting money from them for canteen items, to turning them into a sexual slave."

Riveland noted there were only thirty-three Asians in all of the Oregon State Penitentiary inmate population, so Shaw was in a definite minority. Sixty-six inmates total were doing life without parole in Oregon, 242 doing life with the possibility of parole, and 533 convicted of homicide.

Wolf wanted to know when the last homicide within prison walls had occurred, and Riveland said that had been in 2002. Wolf noted that Oregon cities with a population about equal to Oregon's prison inmate population, roughly sixteen thousand, had a higher homicide rate than within prison walls.

Wolf asked, "In Washington and Colorado, did you have inmates incarcerated with crimes similar to those of Mr. Shaw?"

Riveland answered, "Yes."

"Were you able to successfully manage them?"

"Yes."

On cross-examination Knight asked Riveland, "You've been an expert in fifty trials?"

"Yes," Riveland replied.

"You've been asked by defenses to testify in death penalty cases?"

"Yes."

"With Mr. Shaw, you reviewed his prison reports, but not the thousands of pages concerning his crimes?"

"Correct."

"You can't know what an inmate is doing at all times, correct?"

"That's correct."

"Classification is a prediction?"

"Yes. A celebrity person could be in an isolated area in an Intensive Management area. These are usually for gang leaders."

"Does Mr. Shaw fall into that category?"

"No."

Surprisingly, the defense called Amanda Carpova to the stand as one of their witnesses. Richard Wolf started out by apologizing that she had to be called back to testify. Then he asked her if she recalled being taken to the hospital after being raped and telling Detective Carter that her attacker had said he was sorry for hurting her. Amanda replied, "He wasn't saying he was sorry. In fact, he said he wasn't sorry. He didn't care about my life.

He said he had lost his faith in God and man, and in himself, and he didn't care what he did."

At that point Wolf showed her a report of what she had said to Detective Carter in June 1995. Amanda looked at what she had said, and responded, "I don't remember that part."

"Do you remember Mr. Shaw telling you, over and over, that he was sorry for what he was doing, and he hoped that he would get caught?"

"No, I don't remember that part, but it's possible," Amanda answered. "But he said a lot of different things."

"Do you remember telling the detectives that Mr. Shaw was never particularly crude or crass in a sexual way?"

"I could have said that. But he asked me to put his penis in my mouth. So I don't know what I could have been referring to."

Wolf once again showed Amanda a document of what she had said.

Amanda replied, "I don't know how to answer that. Even if he didn't call me names, he put a gun to my head."

"Before he actually raped you, he laid down beside you and spoke to you?" Wolf asked.

"It was concurrent," she replied. "It wasn't really a conversation."

"Do you remember saying that Mr. Shaw went through varying emotions very quickly?"

"Yes."

"Do you remember telling Detective Stahlman that it seemed as if his brain was trying to process things but couldn't?"

"Yes."

"Do you remember telling Detective Stahlman he would be talking normally, then become very angry and effusive, and then become very needy as if he needed a mom?"

"Yes."

"Did you try to match your conversation to match his?"

"It was kind of scary how quickly his moods changed.

So I would try to match his moods so he wouldn't become angry."

"Do you remember telling Detective Stahlman you thought Mr. Shaw had psychological problems—that maybe he was schizophrenic and had a chemical imbalance?" Wolf questioned.

"Well, I figured if he was doing what he was doing, he had to be pretty crazy or just didn't care about people."

"Do you remember telling detectives that at the time he seemed like a child?"

"Yeah, he seemed like—as though he wasn't used to people he was trying to hurt talking back to him. So it was probably confusing to him."

"Do you remember telling Detective Stahlman it seemed like there was part of him that didn't want to be bad, but there was a part of him that was evil, and he couldn't quite figure it out?"

"Yes," Amanda replied.

"And that he would continually snap back and forth between being angry, confused and needing his mother?"

"He did that until he raped me. And after he raped me, he was just mean the rest of the time."

"After the struggle you described, do you remember him standing against a wall, and he had the blindfold off you and he was holding a gun?"

"He was standing, I was kneeling—and he had the gun to my head," Amanda answered.

"Do you remember telling Detective Stahlman he was possibly sobbing or crying at that point?"

"It seemed as if he didn't know what to do, because he thought people were coming. I think he usually got to kill people, and he didn't get to do that to me. It seemed as if he didn't know what to do at this point, because it wasn't working as planned. He seemed to be confused as to what his next move should be," Amanda explained.

"And that's when you told him, 'If you don't kill me now, that will be a good thing. It will help in all the things you told me about your life and in redeeming your faith in yourself'?"

"Correct."

"You remember saying to the detectives that it seemed to really have an effect on him, and that's when he asked you to come over toward him?" Wolf questioned.

"He made me come over to put his sandals on. And he said he couldn't kill me now, because people were coming. And that if he killed me now, it would be manslaughter, but with me alive if he got caught, it would just be rape."

"Do you remember sliding over to him and wiping the hair out of his face, and asking him to give you the gun?"

"Yes, I do, and then he got mad again."

"Do you remember something specifically about his genitalia that could help you recalling who it was?" Wolf asked.

"I remember thinking it didn't look normal."

"That he had an unusually small penis?"

Amanda snickered at this. "Yes."

McDonnell, on cross, stated, "I want to put this all in context. This all happened after Sebastian Shaw came through your door with a gun, put it to your head and told you to do what he said, or he'd kill you. Correct?"

"Yes."

"He ordered you into the bedroom?"

"Yes."

"He unzipped his pants and ordered you to 'suck him off'?"

"Correct," Amanda anwered very quietly.

"You said he pressed the gun right up to the side of your neck, below your ear?"

"Yes."

"And then he put his penis in your mouth?"

"Yes."

"You started to gag, and he told you, 'You have to do this!'" McDonnell recounted.

"Yes."

"And when you tried to remove his penis from your mouth, he pushed the gun against your neck, and repeatedly threatened to kill you?"

"Yes." Amanda Carpova was becoming teary.

"And then he ordered you to lie on your bed?"

"Yes."

"And that's when he tied your nightgown around your head, so you couldn't see?"

"Yes."

"Then he lay next to you and started fondling your breasts and vagina?" McDonnell inquired.

"Yes."

"And then he penetrated you?"

"Yes," Amanda very softly replied.

"He lay on top of you and asked you to hold him?"

"Yes."

"He attempted intercourse, but he was having problems with an erection?"

"Correct."

"He was becoming increasingly angry because of this?"

"Yes."

"He put his tongue in your mouth?"

"Yes."

"When you moved your head aside, he pushed the gun against you and threatened you?" McDonnell posited.

"Yes."

"He was finally able to obtain an erection and have intercourse?"

"Yes."

"He forced your legs up over your head, and that's when he said, 'I don't care what I do. It doesn't matter whether I'm screwing up your life'?"

"Yes."

"After he raped you, you asked him if he'd ever raped anyone before?"

"Yes."

"What did he say?" McDonnell asked.

"He said no. That I was his first."

"Did he tell you a story about just getting out of jail?"

"Yes. He said he'd just gotten out of jail for robbing a convenience store, but I didn't totally buy it."

"You said his mood changed after he ejaculated?"

"Yes, he became more psycho and angry. It was very scary the rest of the time," Amanda stated.

"He ordered you into the bathroom?"

"Yes."

"Could you see?"

"No, he kept me blindfolded," Amanda answered.

"He ordered you to take a shower?"

"Yes, he wanted me to wash myself. He wanted to make sure that I had washed up all the evidence of him. And he was very angry if I wasn't doing it correctly."

"He gave you a bar of soap and said, 'Wash your crotch really good, and be quick about it!'" McDonnell recounted.

"Correct."

"Then he brought you back into your bedroom and forced you to lay on your bed."

"Yes."

"Facedown," McDonnell said.

"Yes."

"You were still wet from the shower."

"I remember being very cold," Amanda replied.

"That's when he tied your hands behind your back, and your ankles?"

"Yes."

"He attempted to gag your mouth with a T-shirt, but that didn't work?"

"Yes, so then he used a scarf."

"He left the room briefly, came back and then started poking your buttocks?"

"Yes, he said that would be good to do too. It was too bad he already tied me up," Amanda testified.

"He jumped on your back, straddled you and tried strangling you?"

"Yes."

McDonnell took her back, question by question, through all her struggles to stay alive, and then asked, "At some point you were able to get the gag out of your mouth?"

"I was able to make noise, and then he put the gun up against my head. We thought we had heard people. He told me if I screamed, he would kill me. I told him that he was already killing me."

Amanda said there was more struggling as he tried strangling her again, and finally he seemed to become worn-out. "It seemed to me that he wasn't used to fighting so hard. He was breathing heavily and sweating. He backed up against a wall and sat down."

Amanda also said that during the attack she never cried, because she didn't want him to see her cry. She added, "I tried to match his moods and acted as I saw fit at the time. When I didn't act appropriately, he reminded me that he would kill me."

McDonnell asked, "You always tried to act strong and not show any weakness?"

"Yes."

"Have you been diagnosed with post-traumatic stress disorder?" (This is often termed PTSD.)

"Yes. I've been seeing a therapist off and on for eleven years."

After Amanda Carpova's dramatic testimony, Ken Kashiwahara, who had been an ABC newsman in South Vietnam during its final days, was called to the stand as a defense witness. And his story was just as dramatic in its own way, with a country in turmoil and the panicked flight of the refugees, including one man whose attempt to give his baby to someone on the press bus ended in tragedy. Wolf asked how the experience was for Kashiwahara, a veteran newscaster. "For me, this was one of the most terrifying experiences I have ever been through," he answered.

* * *

McDonnell, on cross, asked Kashiwahara, "Have you ever met Mr. Shaw before today?"

"No," he answered.

"Do you have any personal knowledge about the case before this court?"

"I know a little bit, but not much."

"Did ABC help some of its Vietnamese employees escape Saigon?"

"We did."

"Did you keep in contact with other Vietnamese who came to the United States?"

"Not really—though I did stories on Vietnamese refugees."

"Would you say that the Vietnamese that you knew assimilated into our culture fairly well?"

"Most of them did pretty well, though some of them had difficulty."

"Do you know any of them who were ABC employees who had trouble with the criminal justice system?"

"No."

"You have a scholarship for minority applicants for journalism. Any of them Vietnamese?"

"Yes. The very first one was Vietnamese. And he coincidentally was born on April 29, 1975, on Guam as I was leaving Saigon."

The defense's next witness was Dael Morris, an entomologist from Ontario, Canada. She had been a witness at various previous trials over the years for the prosecution and defense concerning insects and their importance to a crime scene. In some cases she'd worked on maggots that had been found on abandoned bodies, and by that means she could get an idea of how long the person had been dead. Her reason for being called for the defense was that she was an expert on fire ants.

Wolf wanted to know if the bites by fire ants could cause serious problems, especially to children. Morris said yes, that did happen, and narcosis could spread to large areas of a person's body, even leading to gangrene, which would cause the loss of a limb. Wolf wanted to know if the ant bite toxins could cause a bad fever. Morris replied, "Yes, there can be systemic reactions or toxic reactions. These can lead to serious neurological effects."

Morris explained that fire ant bites could be very painful, and when one ant was disturbed, many more would come to its aid. There could be tens of thousands of them in a small area. Fire ants had stingers at the tip of their abdomens, and they could also inflict bites with their mandibles. They could sting a person many times, and unlike a honey bee, they did not die after they stung someone. The mandibles would puncture a person's skin and secrete toxins into the wound, while a stinger sprayed a chemical into the wound. All of these chemicals were skin irritants, and they could kill cells where the bites occurred.

McDonnell, on cross, asked, "Where do you live?"

Morris answered that her residence was Ontario, Canada.

"You've come a long way?"

"By modern standards it didn't take that long."

"Do they have entomologists in Oregon?" McDonnell asked.

"You probably know that better than I do," she replied.

"You don't have any personal knowledge that Mr. Shaw was bitten by fire ants, do you?"

"I wasn't there thirty years ago, when he was bitten, no."

"You never examined Shaw for any ant bite marks?"

"No, I haven't," Morris answered.

"You haven't reviewed any medical records on him?"

"There apparently aren't any."

"Isn't it true that the vast majority of people recover from ant bites in a few days?"

"In the literature I've read, if a healthy person is treated, they will recover in about three weeks."

"Only a medical doctor can determine if somebody has suffered long-term effects from ant bites, correct?"

"Yes, it would take a medical doctor to draw a conclusion like that."

"And you're not a medical doctor?"

"No, I am not," Morris confirmed.

Steve McNamara had been ordered by the court in 1996 to run psychological tests on Sebastian Shaw after the incident where he shot up Russ Sperou's room. McNamara testified that Shaw at one point had admitted to a suicide attempt when he was young, and spoke about the abuse from his father. Shaw also spoke about being sexually abused when he was in the third grade by some of his father's friends. McNamara believed Shaw and said, "The norm is that a lot of people lie to me, but I believed Sebastian Shaw. I only note honesty when I think it is correct, and it can be unusual." McDonnell, on cross, asked McNamara if he compared his report to that of Dr. Leung's, and McNamara said no, he didn't have a copy of that.

The next witness, Dr. Leung, testified that when he saw Sebastian Shaw for counseling, Shaw was "having PTSD, loneliness and bottled-up rage." Wolf wanted to know what Dr. Leung's conclusion was after seeing Shaw many times in therapy. Leung said, "It was my opinion that Mr. Sebastian Shaw would need immediate mainstream psychiatric attention in order to deal with his depression and PTSD, specifically addressing the raging issues and hypervigilance. If the conditions were left untreated, the risk of seeing Mr. Shaw get into similar conflicts in the future was quite high, and the outcome might not be as fortunate the next time."

"How does the fact that Mr. Shaw did not share with

you that he had murdered Donna Ferguson and Todd Rudiger, and raped and attempted to murder Amanda Carpova, affect your analysis?" Wolf asked.

"The fact that he did not tell me would not have changed my conclusion about his depression and PTSD. However, it may have affected my conclusion about his personality," Dr. Leung said.

Wolf wondered, "How does one prevent someone like Mr. Shaw from doing something like that again?"

Dr. Leung responded, "There is no way to make certain that someone would not do something in the future. You can only try with treatment. Deal with the depression. Deal with the PTSD. Give him medications and bring down the anxiety. Bring down the nightmares and bring down the rage. All the losses he experienced need to be explored by therapy. The essence is to help the patient to accept all those tragedies that happened to him. I would recommend multiple medications for him. Prison is a safe place to protect him from himself and others. Because of the controlled environment and the inability to obtain alcohol, he should do quite well in prison."

McDonnell, on cross, asked Dr. Leung if he considered himself primarily a psychiatrist, and Leung answered no. McDonnell said, "Clients will lie or embellish things about themselves to help themselves, correct?"

Dr. Leung said that was so.

"They will sometimes omit important information?" McDonnell probed.

"Yes."

"Mr. Shaw told you he would have killed his roommate (Russ Sperou) if he found him?"

"That was my impression," Dr. Leung answered.

"There is a quote from Mr. Shaw in a police report— '*I'm a live-and-let-live kind of guy. But sometimes when people push me, I push back. I have a bad temper.*'"

Dr. Leung agreed that Shaw did have rage issues.

"Did Mr. Shaw ever tell you he had ever been bitten by ants?"

"No, we never touched on that."

"Did he complain of any nightmares from being evacuated from Saigon?"

"No."

"And he did not report to you that he had been sexually abused as a child?"

"No, he did not report that to me."

McDonnell asked, "Wouldn't you agree that many Americans suffer from PTSD?"

"Yes, tens of thousands."

"The vast majority function very well?"

"Ninety-nine percent do," Dr. Leung replied.

"A very small minority of those commit homicides?"

"Yes, sir."

McDonnell got into the aspect of some of Shaw's journals, especially one where he had written, *Damn the creature I have become, for it is a dark beast, just waiting for some unwitting fool to come and release it.*

The words needed no comment by the doctor, and he remained mute.

"Ten years ago you indicated that Mr. Shaw was a high risk?" McDonnell asked.

"Yes, sir."

"Now that you know about the three murders he's committed, wouldn't you agree he's a much greater risk today than what you believed in 1997?"

"Absolutely."

After the jury was gone for the day, Wolf said that they wanted Sebastian Shaw to speak directly to the jurors after both closing arguments had been done. Judge Gernant wondered why they wanted things done that way, and Falls chimed in that it was the way he'd seen things done before. Falls stated that in Oregon the defendant's allocution could be listened to by jurors, but it was not considered as evidence. And once again the defense brought up that Shaw might want to waive his right to any appeal of the penalty, if the jury would vote for life without parole instead of death.

Judge Gernant declared, "Whoa, wait a second! This is something that [the] state has a right to negotiate with you, not me! I don't, and the jury doesn't. If Mr. Shaw gets up there and says he wants to waive his rights to appeals by not getting the death penalty, it has no legal effect. The jury can't grant that, and neither can I!"

Ethan Knight chimed in, saying, "It's not a bargain!"

"It's not a bargain the judge can engage in. The jurors can!" Wolf countered.

Judge Gernant responded, "I'm not going to take that risk if an appellate court down the road says you were wrong, I was wrong and you were incompetent. It's not gonna happen."

When the jurors came back in, they listened to Shaw's various family members talk about him. Shaw's aunt Anna Ho spoke of his early life in Vietnam, his relocation to the United States and verbal and physical abuse by his father. She was very emotional and cried throughout most of her testimony. When Wolf asked Anna how she would feel if Shaw was put to death, she bowed her head and pressed her hands together. Then she said, "I know you have to follow the law," and started crying uncontrollably. Excused from the stand by Judge Gernant, Anna couldn't move and started wailing without respite. Wolf and Falls came forward to help her from the stand. Anna turned toward the jurors and cried out, "Please show kindness to my nephew! Please! Please! If I can take his place and die, I will!"

Wolf and Falls helped her past the jury box. Anna, however, was not through asking for mercy. She dropped to her knees and begged the jurors to be lenient. Shaw was visibly upset by his aunt's demonstration. He turned away and put his head in his hands.

Ly Do also spoke well of Shaw's early years, and asked the jurors for mercy. On cross-examination she admitted to McDonnell that Shaw had done well in school, thus proving he had enough of an IQ to understand what he was doing when he committed his crimes.

McDonnell also got into the issue of her children not wanting to be around Shaw when he got out of the Marine Corps and moved next door to her in Portland. McDonnell asked, "Isn't it true that Khanh Lee and Lan Do didn't want to be alone with Mr. Shaw?"

"No, it's not that they did not want to be around him. I had seen in newspapers and on TV that when a father does bad things to a child, bad things can happen. So I was very careful about my daughters. It was not that I didn't trust him but that I wanted to be cautious," Ly Do replied.

"When Mr. Shaw got out of the marines, he came to live with you, correct?"

"Yes, for a very short time, and I was living in government housing. So he could not stay there for long."

"Didn't Khanh move out when she found out that Mr. Shaw was moving in with you?"

"Yes, but she moved out before he came."

"Didn't she move out because she knew he was coming?"

"Yes, she said she didn't want to be there when he came."

"And the reason she didn't want to be there was because she told you he had touched her inappropriately when she was little?"

"She did not say she was touched that way."

"Isn't it true that when Shaw moved next door, you changed the locks on your doors?"

"Yes."

* * *

Thuha also spoke up for Shaw and told of how loving he had been. Wolf asked her how she felt when she heard about the things that Shaw had done. She replied, "In my heart, and in my soul, I don't understand why he did what he did. Not even from day one to today, when I know all the facts about what happened. Not one time had I seen even one percent of him being evil. You know how sometimes you live with a kid, and they have a bad temper and are very upset all the time? Not once did he act that way to me. None, none, none. Not only with me, but with my kids and with my mom. He was always respectful and never back talked. He never showed an attitude or raised his voice."

Wolf wanted to know how it would affect her if Sebastian Shaw was executed. Thuha replied, "My kids love their uncle. He never did anything bad against them. I lost a brother. I have a bad arm, and sometimes it's numb, so I can't feel it. But I still want it. It is part of my body. I feel that to lose Chau would be like having my arm cut off."

Thuha Tran showed photos of her and her kids at Christmas 2002, a photo they sent to Shaw while he was in prison. She said, "My children and others loved him. He took them places and was very good with them. He was very patient. They had fun with him."

"You know what he's been convicted of. Does it surprise you?" Wolf asked.

She cried, and said, "Yes, it does surprise me. It doesn't seem like the cousin that I know. I never thought he could do anything so horrible. When he was with us, he was so caring. He was totally a different person."

"How would it affect you and your children if Sebastian was executed?" Wolf asked.

"My children don't know anything about that happening. They keep asking when they are going to see their uncle. It would affect me . . ." (Then she cried so much she couldn't say the words in English, so she spoke in Vietnamese and had to be interpreted.) "The things that he did, nobody could believe them. It would be a terrible loss to the family."

Perhaps one of the most powerful witnesses for Sebastian Shaw was someone who was already deceased—his sixth-grade teacher, Suzanne Garman. It was through her widower, Dennis Kuklok, that Suzanne's words were spoken on the stand. Kuklok was very emotional about Suzanne, since she had recently died from cancer, and Kuklok said that he had only met Shaw (whom he called Chau, as Suzanne had) two months previously, but he had heard Suzanne talk about him for years. She called Shaw a special person in her life. "He meant a lot to her," Kuklok said, "and she saved all his letters. When she passed away, I found a box of letters and photos of Chau. She did not do that for her other students. She had schoolwork from Chau and photos of him. I think she even became closer to him when he went to jail. She knew about his arrest and crimes but continued her relationship with Chau, anyway. She felt that he was all alone and needed her help.

"Suzanne wanted me to come and visit Chau in prison, but I had difficulty doing that. I didn't really understand the details of the case, and in some ways I didn't want to. I supported her in every way I could, but I was looking for remorse on Chau's part, and I did not see that. I felt like I could not visit him.

"But Suzanne taught me many things in our life together, and one thing she really taught me was compassion. When you lose somebody, well, I wish I could have supported her more strongly on this. One of Suzanne's favorite sayings was from Corinthians, which begins, *Love is always patient, love is always kind*. She had this translated into Vietnamese, made a watercolor around the saying and sent it to Chau."

Photos of Shaw and Suzanne Garman were presented to the jury. There was a photo of her with him on Mount

Hood, and one of her visiting him in prison. Kuklok told the jurors, "Suzanne was diagnosed with ovarian cancer in April 2001. She had three rounds of chemo and also alternative treatments. She even went to Sweden for a hypothermia treatment, but she died on November 5, 2005.

"Chau sent something from prison to be read at her funeral. A friend of Suzanne's read it, named Priscilla. Some of her friends understood Suzanne's relationship with Chau, and others did not. Her best friend, Dolores, who worked at the same school with Suzanne—when Suzanne visited Chau and worked with the defense team, Dolores would not speak to Suzanne for a year. Suzanne didn't see that she had any other choice. Chau was part of her family. She never had children, and her students were her kids. Some of them were special to her, and Chau was one of them. Suzanne had grown up in a strong family, and you just don't abandon your family in a time of need.

"Even after Sweden, Suzanne kept in contact with friends, and it was clear by then that she would die. We started hospice treatment, with no medical intervention. We were back in October 2005, and there was a five-week period where she was saying good-bye. She worried that Chau would be abandoned. She had no way of contacting Chau in person then. So I wrote a letter to Chau in prison."

On October 18, 2005, Shaw (Chau) was allowed to phone Suzanne Garman at her hospice facility. The defense team played the emotional audiotape of that phone call to the jurors.

Shaw:	*Suzanne!*
Garman:	(In a very weak voice) *How are you, Chau?*
Shaw:	*Hi! How are you? I guess that's a stupid question. Oh, my God! Did you get my letter yet?*
Garman:	*The one you sent a couple of weeks ago?*
Shaw:	*No, the one I sent you yesterday.*

Garman: *Oh, that's too soon.*

Shaw: *I know, I know. Oh, Lord! Dennis (Kuklok) sent me twelve pages of your notes from your trip to Europe. Oh, God! I was expecting good news. The last time I saw you, you were doing so well. And now you've gone down so fast. They said you were dehydrated and malnourished. And basically . . .* (His voice cracked, and he didn't finish the sentence.) *God, I'm so frantic! I put myself in here, and I won't be able to see you before you go. But I got on the honor system and was able to make you a phone call.*

Garman: *On the honor system?*

Shaw: *Oh, man, you sound so weak. I just wanted to speak with you one last time. It's just a medical reality when you are so malnourished. Oh, my God, Dennis said you don't even cry, you're so malnourished.*

Garman: (Very weak) *Mostly, I'm hungry.*

Shaw: *Yeah, yeah. I know you were throwing up all your food. I just want you to know that I miss you and love you a lot!*

(By this point, other inmates in the background were yelling, hooting, cursing and taunting Shaw. The conversation after this point between Shaw and Suzanne Garman was very hard to hear, because of all the noise by other inmates.)

Shaw: *You'll get your Christmas money in December.*

Garman: *No, no, don't worry about that. Don't even send it. It's not important, okay.*

Shaw: *I'm very sorry about my last letter to you. It was very selfish and—*

Garman: *No, no. I love you.*

Shaw: *Oh, God!* (He chokes up with tears.) *I don't know what to say.*

Garman: There will be a celebration for my life. I love you.
Shaw: I need to hang up. There's so much noise in here.

After that audio was played, you could hear a pin drop in the courtroom.

On cross-examination Knight said to Kuklok, "It's clear to all of us that your wife was a tremendously compassionate woman. She cared very deeply for Mr. Shaw, didn't she?"

"Yes, she did," Kuklok answered.

"And considered him to be a part of her family?"

"Yes."

"She did everything she could to make a difference in his life?"

"Yes."

"Did you know that when Mr. Shaw posed for his picture with her in 1997, he had already killed three people?"

"Yes."

"In 1997, did he tell you that he had killed three people?"

"No. I wasn't there."

The defense had one more witness, Dr. William Sacks, who was a director of child psychology, and who studied the plights of Southeast Asian refugees, especially children, and how they adapted to their new lives in the United States. He particularly studied the plights of children from Cambodia and South Vietnam, who had escaped war-torn countries. Sacks had read many documents on Sebastian Shaw—Shaw's work records and military records, his 1996 psych reports, Department of Corrections records and records on his father, Van Ho.

Of refugees in general, Dr. Sacks said, "It's important as to when you become a refugee, at what age. You face a whole host of stressors, including new foods, different weather, different attitudes toward people, and you usually end up at the lower socioeconomic rung on the ladder. It takes a lot of energy and effort to reintegrate into a society with different values. The kids we studied from Cambodia talked a lot about those stressors, particularly in their first year of readjustment. As we followed them over time, most of them were successful integrating into our culture.

"The kids we saw all had the first six or seven years of normal life before Pol Pot struck, killed their families and put them in concentration camps. So they had enjoyed six or seven years of normality in child development. Those kids did very well overall."

Wolf asked why the early years were so important to a person's development. Sacks answered, "During those first years a child learns to trust people. It gives a sense of hope and optimism about the future." Wolf wondered if there were things that Dr. Sacks had read that indicated problems for Sebastian Shaw in his early development. Dr. Sacks replied, "Yes, and I've been an expert witness in three capital cases on refugees who have murdered. Those cases were different than people who just ended up becoming antisocial. And all of them had something very bad happen to them in the first two years of their lives. There was trauma. There was loss. They got off to a bad start. They were abandoned by parents because of the war. They never learned a sense of trust and sense of who they were. That set the stage for the second stage, which was that they never did well in resettlement and adapting to our culture. They didn't seem to know how to do that. When I looked over the records of Mr. Shaw, I found that he seemed to qualify for those things. He lost his mother when he was an infant, and was taken care of by a paternal aunt. He had the experience of being bitten by red ants before he could even walk.

"As Shaw looked back on those things, his sense of being an outsider seemed to develop. His aunt and cousins tried to take good care of him, but the injuries to his legs and the scars and the pain all made it hard for him to feel nurtured. When he came to this country, he lived for a while with his father, and that was part of the stress. He saw his father abuse women, and a lot of domestic violence. When he moved to Oregon, he was regularly beaten by his father with belts and boards. He was left out in the cold when his father went to work or out drinking. He went to a neighbor Vietnamese woman who took him in.

"On the surface he seemed to be reasonably happy, and he did reasonably well in school. The coup de grace came when his dad threw him out of the house at the age of seventeen because he refused to go to work at midnight to help his dad with his janitorial job."

Wolf asked if any of those traumas could have an effect on someone in their adult years. Sacks replied, "Any one of those can. When you have a progression of them, they can become more than the sum of their parts. A combination of an early loss and poor family relationships—they tend to snowball."

Wolf asked if Dr. Sacks thought that Sebastian Shaw was someone who could be controlled in prison with medication and therapy. Dr. Sacks answered, "Yes."

On cross-examination Knight asked, "You've never spoken to Mr. Shaw, correct?"

"Correct," Sacks answered.

"You've never evaluated him?"

"Correct."

"Have you looked at all the reports or just excerpts?"

"I mainly looked at the Amanda Carpova case."

"When was the last time you looked at the Jay Rickbeil case?"

"[For about] forty-five minutes this morning."

"Where in any report does it state that Shaw was sexually abused?"

"It was from a 1996 report."

"And out of thousands of pages of reports, that's the only instance of sexual abuse?"

"Yes."

"And that was a self-report by Mr. Shaw?"

"Yes."

Knight asked if Pol Pot's regime in Cambodia was one of the most murderous in the history of mankind. Dr. Sacks agreed that it was, and that out of a population of around 7 million, between 1 and 2 million people had been murdered. There was state-sanctioned murder of monks, civil servants, landowners and anyone with Western learning. They turned children into informants on their parents and caused mass starvation.

Knight had Dr. Sacks agree that most of the fighting in Vietnam was in the rural areas—Saigon only experienced it in 1968 and in 1975—and Shaw had lived in a suburb of Saigon. Knight asked, "The refugees from Saigon, they didn't suffer nearly the amount of trauma as the refugees from Cambodia?"

Sacks replied that was true. He also agreed that Shaw had done well in grade school, and that lots of people in America suffered from PTSD, but they did not turn into killers.

"It would be a very tiny group who committed homicide?" Knight asked.

"Yes."

"It would be an even smaller group that committed multiple homicides?"

"Yes."

"If Mr. Shaw was suffering from PTSD, would that justify the murder of Jay Rickbeil?"

"No."

"Is there anything in the material you read that shows that Mr. Shaw does not know right from wrong?"

"No."

* * *

The defense had called the last of their witnesses, and the jury was excused, as the defense and prosecutors hammered out the thorny problem of just how Sebastian Shaw was going to speak to the jurors. A defendant was required by law to write out what he was going to say, but during a review of the text, Judge Gernant would have to be very careful about what he edited out of the manuscript. "The scary part is, no matter how well we've done in this case up to this point, the supreme court is not adverse to reversing the decision if an error is made at this point. The less said about it (the written statement by Shaw), the better," Gernant said.

Wolf spoke up and said that he wanted the jurors to "give Mr. Shaw's allocution as much weight as they wish." The prosecution didn't have any argument with that statement. The curveball in all of this was that Sebastian Shaw might say to the jurors that in exchange for not giving him the death penalty, he would waive all his rights to appeal the penalty phase of the trial. Wolf added, "He can say to the jury, 'I'm not going to get in the way of that.'" (In other words, no appeals.)

Judge Gernant heaved a big sigh and said, "I guess the jury is just going to have to make of that what they can. I still think it is of no legal value. I don't have the right to limit his sentence on rights of appeal, and I don't think anybody does—except him negotiating with the state."

"I would not object to the defendant saying he would waive his rights to an appeal. But I just don't think it's binding," McDonnell replied.

Judge Gernant responded, "I guess if he does bring it up with the jury, it goes to a trait of character."

McDonnell quickly replied, "I disagree with that. It's a promise to do something in the future, it's not something he's doing now. It's not like *Rogers* versus *State,* where a judge imposed a sentence. Here a jury is imposing sentence."

Judge Gernant asked, "So what happens if I agree

with you that he accepts this waiver with knowledge and intelligence?"

"Well, then the victims' families will know he will go to prison for life and not start an appeals process to overturn sentencing down the road. The case is final. It's done and over. And there will be no additional cost," Wolf replied.

McDonnell responded, "It's improper to say you're saving money. That can't come in."

"It makes a difference if he sucks it up and agrees to do life without parole. No more examinations," Wolf said, however.

"But he's doing it, anyway, right now—two life sentences," Judge Gernant replied.

Wolf: *But without this waiver he could appeal this conviction and the sentence and cause us to come back five years from now and have all these people brought back in here, traumatized because of that appeal. This is an indication of . . .*

Gernant: *Well, what would you say if the state argued that if the death sentence was imposed, Mr. Shaw would be taken out of the general population, and essentially be in solitary confinement while he made his appeals?*

Wolf: *I see that as apples and oranges. What we're offering shows an aspect of character, which is relevant to the questions jurors may consider.*

Gernant: *But you want them to know the impact of a life sentence. Why should they not know what the impact of a death sentence should be?*

Wolf: *I don't see how one argument leads to another.*

Gernant: *Just as a matter of fairness is all I'm suggesting.*

McDonnell: *The jury is going to believe the waiver is*
            binding, but I just don't know that it is.
Gernant: (To Wolf) *You want the court to become*
            involved in this, and I don't think that is
            correct. So I'll allow Mr. Shaw to put on
            paper what he wants to say. It's not part of
            your closing, and then let him speak his
            allocution.

That finally accomplished, the defense and prosecution now battled who, if anybody, was going to be able to
review what Shaw wrote before he spoke to the jurors
during allocution. Wolf said it was up to the court to read
what was written, but not the prosecution. Judge Gernant
responded he couldn't imagine reading it without comment from the prosecution. Wolf went back to *Rogers* v.
State, which spoke of the prosecution never reviewing a
written statement of allocution by the defendant. Mc-
Donnell jumped in and said that he was worried that Mr.
Shaw was going to say that he had objected to his relatives
being brought in to speak on his behalf in court. It made
Shaw look saintly for trying to exclude his relatives.

Wolf responded, "Yes, but that's true. It's important to
him. Back in 2004, there was a motion to relieve me as
counsel by Mr. Shaw. We were at loggerheads over this
issue. As his lawyer, it was up to me to make sure the jury
had all the relevant evidence concerning his life. I told
him he had a right to allocute during the penalty phase,
but which witnesses were to be called fell to me as his
lawyer. He indicated in the light of that he did not wish
to retain me as his lawyer. You (McDonnell) asked him
on that day if he wanted to speak to the jurors. And he
said, 'Well, what I've done with my crappy decisions—
evil, malicious things I did on my own—I feel that my
family have no place in it. They are decent, law-abiding
people, and they have kids and stuff, and jobs to go to,
and bills to pay. They really don't know anything of what

I did. I was just doing what I did all on my own. In the day of media coverage, I don't feel I want to subject my relatives to that.'

"You (Judge Gernant) asked Mr. Shaw, 'Do you have any concerns about Mr. Wolf's ability during the penalty phase?' And he answered, 'I have some concerns about witnesses and stuff.' And you (Judge Gernant) said, 'Okay, I'm not going to remove your attorney at this time.'"

"Well, I think it reflects his character back then, because he didn't want to bring his relatives in to say what they said," Judge Gernant replied.

Falls joined in at that point and stated, "From what I've read, Mr. Shaw would submit his written statement to us first, and if we find anything that would draw objections, we'd have him rewrite those parts. This can be a kind of catharsis. Kind of the opposite of what I'll do in closing."

"I will not comment on that," Judge Gernant quipped.

There was so much work to be done on getting the jury instructions lettered, just so, that the defense and prosecution came to court over the weekend. Very small words such as "either" and "or" were debated, assessed and decided upon. At least there was one moment of levity in the proceedings when Richard Wolf said, "I wonder if the prosecutor will be so kind as to share the photo projector?" McDonnell shot back, "As long as you thank me in front of the jury." Wolf laughed and promised that he would do so.

Wolf said at one point, when only the defense and judge were looking over Shaw's allocution statement, "If Amanda Carpova is in the gallery, Mr. Shaw intends to turn toward her and say, 'I apologize to you.' If she is not in the gallery, he will say, 'I apologize to her.'"

Then Judge Gernant spoke up and said, "What about this statement? It says, 'As to Todd Rudiger's mother, thank you for your forgiveness. I'll try to be worthy of it.' When was that said?"

"I think Mr. Shaw garnered that from reading an article about Todd's mother," Wolf replied.

Sebastian Shaw, who was listening to the conversation, spoke up from the defense table and said, "Your Honor, at the time of the trial (the 2000 plea agreement), I apologized to the family, to Todd Rudiger's mom. She said, 'I accept your apology.' I know that was, in effect, to get on with her life and not hold bitterness. I can only be thankful for her."

After that was said, Judge Gernant read more of Shaw's allocuting statement and said, "Here is the only line I have a question about—*I thought I heard you express forgiveness and I will try to be worthy of that.*' It's Mr. Shaw's perception. But you should alert Mr. McDonnell to that, so he doesn't come unglued. He should listen to the audio disc to make sure that is on there."

Falls said, "He wasn't there. It was a different prosecutor then."

Judge Gernant then responded, "Well, then it is what Mr. Shaw thought he perceived."

19

Decision

On May 1, 2006, closing arguments were ready to begin. Before that occurred, Judge Gernant spoke to a photographer for the *Oregonian* in the gallery and said it would be all right to photograph the proceedings but not to take any photos of Sebastian Shaw's restraints. Judge Gernant also asked the prosecution whether they intended to use the words "serial killer" in relation to Shaw in their closing arguments, since the defense objected to those words. McDonnell replied, "No, but I think he meets the definition of a serial killer."

Then Wolf asked whether jurors could come up and speak to the defense, the prosecution or judge, after rendering their decision. Judge Gernant responded, "I think that raises a substantial risk of creating multiple issues. I don't think we should do that."

"These cases are often extremely emotional for jurors," Wolf replied.

"Well, I don't know what kind of money we have for counseling, but as for them talking to me or the attorneys, I think that is risky," Gernant responded.

Wolf persisted, however, saying, "In my experience it's often helpful for jurors to talk afterward."

"Has your experience ever included a capital murder case?" Judge Gernant asked.

"Not in my case. But in a different one here in the court, jurors met with the judge, defense and prosecution afterward, and a couple of jurors went out to dinner with counsel."

"Was the death sentence imposed?" Gernant wondered. Wolf replied, "No."

"That makes it a different category. Do you know of one that occurred after a death sentence was imposed?"

"In a case I did in Clackamas County, the judge instructed jurors that they could talk to the judge and attorneys after their decision," Falls chimed in.

Judge Gernant replied, "I'm not going to set up anything formal for jurors to talk to attorneys afterward."

"While I would love to hear from the jurors afterward, my cynicism is that people would interrogate the jurors to find misconduct," McDonnell observed.

The jurors were brought in at 9:10 A.M., and Judge Gernant told them not to turn the pages forward on their instructions, especially the last page. The reason for this was that on the last page was an explanation about how they were to view Sebastian Shaw's allocution, and they didn't know he was going to speak to them at that point. Mark McDonnell finally began his closing argument at 9:24 A.M. He started out by saying that in the guilt phase they learned that Sebastian Shaw was a cold-blooded killer. McDonnell declared, "He killed for the sheer pleasure of it." Then he added that Shaw had kept a diary over a fifteen-year period, and on one date he'd written: *I've been thinking about murder lately.* McDonnell said that Shaw went on to write about the rape and murder of victims.

McDonnell told the jurors that they needed to make the appropriate decision about Shaw, and that decision should be death. If they chose death, Shaw would be isolated from the rest of the general population at the Oregon State Penitentiary, where he could not attack them. If they chose life without parole—he was already serving that for the murders of Donna Ferguson and Todd Rudiger—McDonnell declared, "It will be as if the Jay Rickbeil murder trial never happened."

Then McDonnell went down the questions about the sentencing phase, and asked what was Shaw's state of mind before killing Jay Rickbeil. He answered that question by saying that from Shaw's diary they knew that he had murder on his mind. McDonnell added that from the other murders, and attempted murder of Amanda Carpova, they knew how Shaw operated—with the intent to break into someone's residence to commit crimes and murder. Amanda Carpova was to have been one of his murder victims, but by luck—and her desperate fight for life—she survived. Even Jay Rickbeil had struggled desperately to save his life, even though he was wheelchair bound. Rickbeil actually grabbed the knife blade, trying to keep it from his chest area.

McDonnell said that Shaw wrote about going to a university and killing people, and that he kept a "murder kit" in a car he had stolen. McDonnell showed the jurors photos of that murder kit, one by one: *The Anarchist Cookbook*, duct tape, rope, surgical gloves and a book on anatomy that showed where mortal wounds could be inflicted, along with all the rest of the items.

In another part of his journal, Shaw had written on December 26, 1994: *What causes me to have such strange heros? [sic] They are all killers in one form or another. For these anti-heros [sic], so full of self-loathing that death becomes nothing. The true reality to them is like dirt under a fingernail.*

McDonnell said that Shaw was obsessed with rape. On February 24, 1990, he wrote about trying to stay up until 3:00 A.M. to watch a movie that *had a great rape scene in it.* Then he added, *This is a very weird subject with me. It turns me on as much as voyeurism.*

In June 1990, Shaw wrote about being over a friend's house in Mt. Angel, where the friend had three beautiful daughters. *It was all I could do to keep myself from raping all three of them,* he wrote.

McDonnell told of the pornography found in the car Shaw had stolen, and in his room at the Danmore Hotel: comic books about tying up women, forcing them to do oral sex; then they were chained and bent over for anal sex. There were also tales of women forced to endure torture and branding. McDonnell said, "It is despicable material, and in the hands of Sebastian Shaw, it is frightening. Unfortunately, for Donna Ferguson and Amanda Carpova, he acted out his fantasies."

There came the question of whether Jay Rickbeil had done anything to contribute to his own death. McDonnell challenged any one of them to come up with a reason why a wheelchair-bound man in his own apartment would somehow be responsible for his own murder. McDonnell said that the question to them was not if bad things had happened to Shaw in his early life, but whether he was responsible for Jay Rickbeil's murder on July 2, 1991. There were even notes to Shaw's own character, written by him in a journal. On September 6, 1994, he had written, *I don't know when disillusionment set in, but boy when it did, did it ever. I have in my mind a searchlight. But I can't see it anymore on my horizon. I lost allegiance to my God.*

McDonnell told the jurors that Shaw had no empathy for his victims, and no regrets. He had told Amanda Carpova while raping her, "I don't care what this does to you. I don't care if it screws up your life." McDonnell emphasized one of Shaw's journal entries from November 12, 1995, after he had already killed Jay Rickbeil, Donna Ferguson and Todd Rudiger. Shaw wrote, *I have no regrets.*

McDonnell also said that Sebastian Shaw was manipulative and a liar. He sobbed while talking to Dr. Leung about feeling bad because he had interpreted things incorrectly for his stepmom, and she ended up having to pay back the government on fraud charges. But his stepmom didn't remember this incident at all. As far as nightmares went, Shaw had even told Dr. Leung, "I'm not losing sleep." Shaw had said that to Leung after he had already killed Todd Rudiger, Donna Ferguson and Jay Rickbeil. And in another journal entry he wrote, *I have no real nightmares. When you are a monster, what dreams are capable of scaring you?*

McDonnell said that ABC newsman Ken Kashiwahara was a great storyteller, and he had obviously gone through a horrendous experience in the last days of South Vietnam. McDonnell even admitted that it had to have been traumatic for young Sebastian Shaw to be helicoptered off the roof of the American Embassy in Saigon. But nowhere in his visits to Dr. Leung, in 1996 and 1997, had Shaw mentioned any problems stemming from his childhood on that account. In fact, McDonnell quoted Shaw once again from Shaw's own journal: *"My troubles are my own fault."* And McDonnell said that PTSD did not excuse the murder of Jay Rickbeil. There were refugees from Cambodia, who as children lost both their parents to genocide, but they did not become murderers.

McDonnell spoke about Shaw's relatives, and agreed that their love for him and grief was real. McDonnell said, however, that only showed that Sebastian Shaw had people around him who loved him, and how did he repay them? With shame. "Sebastian Shaw's relatives did not kill Jay Rickbeil. Sebastian Shaw did!" McDonnell said that Shaw's relatives couldn't believe the boy they knew could have done such terrible things. But they hadn't seen a photo of Jay Rickbeil as he lay halfway out of his wheelchair, with his throat slashed so badly that it nearly severed his head from his body. They hadn't seen a photo of the nude body of Donna Ferguson, a gag placed in her mouth by using her own panties, with her throat cut. They hadn't seen a photo of Todd Rudiger as he lay on the floor, his hands and legs bound, and his throat slashed. They hadn't heard the "chilling testimony" of Amanda Carpova. And McDonnell said that they shouldn't have to see and hear all that—they hadn't committed the crimes, Sebastian Shaw had.

McDonnell asked once again: what type of person deserves the death penalty? And he added that one juror had told him the perfect answer during voir dire: "Only the jury can decide that." Given all the evidence they had, and the fact that Jay Rickbeil was a paraplegic sitting in a wheelchair in his own residence, there could only be one reasonable decision to be made, and that was that Sebastian Shaw, who they had already said was guilty of the crime, should be put to death. "Sebastian Shaw is every woman's worst nightmare. He is the worst nightmare for anyone who loves another person. Society has a right to stand up and say to Shaw, and others like him, 'You simply cannot kill innocent people indiscriminately.' Deliberate murder is not a triviality. It is not like dirt under a fingernail."

Even before the defense started their opening argument, Judge Gernant told them that they had a two-hour limit in which to speak. Richard Wolf was incredulous, and said, "I have a limit as to how long I can argue for my client's life?"

Gernant replied, "Yes, the court of appeals has set a limit of two hours."

Wolf replied, "I can't guarantee that right now. I want to know if I'm not done in two hours, will the court close off my argument in the sentencing phase of a capital case?"

Judge Gernant responded, "Well, I didn't imagine you would go to two hours."

Wolf said that he could, and he might even speak longer than that. Gernant replied, "Well, as far as I know, that time limit goes to every type of case. But I will study it. I don't want this case overturned on that issue."

That being said, and with a possible time limit hanging over his head, Richard Wolf began by telling the jurors that thirty-one years ago, a child rode aboard the United States naval vessel *Blue Ridge* without a father or a mother. He had just been evacuated from the chaos of Saigon, and he was sailing into an uncertain future. Then Wolf told the jurors that he wanted them to know right off the bat that he wouldn't be brief in his attempts to sway them to vote for life without the possibility of parole, instead of death, for Sebastian Shaw.

Wolf said that the prosecution had the luxury of knowing that no matter what the jury did, Sebastian Shaw would spend the rest of his life in prison. So, according to Wolf, the prosecutors thought, "Why not take a shot at the death penalty?" Wolf said the execution of Shaw would not bring back Jay Rickbeil. Shaw's death might give Rickbeil's family a fleeting feeling of retribution, but they could only hold on to those feelings for so long. Wolf said the circumstances of Shaw's life required them as jurors to use "their reason and moral judgment" to allow Shaw to live behind bars until his natural death.

Wolf stated that in the last five years he and David Falls had spent untold hours getting to know Sebastian Shaw and his extended family. They had shared meals with his family and friends, and Wolf said that they as jurors would do irreparable harm to those people if, out of vengeance, they decided to execute Shaw.

Wolf added that all the emotions they'd seen displayed by witnesses on the stand over the previous month were genuine, and that neither he nor Mr. Falls had ever attempted to manipulate the jurors. Then he said that if on any question before them, if even one juror answered no, then a life without parole was what Sebastian Shaw would receive. The prosecution had to prove those things beyond a reasonable doubt, and reasonable doubt was defined as "an honest uncertainty." This could even be a moral uncertainty.

Wolf gave an example about an intentional act—that one of them would be in a grocery store, see the candy aisle and decide to buy a Mounds bar. That was an intentional act. A deliberate act was different, he said—one of them drove to the store with the deliberate purpose to buy the Mounds bar. In the Rickbeil case, Wolf said, Shaw's killing of him was "intentional" but not "deliberate." Wolf argued that Shaw knew Jay Rickbeil and that he had gone to his apartment on some business. A fight had suddenly occurred and Shaw killed him. This was very different than going to Jay Rickbeil's apartment with the deliberate forethought of killing him.

As far as Amanda Carpova went, Wolf said, Shaw made a conscious decision not to take her life. Wolf added that it wouldn't have been hard for Shaw to go into the kitchen, grab a knife and slit her throat, but he decided not to do so even though he knew the risk of her identifying him later would be great. Wolf declared that they knew Shaw struggled with this, because of his conversation with Amanda Carpova. Wolf argued that the state had already made a plea on Amanda Carpova's case for life without parole, but now they were trying to get it in the back door to execute him for the same crime.

As far as being a continuing threat to society, Wolf said, the prosecution had to prove beyond a reasonable doubt that Shaw would commit a new crime while in prison. The way things stood now, Wolf stated, the prosecution was asking them to put Shaw to death for crimes "he might commit in the future." But the justice system did not work that way. Even the items the prosecution produced from the shooting up of Russ Sperou's room, to the so-called murder kit from the stolen car, had been part of the plea agreement in 2000. Those things could not be brought up now, Wolf said, because they constituted double jeopardy.

Wolf declared that even in prison Shaw had the right to defend himself, and that is what had occurred during his two altercations behind bars. As far as ever committing new crimes out in society, that was never going to happen, because Shaw was not eligible for parole. Wolf kept pounding this point home—Sebastian Shaw was never going to leave prison if they voted for life, rather than death.

Then, bit by bit, like stacking bricks to make a wall,

Wolf told of incident after incident in Shaw's young life in Vietnam and in the United States where he received trauma, abuse from his father, and even made a suicide attempt. Wolf read the entirety of Shaw's story about a fictional soldier in a country as the country collapsed amidst chaos and fear. Everything Shaw had written about, Wolf said, a juror could find as a mitigating circumstance to spare Shaw the death penalty.

Wolf then said that the prosecution had read various parts of Shaw's journals, but they failed to read from others. On December 26, 1994, Shaw had written in his journal that it was sad that his only accomplishment for the day was to buy new bags for his vacuum cleaner and batteries for his answering machine. Shaw felt a sense of sorrow for the *blind alley* that he was in. Then Shaw spoke of being forced out of a relationship: *It's a bad thing for an Asian lady to be cohabitating with a male. I really don't know what the real reason is behind my eviction notice. It could be that I'm an inadequate, inexperienced lover.*

This woman remained somewhat of a mystery (it might have possibly been the Chinese woman to whom Ly Do had referred), but Shaw spoke of how her kids ran wild when she went away to work. And in her absence he broke a toy gun he had given them for Christmas, after telling them to never point it at anyone and pretend to shoot them. Shaw added: *Amazing how hypocritical we can be in our teaching of children. Could I actually be a successful father, when I have almost no morals?*

Wolf pointed out that in various parts of his journal, Shaw was seen to be struggling with the good and bad side of his nature. He didn't look back and make excuses, but rather he looked at things as they were. Wolf said, "We know how those events of his early life piled up to have a profound and traumatic effect on him." Then Wolf brought up the image of a cartoon that depicted a person with a devil on one shoulder and an angel on the other. Both the devil and the angel were whispering into the person's ear. Wolf said that the cartoon image summed up Sebastian Shaw's life from 1991 to 1996. It was in 1996 that he began to get therapy and take Paxil, and he had not raped or murdered since then.

Wolf asked where was the prosecution psychiatrist to say that Shaw presented a future danger. They hadn't brought one to testify. While in the penitentiary Shaw would constantly be monitored and given medication to combat his anger and depression. Wolf contended that with a life in prison without possibility of parole, Sebastian Shaw would never again be a threat to public safety, and that mercy—not vengeance—was within each juror's grasp.

On rebuttal Ethan Knight spoke of each and every question the juror would be asked on the instruction form. Number one concerned whether it was a deliberate act or not, and Knight said the only conclusion was that it had been. According to Knight, Sebastian Shaw had gone into Jay Rickbeil's apartment with one thought in mind—and that was to kill him.

Number two addressed the question of future danger. He said that past history showed how Sebastian Shaw reacted whenever he became angry at some incident. When he got into a fight with an inmate, he threatened to kill by stabbing him in the neck with a pencil. That was a vivid image. Shaw had murdered his victims by slashing their throats. And Knight said, "Sebastian Shaw kills because he enjoys it!"

The third question was about provocation. Knight said for the jurors to use their common sense on that one. He asked what provocation could a paraplegic in a wheelchair have to cause his own death in such a brutal manner.

On the fourth question, should Mr. Shaw receive the death penalty, Knight again asked them to use their common sense about mitigating circumstances. He said that some parts of Shaw's story were compelling and interesting, but that everyone had losses and hard times. Knight added that it was very interesting to listen to

Shaw's relatives and Ken Kashiwahara talk about the fall of Saigon, but that had nothing to do with Jay Rickbeil's murder. Knight asked how being baptized into the Catholic Church in Mt. Angel, serving in the U.S. Marines or taking courses at a community college could possibly be mitigating circumstances for a cold-blooded murder. "The choices Mr. Shaw made put you in a position for voting for death."

Knight said that Shaw supposedly loved his family, but he was the one who had done things so they had to come be witnesses and feel a sense of shame in front of the jury. Knight declared that Suzanne Garman was an amazing woman, but even she was a reason to vote for death. "How lucky Sebastian Shaw was to have her, and what did he do despite her? He murdered. He is who he is, despite their best efforts. That is what is so alarming."

Knight said that despite seeing Dr. Leung in 1996 and 1997, Shaw's room at the Danmore Hotel had books on torturing and raping women and photos of dark-haired women on his walls; it also contained ski masks, duct tape and rope. "One thing you need to know about Sebastian Shaw," Knight declared, "his murders were premeditated even before he picked out his victims. Because he was, is and, sadly, will be a murderer. And that's why he alone has left you no other choice but to vote for death."

After the prosecution and defense were done with their closing arguments, it was time for Sebastian Shaw to speak directly to the jurors. In a low, calm voice, he began, saying that all jury service was a civic duty, but there could be none more stressful and important jury duty than being a juror on a death penalty case. He thanked them for being jurors in his case, and admitted that the evidence presented against him by the prosecution had to be "a nightmare" for them. Shaw said that in his previous case, he apologized for his acts against Todd Rudiger, Donna Ferguson and Amanda

Carpova. He said he knew his apologies were woefully inadequate, but he didn't know any other way to show how sorry he was for what he had done.

Shaw told the jurors that to relive all his misdeeds was both painful and humiliating. Even then, he said, he knew it didn't compare to the pain suffered by his victims or their surviving family members. Shaw stated, "I could see you cringing as Ms. Carpova told of my actions against her. I was cringing at her having to sit up there and relive those moments all over again. Although she must carry the effect of what I did to her, every day, I couldn't help but see the strength and courage she displayed to you—the same as she had on June 1, 1995." Shaw said that because of the way Amanda Carpova acted that day, he could not kill her, even though he felt at the time it might come back and lead to his eventual arrest. He added that his decision not to kill her was one of the best decisions he had made in a long time.

Shaw asked for, but did not expect to receive, forgiveness from Donna Ferguson's and Todd Rudiger's parents and friends. Then he said that his father had beaten him and treated him badly, but he was not the only one to suffer those things in childhood, and it did not excuse his crimes. He asked why he had gone wrong, and added that he wasn't there to justify why he had killed Jay Rickbeil, but rather to try and explain to them why that had occurred. Shaw said that in the 1980s, while in the marines, sexual harassment was a new issue just being discussed. He didn't know that when he made jokes and used sexual allusions, some females would take offense at that. In the Marine Corps, those kinds of jokes were done all the time. So, in the private sector, he was surprised at various times when women at work would accuse him of sexual harassment. He thought he was just being friendly, but they did not take it that way.

Shaw stated that he had always been fascinated with movies, and on one boring day in the summer of 1991, he had called up a woman at work at Paragon Cable and made a joke, using one of the lines directly from the movie *The Terminator.* The line was when Linda Hamilton's character answers a phone call intended for her female roommate. The roommate's boyfriend, not knowing it was Hamilton, said, "First I'm gonna tear off your buttons with my teeth," and Hamilton giggled at that.

Shaw said when he used the line, he thought the woman who was his friend at work would just laugh it off as a joke. When she actually turned him in to the personnel supervisor, he was stunned. Shaw declared, "I was not trying to be hostile or vicious to her, and I could not understand at the time why someone who I knew for a while, and drank coffee with, would do such a thing. It struck me as a sucker punch out of a clear blue sky."

The second incident, concerning Shirley Philip, also came as a surprise, he said. Shaw said in the past they had talked about things of a sexual nature, and one day he told her that a porn star was going to be at an adult bookstore nearby, signing autographs. Then the conversation drifted to streetwalkers, and Shaw told her she shouldn't judge them if she had never been in situations such as they experienced. Shaw said the conversation had not been crude or crass. When Philip also spoke to the supervisor of sexual harassment by Shaw, he said he was absolutely stunned.

Interestingly enough, Shaw denied having anything to do with the satanic balloon incident. He said that he had listened to his share of Black Sabbath, Ozzy Osbourne and Judas Priest, but he had never drawn a satanic face on a balloon at home or at work. He said he used to blow up balloons at work out of boredom and bat them around. Someone there who didn't like him must have drawn a satanic face on the balloon and left it on Shirley Philip's desk, along with a satanic message. Shaw claimed to have not written that message.

When he was called into Linda Aday's office that afternoon, he was shocked by the allegations, and he left Paragon Cable in a very bad mood. He went out drinking and later to Jay Rickbeil's residence. Shaw left out any details about actually killing Rickbeil, but he did apologize to Rickbeil's sisters and family for their loss. Then he began to sniffle. Shaw said that on that day, and many others, he felt the whole world was against him. All he felt was "heartache and distress." Getting closer and closer to the verge of tears, he said that if his religious faith had been stronger, he might have resisted the urges that overwhelmed him then. Shaw added, "You may wonder what someone feels when they commit a cold-blooded murder. I don't know what others have felt, but I immediately felt damned."

He said that having broken the tenet "Thou Shalt Not Kill," he felt doomed and destined for hell. He said that after the first murder it didn't matter what he did, because he was going to hell, anyway. And he agreed with Mark McDonnell—after the first murder it was easier to do a murder the second time. Shaw said he wasn't telling them this as an excuse, but rather as the truth of how he felt at the time.

Then Shaw added that he believed God was a forgiving God. He said in the Old Testament view, God was a wrathful God, who put whole cities to the sword. But he declared in the New Testament view, he believed God was a God of forgiveness by the grace of Jesus Christ. He said Jesus even forgave the ones who crucified him. Shaw stated that he was once at a sermon where a priest asked the congregation if they believed Hitler, Stalin and John Wayne Gacy were in heaven. Most of the congregation didn't believe that and were angry at the very suggestion. The priest, however, said that Jesus Christ had died for all of mankind's sins. Shaw said that for a while he had lost his faith in God and religion, and he had even told Amanda Carpova so. Now, however, he prayed for strength, forgiveness and peace. He said he would struggle with those things until the day he died.

Shaw spoke of his "squabbles" with fellow prisoners, and he said that when he was bullied, he had always been taught to stand up for himself. He said he would try to turn the other cheek if attacked in prison again, but he couldn't promise them that. He did say that he would never provoke another inmate, and that he would take his Paxil to ensure that he was not filled with anxiety and rage.

Shaw apologized to his own family "for the shame I have brought on them. I told my lawyer, they should not be brought into this mess I created. I wanted to spare them the pain and trauma of being a witness in this courtroom."

Then Shaw played the card that both the defense and prosecution wondered if he would play. He said directly to the jurors, if they voted for life without parole, instead of death, he would not appeal his guilt or his sentence. Shaw declared, "I want this case to end for everyone. I do this (waiving the appeal) clearly and voluntarily of my own accord, without any threats being made to me by anyone, or by any promises being made to me by anyone. I'm sorry you have been placed in this position. I want you to know that whatever decision you reach, I'm certain it will be a correct and just one. Thank you."

The jury was then sworn in by a court staff member, and they went in to deliberate at 3:30 P.M., on May 1, 2006.

At 2:50 P.M., on May 2, 2006, Judge Gernant, the defense lawyers and prosecution got word that the jury had reached a decision about life or death for Sebastian Shaw. Since the jury was coming back relatively quickly, that did not bode well for the defense or Sebastian Shaw.

At 3:00 P.M., the jurors filed back in and sat in the jury box, which had been their home away from home for more than a month during the penalty and sentencing phases. At 3:02, the foreperson handed a note to Judge Gernant, who read it and asked if this was their verdict. They said that it was. Judge Gernant read that on the first question to the jurors, their answer was yes, to death being imposed. On the second question, the answer was yes. On the third question, the answer was yes. On the

fourth question—should the death penalty be imposed—
the answer was no.

There was an audible gasp from the defense table.
They were truly stunned that they had prevailed.

Judge Gernant thanked the jurors at 3:04 P.M., and they
were dismissed. The Jay Rickbeil murder trial was over—
after starts, stops, acquittals and day upon day of testimony.

Jay Rickbeil's sister had no comment after the decision, but Jay's mother was furious. She told an *Oregonian*
reporter that now Shaw had no incentive to tell about
the other murders he had mentioned. "He got away with
it! It's all an act. He's a maniac! It's like the detective in
the case once told us, 'It's like talking to a reptile.'"

And so the Jay Rickbeil trial was over, or almost over,
because Judge Gernant had to officially pronounce sentencing upon Sebastian Shaw. And when Judge Gernant
did so, some of his comments were almost as astonish-
ing as the ones he had uttered on the day two years
before when he had acquitted Shaw of the crime. Judge
Gernant declared that he had been "looking forward to
the jury giving me the authority to pronounce a sentence
of death on this defendant." Gernant then added that he
supposed some of his friends would be surprised to hear
that, but he wasn't opposed to the death penalty in prin-
ciple. "If the people want it, they are entitled to have it."

Then Gernant brought up the terrorist Zacarias Moussaoui's trial, which had concluded that week as well, where
a jury gave Moussaoui life without parole rather than
death. Gernant said in both cases, the verdicts were surprising. "Rather than justice tempered with vengeance,
they have seasoned it with mercy. And who among us can
say that they were wrong to do that. In exercising their
earthly power, they have exercised it, according to Shakespeare's Portia, in a way most fit to an Almighty Power."

Then turning directly to Shaw, Judge Gernant declared, "Mr. Shaw, you have killed three people. You have

tried to kill two others. You have raped two young women. Yet even in the state's carefully presented case you look like just an ordinary guy. But your very ordinariness, coupled with your extraordinary crimes, is what makes you so dangerous. It is what chills to the bone those of us who have through this courtroom been witness to your deeds.

"Even the state, in its meticulous presentation of a difficult case, did not call you a monster. They figured you out. Beside whatever else you may be, in their simple phrase, you are someone who kills. Most of the time in everyday life, you are an everyday person. But when you get upset, you kill. And you have killed again and again and again."

Gernant thanked all the attorneys who had worked on the case for the past many years, and once again mentioned that it was he who had created a major roadblock when he dismissed the case the first time. He said that some doubted the wisdom of trying to seek a death penalty on someone who was already serving two true life terms. He praised Knight and McDonnell for their persistence and professionalism.

Then Judge Gernant also praised the defense team of Wolf and Falls. He said, "Defense attorneys in capital cases take on a task, as Clarence Darrow once called it, of being attorneys for the damned. Sometimes victims and the public misunderstand their role. Prosecutors and judges never misunderstand. Defense attorneys are as necessary, as indispensable, to the pursuit of justice as any prosecutor or any judge."

Turning again to Shaw, Judge Gernant pronounced, "Sebastian Shaw, for the intentional and deliberate and unprovoked killing of Jay Rickbeil, for his aggravated murder, and based on the jury verdict rendered a week ago, you are committed to the custody of the Oregon Department of Corrections for the rest of your natural life. This sentence is imposed consecutively to those that you are presently serving."

No one had ever thought of Sebastian Shaw and

William Shakespeare somehow combined in the same phrase. Yet, it was now part of a court record. After the sentencing, alternate juror, Shirley Minor, spotted Mark McDonnell and Ethan Knight in the hallway of the court and spoke to them. Three other jurors were nearby, and she told those jurors that McDonnell and Knight wanted to talk about their decision. Richard Wolf and David Falls were also nearby, and they wanted to listen in. So everyone convened to the deliberation room, where the jurors had decided Shaw's fate.

The three jurors, besides Minor, were Joanna Roork, Francis Maderos and Anita Mayhew. According to an *Oregonian* reporter who talked to those people later, the attorneys wanted to know why the jurors had voted the way they did, but, in essence, the jurors turned the tables on the attorneys by asking why certain information had been withheld from them. In particular, they were angry about the fact that they had just learned, and it's not apparent from whom, that Shaw had claimed to have killed ten to twelve other people besides the ones they knew about. Roork, who had not voted for death, said, "I just felt for those other people that are out there. They may not know where their loved one is. They may not know what happened to them!"

McDonnell piped up and said that they had wanted to make a deal on this with Shaw on the other cases, but he wanted immunity. This brought a round of debate between the prosecutors and defense once again.

"No, no, no!" Falls said. "You weren't willing to do that."

"Yes, we were!" McDonnell responded.

"No, that's not true!" Wolf said.

Roork, who was becoming agitated by this round of bickering, exclaimed, "Let's not argue! We're already stressed out!"

Shirley Minor, however, said, "I want them to argue in my presence. I want to learn something from this!"

So each attorney gave a version of what had happened in the 2000 and 2001 negotiations with Sebastian Shaw.

McDonnell said that he was willing to grant immunity on the unknown cases—only if Shaw talked first. Shaw's attorneys at the time were only willing to have him talk if the immunity from death was in place. And so it went—round and round—never quite coming full circle. Because they could not hammer out a deal, the Jay Rickbeil trial had gone to a jury, and those jurors never heard the statements Shaw made about possibly killing ten other people. Inevitably in the Rickbeil trial, the cards had turned up in Shaw's favor with a vote of life without parole instead of death.

One of the more interesting reasons for voting no for death came from juror John Grimsbo. He said, "At first, I was ready to throw the switch. But then I got to reading the diaries again. Society could benefit from him getting studied a bit."

Sebastian Shaw had just escaped the death penalty for the third time, but he was not quite out of the woods yet. Just as the Jay Rickbeil trial came to its conclusion, the matter of whether he had murdered Jenny Lin in Castro Valley, California, in 1994, was just heating up.

20

Jenny

On May 25, 1994, Jenny Lin, of Castro Valley, California, turned fourteen years old. Her father, John, videotaped her birthday party, and Jenny laughed as she received a troll doll, among other gifts. She also got the complete collection of stories by author Douglas Adams, a writer she enjoyed. A quiet girl, she, nonetheless, had lots of friends in school, got good grades and was an accomplished pianist. Jenny had carried a 4.0 grade average for six semesters in a row and one day dreamed of attending Brown University in Rhode Island. That spring, Jenny won an Outstanding Musician Award from the Castro Valley High School, even though she was still only in Canyon Middle School. She also played viola with such an accomplished style that she participated in the community orchestra. In fact, on May 20, 1994, Jenny had played with that orchestra at the Redwood Chapel in town, and her proud father videotaped the performance.

May 27, 1994, was just a typical day for Jenny and her family at their home on Pineville Circle. At 7:40 A.M., John drove Jenny to school, where she spent a normal day in classes. At 2:20 P.M., Jenny boarded the school bus for the trip back home, and it let her off about a half block away from her house, around 2:45 P.M. Jenny's home on Pineville Circle was in a new development, and there had been almost no crime up in the area, even though a lot of transient workers moved back and forth through the new development.

Jenny's usual routine after school was to watch televison for a while and then to do her homework before her parents came home from work. Jenny had an older sister, Rhoda, but she was away at college, attending Stanford University.

Around 4:45 P.M., one of Jenny's friends, Sarah Lester, called her and they talked until 5:25 P.M. John Lin attempted to call Jenny at 5:30 P.M., but got no response. Around this same time, next-door neighbor Ivan Wong noted that his dog started barking. It carried on for a while, though the reason for its barking was not apparent.

At 6:45 P.M., John Lin returned home from work, but his daughter did not greet him as usual. John walked up to a bathroom on the second floor, and was startled by a horrible sight. Lying on the floor, almost completely disrobed, was Jenny. She had been stabbed multiple times, and blood had pooled around her body. Jenny was lying on her stomach on the floor, and when John turned her over, it became obvious within moments that she was dead. There was a gaping wound in her neck, and other stab marks on her body. She had been bound with duct tape and a gag placed in her mouth.

John Lin immediately called 911, and sometime between 6:45 and 7:00 P.M., sheriff's deputies arrived on the murder scene. One of the first there was Officer Mike Godlewski. The officers took an initial look around before detectives arrived and noted the stab wounds, the largest one being to Jenny's neck. There were no signs of a struggle or robbery, but the officers did note a downstairs window that had been broken. They surmised the intruder had entered the house at that location. There was also an unlocked sliding door, by which the assailant might have made his exit after murdering Jenny.

It wasn't long before news agencies got wind of the murder on normally quiet Pineville Circle, and sheriff's spokesman Jim Knudsen told them that detectives were going to work through the night on the case. In fact, the detectives went over every square inch of the house and also canvassed neighbors about any suspicious activity they had observed between 3:15 and 6:45 P.M. Ivan Wong told them about his dog barking in the late afternoon, and one woman added that she'd seen a suspicious person loitering in the neighborhood. She described this person as "Asian, with a stocky build, and wearing a puffy dark-colored coat."

Neighbors began talking to the media about Jenny, and Sophia Limnios said, "I saw Jenny walking home from school a lot. She was the kind of girl who stopped to say hello. She used to walk her husky dog through the neighborhood. My God! Who did this?"

John Lin told the detectives that Jenny had lived a very orderly life. She got on the school bus for the ride home and rode it on a winding road that led up to the new development. She was dropped off a half block away from home, at around 3:15 P.M., every school day. She usually watched television for a while and then did homework. On the day he returned from work to find her on the floor, John discovered that the television was still on, as if Jenny might have been interrupted at that point by the intruder.

Looking at the immediate area, detectives wondered if the killer might have come over the hills behind the house, unseen, and left the same way. They did discover an unknown shoe print on the back deck.

Speaking of the new out-of-the-way development, one neighbor told the media, "You probably have to have a two-income family to live here. Most homes are vacant during the daytime because both parents have to work." That was, indeed, the case for Jenny's parents—her dad worked at the Federal Reserve Bank in San Francisco, and her mother at a Mervyns clothing store.

Castro Valley students were naturally scared after the vicious attack, and it was noted that two days before Jenny's murder, a stranger had molested a girl right on campus on a basketball court. The high school had warned the students to be on the lookout for a "Pacific Islander in his twenties." He had a potbelly, a moustache, a goatee and a blue trench coat. This man had been harassing girls for a week.

As far as Jenny Lin went, Canyon Middle School principal Allen Honda stated, "She was a phenomenal girl and a friend to everyone. She was extremely bright and had a good sense of humor. I'm shocked by this! She was a great, great kid."

Since it was a long weekend holiday, Honda said, counselors were going to be available when school commenced once again on Tuesday. Teachers would also be walking down the hallways with walkie-talkies, looking for kids who might need help.

Few details about the crime came out in the media, but among these were the facts that an autopsy revealed that Jenny had died of multiple stab wounds, but there had not been a sexual assault. It was wondered if Jenny's father, arriving home when he did, might have scared off the assailant before he sexually attacked her. Lieutenant Nelson, of the Alameda County Sheriff's Office, repeated the theory that the assailant probably came in through a broken downstairs window, and added, "We don't think Jenny voluntarily let someone into the house. We think she was taken by surprise."

The Lins did a walk-through of the entire home with detectives and didn't notice anything missing. For that reason, Nelson said, "There is no apparent motive at this time." He also asked the public for its help in finding Jenny's killer. Neighbors in the development met in the community clubhouse to discuss forming a crime prevention committee and a Neighborhood Watch program.

On June 1, 1994, a new and strange twist surfaced in the case. The *Hayward Daily Review* printed an article, GIRL'S WOUNDS SEEN AS MESSAGE. Within the article were the lines: *Jennifer Lin's wounds might have sent a message, but police said they can't figure out why it would have been directed at a respectable, hard-working family. Lt. Nelson related, "It does not appear to be a random act. The murder seems to be what the person went there to do. Jenny was the target."*

John Lin was, of course, devastated by what had happened. "Jenny's death has shattered my family. The home is supposed to be our shelter, our place for love and warmth. But now the shelter is broken, the love is gone, and it only feels cold and scary. We are a simple, hardworking family. We never did anything to hurt anybody. We don't understand why this happened to Jenny."

Students at Canyon Middle School were very frightened by the murder, and many of them instituted a buddy system, where two or more of them would walk to and from school together. One student, Erin Taylor, stated, "It's scary that there's someone like that in Castro Valley."

By now, the detectives were canvassing the entire area, asking anyone if they might have seen anyone suspicious, especially on Friday, May 27. Some people commented about a white male they had seen, who was wearing motorcycle clothing and distributing leaflets in the area. And a strange occurrence had happened to John Lin two weeks before the murder. He had gotten off a Bay Area Rapid Transit (BART) train and was at the station when a man approached him and said, "I have a proposal for you. I've got your daughter." Lin, at the time, thought the man was homeless and delusional. He called home, anyway, and found that his daughter was all right. There were no further threats, and John never saw the man again.

Lieutenant Nelson also brought up a possibility that the Lins had been targeted by mistake by criminals who were after a different Asian family. Just why Nelson brought this up, he didn't expand upon at the time.

Jenny Lin's memorial service was held on June 2, and

friends and family couldn't hold back their tears at the service. Fourteen-year-old Sam Lee, who was a friend of Jenny's, shook so much at the podium while trying to read from a script about her that he couldn't finish his speech. He stated, *"Jenny couldn't wait to get into high school. She had so much to look forward to."* At that point Lee was so emotional, he couldn't continue and sat down.

Many other people in the audience were crying as well, as Jenny lay nearby in a flower-bedecked coffin. There were rings on three of her fingers, and a silver bracelet on one wrist. Stuffed animals and her viola lay in her coffin beside her—the same viola she had been playing since she was three years old.

Thirteen-year-old Sarah Lester, the girl who was the last to speak with Jenny on the phone, recalled one incident about her when Jenny looked up at the clouds in the sky and said, "It looks so peaceful. I'd love to live up there." Lester declared, "She never knew she'd live up there so soon."

Lester then added that Jenny had lots of friends with whom she talked on the phone. "You knew if you called her, and she answered on the second ring, she was talking to someone else at the time."

John Lin was so distraught, his statement had to be read by the Reverend Dale Hummel. Hummel read to the audience, *"My dearest daughter, Jenny. There are so many things I miss about you. Playing tennis, swimming laps, watching Jerry Seinfeld on TV, going to the Valentine's dance with you. I miss you."*

Jenny's much older sister, Rhoda Lin, said, "Jenny knew how to live more than anyone I know. She seemed superhuman to me. There was no mean streak in her, and she didn't know how to hate."

Jenny's mom, Mei-Lian Lin, stood up and accepted school awards that Jenny would have been given at the end of the school year. Among the awards was a Golden Apple Award, the highest academic honor at Canyon Middle School. Then the Castro Valley Chamber Orchestra played at the memorial service. So did Jenny's music teachers, Charlene Welch on the piano and Brian Welch on viola. A slide show accompanied the music and showed photos of Jenny, from the time she was a baby to her last birthday, only two days before she was killed.

Reverend Hummel told the audience, "Jenny has taught us parents not to take anything for granted. She taught us to take down our fences and know our neighbors. What we have in common is our children, and we need to work together to protect them. To put away prejudice, to put away politics, to ignore pessimists."

After the memorial service a local real estate developer, Dan Hancock, of Shapell Industries of Northern California, pledged $20,000 for information leading to the arrest of Jenny's killer. He said, "It happened in our project and it was a family that bought their home from us."

Alameda County sheriff's detectives were still working around the clock on the case. A state specialist in Asian gangs was called in to see if the stabbing was ritual or cultural. Even the FBI was called in to do a profile of the killer.

Once again, newspapers in the area noted that children were afraid, and five hundred people showed up at the community clubhouse to discuss the children's fears and what could be done about them. A sheriff's officer told the audience how to answer children's questions: "What if the bad guy comes back?" or "What if the robber shoots through the door?" Then he told of commonsense things to do, such as not taking shortcuts from school, using the buddy system, having a secret code in place in case a child was kidnapped—so they could relate it to the parents—and also setting up "safe houses," where children could go if they were afraid of someone or felt threatened.

The officer asked the kids a rhetorical question: "If you come home and see a window broken at your house, do you enter it?" The kids replied in unison, "No!"

* * *

Unfortunately, as it had been for Todd Rudiger's parents and Donna Ferguson's parents, all the detective work and leads for the Lins seemed to go around and around, and never quite led to a suspect. Then a very odd thing happened. Dean Campbell's house was broken into in nearby San Ramon, and the culprit seemed to have entered by breaking a downstairs window. The Campbells' car was stolen, and so were two .22 rifles. Months later, up in Portland, Oregon, Sebastian Shaw was found sleeping in the stolen car and arrested. When he later asked for some of the items back, Officer Terry Long decided to photograph all the items from the car and Sebastian Shaw as well. It was perhaps more than just a coincidence that Sebastian Shaw had a potbelly, wore a moustache and a goatee, had a black cap and was mistaken by Amanda Carpova and her neighbors as a Pacific Islander rather than Vietnamese.

The items in the stolen car, of course, contained what Officer Long would later call a "rape/murder kit." These included ski masks, duct tape, books on anatomy, pepper spray and a sock with a lead weight inside it. Also included was *The Anarchist Cookbook* and a book on how to make keys. Officer Long passed these items on to the Alameda County Sheriff's Office, and Sebastian Shaw became a "person of interest" in the Jenny Lin murder.

A year after Jenny's murder, her room was exactly as she had left it. There was a backpack still stuffed with books, a poster of *The Lion King* on a wall and her favorite teddy bear, "Pepper," in the room. Jenny's viola case was still propped up against the piano. John Lin told *San Francisco Chronicle* reporter Henry K. Lee, *"I can't believe that a person so loving could attract anyone so evil, so cowardly. She was defenseless. Someone broke into a house that was supposed to be a safe and sacred place."*

Since 1994, the Lins had created the Jenny Lin Foundation, with the help of Polly Klaas's father, Mark

Klaas. It is an organization dedicated to promoting child safety and keeping unsolved murders in the public eye. On the one-year anniversary of Jenny's death, the Lins put together a slide show at the First Baptist Church of Castro Valley. While slides of Jenny's life were shown, Elton John's "Circle of Life," from *The Lion King* movie soundtrack, was played.

Mei-Lian Lin dabbed at her eyes as slides of Jenny playing the piano, dressed in an Indian costume, and with her sister, Rhoda, were portrayed. Mei-Lian stated, "We promised ourselves we would be strong. Otherwise, we would not survive. That is what is holding us together."

Pat Lee, whose sixteen-year-old daughter was a friend of Jenny's, said that her daughter had been traumatized by the murder, and was still afraid to be home alone. And ACSO sergeant Casey Nice said, "I'm going to pursue this case until there's nothing left to pursue. These cases never end, so it will never be closed until someone is arrested."

By now, hundreds of leads had been tracked down, and even the FBI had been consulted. Yet, nothing seemed to get the authorities closer to who had murdered Jenny Lin. There was only one slim clue that a neighbor had seen a "short, stocky Asian man in a dark jacket and dark baseball cap" in front of the Lins' home on the day of the murder.

And so it went, year by year, with a case that seemed as if it would never be solved. In 2003, the Lins went to the Comcast Cable Company offices in nearby Hayward, California, to tape an episode of *Best Kept Secrets,* a community-oriented program. Normally, these programs were about people in the community with lighthearted episodes. This time, however, host Winnie Thompson explained, "The Lin family's dedication to students and youth music programs made them seem a perfect fit for the show. Through the years they've sponsored musical events and concerts and safety fairs. Jenny was such a likeable, brilliant and talented little girl. They have dedicated their lives to carrying on Jenny's spirit."

Polly Klaas's father also joined the Lin family in the studio. John Lin said of Mark Klaas, "We've had a similar experience. He's been a tremendous help to us." In fact, Mark Klaas was a former Hayward resident and graduate of Mount Eden High School from that city.

By 2003, Sergeant Scott Dudek, of ACSO, was the lead investigator on the Jenny Lin case, and Dudek said, "Since it's a local show, we can target the local community. Hopefully, people can come forward and give us tips, even seemingly insignificant ones." Dudek added that no one could tell ahead of time which tip was going to be the one that changed everything. Every bit of evidence had to be looked at—no matter how small.

In an odd turnaround of events, it was the Jenny Lin case and Casey Nice's comment to Detective Mike Stahlman about Sebastian Shaw and the stolen car from San Ramon that had been crucial in the Donna Ferguson and Amanda Carpova cases. It was Casey Nice's reference to a guy named Sebastian Shaw, who had stolen that car, that pointed Stahlman and Bocciolatt in the right direction.

The Jenny Lin case, however, lay dormant for many years—just one more unsolved cold case in Alameda County. And then Sebastian Shaw was arrested in 1998 for the rape and murder of Donna Ferguson, and the rape and attempted murder of Amanda Carpova. These cases had a lot of similarities to the murder of Jenny Lin, and both the Portland detectives and Alameda County sheriff's detectives started looking at the Lin case very carefully once more. The case got a new lease on life with ACSO sergeant Scott Dudek and Detective Mike Godlewski.

Detective Godlewski, in fact, had been the first uniformed officer on the murder scene on May 27, 1994. Years later he was a full-fledged detective in the Crimes Against Persons Unit, along with Scott Dudek. Godlewski stated, "I know that John Lin was looked at as a suspect early on, but I could tell within two minutes that he hadn't done it. He was absolutely devastated by his daughter's murder."

The detectives amassed more and more information about the similarities between the Ferguson, Carpova and Lin cases, and Sebastian Shaw's MO in rapes and murder. They put together, bit by bit, a very detailed account to present to the district attorney's office for an arrest of Shaw for the murder of Jenny Lin. Almost every page had an accompanying photograph. The detectives started out by presenting a short biography of Jenny and her family, and then moved on to the day of the crime. They showed all the items in great detail that were used to bind Jenny and just how much of each item was used. With computer drawings they showed where the bindings had been placed and where all the knife wounds had been inflicted as well. The computer-created depictions were very precise and very graphic. One showed how Jenny had nearly been decapitated by a savage knife wound to her neck and throat. It was hauntingly similar to a photo of the knife cut that Sebastian Shaw had used to kill Jay Rickbeil.

Explaining how the Lin home had been entered by the intruder, the report and photos depicted the point of entry as a sliding window on the west side of the house, which had been broken with a brick. The window had been broken near the latch, and laboratory analysis revealed that it had been broken from the outside in. A potted plant had been knocked to the floor when the intruder entered the room. Processing of the windowsill and the potted plant proved negative for fingerprints, but it was determined that a brick had been removed from the dog run area and used by the intruder.

An examination of the sliding glass door outside the upstairs master bedroom indicated that the lower half of the sliding glass door had been unsuccessfully pried with a large tool of some sort. The detectives surmised that the intruder had initially tried to come into the house by that means. Tool markings were found in some areas of the door frame, and these marks were consistent with a tool that had a flat-tipped surface. The contact surface of the tool appeared to have been approximately a quarter inch in width.

It was also noted that the remote control to the downstairs television was discovered on the floor of the master bedroom upstairs. Sergeant Dudek wrote: *It is our belief that Jennifer heard a noise in this area and went upstairs to investigate with the remote in her hand. At this point she discovered the suspect and she dropped the remote.*

In the backyard area several footprints made by someone wearing Gorilla-brand-type boots were discovered. These footprints were found on the stairs leading to the sliding glass door outside the master bedroom. A similar boot print was also found outside the rear fence, along a trail that ran behind the homes. Later the investigators determined, through an FBI shoe expert, that the dimensions were of a 7½ boot size. It was also noted that during an early neighborhood canvass in 1994, Mrs. Georgette W. was out watering her roses when she saw a "short, stocky Asian male," with a "puffy black coat, wearing a black baseball cap," standing in the driveway of the Lins' home.

Dr. Henry Lee, famed forensic investigator who had worked on the O. J. Simpson case, among others, was consulted by Dudek and Godlewski on the Lin case, and Lee examined the photos taken of Jenny after the murder. He noted the blood smears on her buttocks and concluded the blood smears were handprints consistent with a suspect trying to anally penetrate Jenny. Dr. Lee also examined the knife wounds and surmised that the knife was double-edged and probably seven or eight inches in length, and lacked a conventional hilt. The lack of any hilt impression on Jenny indicated the lack of a hilt on the knife.

Then the detectives wrote of the burglary that had occurred at Dean Campbell's home in nearby San Ramon, sometime between May 30, 1994, and June 14, 1994, while the Campbells were on vacation. Entry was gained into the home by an intruder who broke a downstairs bedroom window. Once the window was broken, the

intruder gained access by opening a latch to the window
and crawled inside. The Campbells' 1978 Pontiac Bonneville was stolen from the driveway, and two rifles,
binoculars and a six-pack of malt liquor were also stolen.

The detectives noted that on August 30, 1994, Sebastian Shaw was arrested in Portland, Oregon, while sleeping in the Campbells' stolen car. Detectives Stahlman
and Bocciolatt later determined that the license plate on
the stolen vehicle was actually taken from a parking
garage near the California State Court of Appeals in San
Bernardino, where Shaw had just been fired in 1994 for
harassing women there. Shaw remained in custody for
less than a week for the stolen vehicle, and when Contra
Costa County and Multnomah County failed to prosecute him for the stolen car and rifles, he was released.
Upon his being released, Shaw requested items from the
car be returned to him.

An inventory of the items found in the car was taken,
and those, of course, included a blue gym bag, binoculars,
duct tape, flex ties, latex gloves, a hammer, a screwdriver,
a knife and a ski mask. There was also a black sock with
weights inside it, rendering it as a weapon, and there was
duct tape on the sock. Strangely enough, there was also a
child's white recorder inside. (A recorder is a musical instrument like a flute.) Miscellaneous shoes, boots, rifles
and a handgun were also noted to be in the car. A receipt
from an ATM proved that Shaw had been back in the Portland area on June 7, 1994. A photo of a young Asian
female was also found in Shaw's wallet. Although investigators never did find out who she was, the photo bore a resemblance to Jenny Lin.

The detectives next presented a bio of Shaw, starting
with his younger years in Vietnam, his move to the
United States with his aunt and cousins, and the trouble
with his father, Van Ho. They reproduced some of the
entries from Shaw's diary, such as a statement from November 12, 1994: *I've been thinking of murder lately.* There
also was noted a statement written on that same day by

Shaw: *No one knows my secret and it is to my eternal shame that I shall probably keep this secret until my grave.* Also reproduced was Shaw's statement attached to the satanic balloon at Paragon Cable: *Death is too final, so to live and suffer before dying, that's damnation.*

The detectives wrote of the pattern of Shaw's murders: how he would be fired from a job and then lash out at someone who had no connection to his being fired. This had happened in 1991 when Shaw was fired from Paragon Cable. He had gone out that same afternoon and murdered Jay Rickbeil in Rickbeil's apartment. In 1992, Shaw had been let go from the Pinkerton Agency, and he murdered Donna Ferguson and Todd Rudiger within days. The detectives posited that Shaw had done the same thing in 1994, after being terminated from Guardsmark for his harassment of women at the court of appeals, where he had worked. Within a short period of time, from the date when he was released, they surmised Shaw had driven north and murdered Jenny Lin in her home.

A psychologist's report on Shaw, after the Oregon murders were discovered, related: *Sebastian Shaw is an anger-retaliatory rapist. He offends because he possesses an intense hatred of women which leads him to depersonalize them and attempt to control and humiliate them.* It went on to say that he set the stage for the homicides by putting himself in situations where he would be rejected by a woman or fired from jobs.

Sergeant Dudek and Detective Godlewski wrote that Shaw had given Barbara Phillips-Crawford a knife sometime in 1992, and even showed her how to cut someone's throat with the knife. Discussing the Amanda Carpova case, they noted that Shaw caught her by surprise in her apartment, much like he might have caught Jenny Lin by surprise. The detectives noted how Shaw had used electrical cord and telephone cord to bind Carpova's hands and legs, just as had been done to Ferguson and Rudiger. Carpova stated later that her attacker seemed to know what he was doing, and she believed he had done this before. Carpova had been gagged with a scarf, and Jenny Lin had been gagged with an item in her house. Donna Ferguson had been gagged with her panties.

One bit of very damaging evidence against Shaw came from an interview of a fellow inmate at the penitentiary, where Shaw was being housed. This inmate was not the same one who had tipped off law enforcement agents about Shaw's declarations in 2000. This new inmate and tip occurred in 2006, and never made its way into the Jay Rickbeil murder trial. The inmate told authorities that Shaw had told him that he'd committed several murders in several states in the West, and possibly one on the East Coast. Shaw expressed that he liked to bind his victims with duct tape, then sexually assault his victims. He liked anal sex and oral sex as well. Shaw told the inmate that he would steal cars and switch their license plates to avoid detection. Shaw told the inmate that he liked to cut and stab his victims to death. He declared that he changed his pattern of stab wounds so as not to be easily traced from one crime to another.

Shaw added that he always changed his MO a little bit to throw off detection. Shaw spoke of killing a female in Daly City, California. (He may have been lying about this, though, since investigators could not find a female victim in the time period spoken of. Or, possibly, Shaw may have confused Daly City with Castro Valley.) Shaw told the inmate that on one occasion he had used a six- to eight-inch knife to cut off the victim's clothing. Shaw said that he liked Asian females, and that he immediately got rid of clothing he wore after the murders because they might have become bloodstained. What made this report from the inmate so compelling was that he spoke of things not reported in any newspaper at the time.

The detectives also wrote of going to the prison in Oregon on January 9, 2006, and speaking with Shaw in person. Once again, Shaw, as he had done with Detectives Higgins and Stahlman, said that if they made a package deal where he could serve the rest of his time in federal prison, he would tell of at least ten people's murders that he hadn't been arrested for. Then Shaw asked what murder they were investigating, and the detectives said it was the murder of a young Asian female in Castro Valley, California. Shaw didn't know where Castro Valley was, so they told him. They said, "The one near where you stole a car in 1994." Shaw's only reply was "Oh, okay." He didn't deny that he had done it. In fact, it sounded like an admission that he knew what they were talking about. Just before the detectives left the interview, Shaw spoke up and said, "I've wanted to kill ever since I was seven years old and saw the movie *The Texas Chainsaw Massacre.*"

The detectives concluded their report with many comparisons between the Jenny Lin murder case, and those of Jay Rickbeil, Donna Ferguson, Todd Rudiger, plus the rape and attempted murder of Amanda Carpova. They started out by saying that Shaw, by his own admission, was a serial killer who may have murdered more than ten victims. Jenny Lin was murdered on May 27, 1994, and a vehicle was stolen in San Ramon by Shaw, 11.6 miles away from the Lin home, shortly after the murder. Around the same time, Shaw showed up in Stockton, California, at a relative's home, and he spoke of being fired from Guardsmark. He often murdered after being fired from a job.

Showing photos, side by side, the detectives indicated the lower-floor windows where an intruder had broken into the Lins' residence and the Campbells' residence. Showing a photo of the screwdriver among the items Shaw claimed were his in the stolen car seized in Portland, they revealed that the screwdriver was a quarter-inch-blade type, the same type that had caused a quarter-inch groove on the sliding door of the Lins' home. Showing a photo of Shaw at 220 pounds in 1994, and height of five-six, the report noted that a neighbor of the Lins spotted *a short, stocky Asian male in their driveway* on the day of the murder.

Knife wounds on Jenny Lin were thought to be from a double-edged knife with no hilt, the same kind of knife recovered in the stolen vehicle. Both the gags on Donna

Ferguson and Jenny Lin had been secured in place by bindings. *Dr. Henry Lee stated in a report that it appeared Jennifer Lin was sexually assaulted in her anus based on handprints on her buttocks. The autopsy did not reveal any trauma to Jennifer in this area.* The report also stated that Amanda Carpova said that Shaw's penis was so small, she didn't even know she was being penetrated by him.

Photos, side by side, showed panties stuck in Donna Ferguson's mouth and secured by a bathrobe sash, and a gag had been stuck in Jenny Lin's mouth and secured by duct tape. Every one of Shaw's victims, except paraplegic Jay Rickbeil, had been bound. Todd Rudiger, Donna Ferguson, Jenny Lin and Amanda Carpova were all bound at the ankle area, and then farther up the legs. Both Jay Rickbeil and Jenny Lin suffered massive knife wounds to the neck, which nearly decapitated them. The clothing on Donna Ferguson and Jenny Lin were both cut off by the use of a knife, after they had already been bound. Dr. Lee was certain that the assailant of Jenny Lin cut her throat from left to right, as had been done on Jay Rickbeil. This would have been done by a right-handed person, as Shaw was. A recorder (musical instrument) was found in Jenny Lin's room, and Shaw was found in possession of a child's recorder, although it hadn't belonged to Jenny. The question was asked, "Why would Shaw, an adult, have a child's recorder in his possession?" A psychiatrist stated that some serial killers liked to keep mementoes that remind them of their murder scenes.

The detectives noted that Shaw carried rolls of duct tape and often used them on items. Forty-five feet of duct tape had been used to bind Jenny Lin before she was stabbed to death. During his Marine Corps training, Sebastian Shaw had learned how to stab someone to death with a bayonet and a knife.

With its thorough and detailed manner, along with the abundance of photos, the report was a very potent and profound testament that Sebastian Shaw was indeed the person who had murdered Jenny Lin in such a brutal

manner. ACSO commander Greg Ahern announced in
May 2006, "Shaw's been a person of interest in this case
for a very long time. Because of the convictions in Oregon
and the trial (for Jay Rickbeil), we didn't want to interfere
with their investigation or interfere with the trial."

Jenny's mom, Mei-Lian, stated, "We have mixed feelings. We feel relieved that a suspect has been named, but
we are still very hurt by this. We have no idea how he
found Jenny. We think he is a sick man. We are grateful
that the sheriff's office never gave up the search for who-
ever is responsible for Jenny's killing."

However, there was one huge problem—Alameda
County district attorney Tom Orloff, for whatever reason,
chose not to prosecute the case. It was hard to say how
much the Jay Rickbeil trial influenced him in his decision.
If a jury up in Portland would not sentence Sebastian Shaw
to death for killing a paraplegic in cold blood, what chance
was there that an Alameda County jury would do so for a
fourteen-year-old girl's murder that was based on circumstantial evidence? Granted, there was a lot of circumstantial evidence that pointed to the fact that Shaw had
murdered Jenny Lin—and both Sergeant Dudek and Detective Godlewski were sure that Shaw was the killer. Orloff,
however, may have wondered what good it would do to
have Shaw receive just one more sentence of life without
parole, when he was already doing life without, up in
Oregon.

This decision left the Lin family with no conclusion or
sense of justice for Jenny. To have the case remain officially "unsolved" left a very bitter taste in their mouths.
Jenny was a sweet, gifted, totally innocent child, who de-
served that her cold-blooded killer be brought to justice.
Anything less was not adequate, as far as the Lin family
and detectives were concerned.

In the spring of 2008, Sebastian Shaw went about his
normal routine at the Oregon State Penitentiary. Up early

for breakfast, milling around with the general population in C Block, and always worried that someone would "dis" him, or worse, for being a "rapo," Shaw's days were unvaried, dull and occasionally filled with fear that he would be attacked by another inmate. Once in a while he was allowed to go to the library, and as Detective Stahlman noted, "Shaw checked out books mostly on science and mathematics. In fact, he checked out books that no one else had for a very long time."

Sebastian Shaw may have "dodged a bullet" as far as the death penalty was concerned on the Donna Ferguson, Todd Rudiger and Jay Rickbeil cases, but the Jenny Lin case hung on the distant horizon with piles and piles of evidence and thousands of pages of reports. Just because District Attorney Tom Orloff would not prosecute the case didn't mean that his successor would not. And Alameda County juries had shown in the past that they were not adverse to handing down a death penalty. In 1997, a young pretty Filipino woman named Vanessa Lei Samson, who had been kidnapped only a few miles from where Jenny Lin had lived, was sexually tortured by James Daveggio and his girlfriend, Michelle Michaud. After torturing Vanessa, they both strangled her to death. Arrested for the crime and convicted, both Daveggio and Michaud received the death penalty from an Alameda County jury. Michelle Michaud became only the third woman on California's death row at that time.

If a jury was willing to convict those two for the murder of Vanessa Samson, based on circumstantial evidence, what chance would Sebastian Shaw have against a stack of circumstantial evidence—as the detectives had noted: *You can only have so many coincidences, when at some point they are no longer coincidences.*

Sebastian Shaw might have been trapped in a dull, rarely changing routine of prison life in 2008, but it wouldn't have been unusual if every so often he gazed southward toward California and wondered whether death for him hovered down there, like a dark cloud that would not go away.